Surviving Sacrilege

Surviving Sacrilege

CULTURAL PERSISTENCE IN JEWISH ANTIQUITY

STEVEN WEITZMAN

HARVARD UNIVERSITY PRESS
Cambridge, Massachusetts
London, England *2005*

Printed in the United States of America

Library of Congress Cataloging-in-Publication Data

Weitzman, Steven, 1965–
Surviving sacrilege : cultural persistence in Jewish antiquity / Steven Weitzman.
p. cm.
Includes bibliographical reference (p.) and index.
ISBN 0-674-01708-0 (alk. paper)
1. Jews—History—586 B.C.—70 A.D.
2. Judaism—History—Post-exilic period, 586 B.C.–210 A.D.
3. Jews —Identity. 4. Jews—Civilization—To 1500.
5. Cultural property—Protection—Palestine—History— To 1500.
I. Title.
DS121.65.W46 2005
305.6.6′96′09014—dc22 2005040236

Contents

Acknowledgments

This book would not have been possible without feedback, advice, and encouragement from many friends and colleagues, most especially John Efron, Constance Furey, Lisa Hughes, Mitch Merbach, Saul Olyan, Alvin Rosenfeld, Michael Satlow, Jeffrey Veidlinger, and Mary Jo Weaver. At a moment when I was uncertain whether the book would get a chance to find an audience, David Brakke and Robert Orsi stepped in with encouragement and help, acts of friendship for which I will always be grateful.

I also wish to thank the Yad Hanadiv/Barecha Foundation, the American Council of Learned Societies, and Indiana University for funding a leave in 1996–1997 that allowed me to initiate the research reflected in this book. The project took a little longer than expected, evolving considerably in the interim, but I hope the results partially validate the investment of these wonderful institutions.

It has been a pleasure to work with Peg Fulton of Harvard University Press, a delightfully receptive and supportive person. I am indebted to her, to the outside readers who reviewed the book and offered helpful advice, and to the others at Harvard University Press who have worked toward the book's publication. Helping to prepare the manuscript and double-check references were two outstanding students, Ellen Muehlberger and Marie Harf. As I reflect on my association with them, I take great pride in having been their teacher. I am also indebted to Susan Yates and Michael Hoffeditz for their expert editorial interventions.

In citing primary sources, I have tried to use readily accessible translations whenever possible, albeit with an occasional revision when my argument demands it. Citations from the Hebrew Bible, New Testament, and apocryphal literature are according to the New Revised Standard Version; those from classical literature are usually from the standard Loeb edition. Almost all of the research reflected in this book appears here for the first time, except for the middle section of Chapter 6, published as "Myth, History and Mystery in the Copper Scroll" in Hindy Najman and Judy Newman, *The Idea of Biblical Interpretation: Essays in Honor of James Kugel* (Leiden: Brill, 2004, 239–55). I thank Brill Academic Publishers for giving me permission to reuse this material.

Although they are not aware of what they have contributed to this book, my sons Yosef and Hillel have had a deep influence on its formulation, fueling the optimism the reader may detect between its lines. I am most thankful to and for my wife Mira Wasserman. It is hard to imagine a muse working more persistently on an author's behalf than Mira did in helping me to develop my writing, and no words can express my gratitude. As a rabbi, she has been deeply committed to keeping the religious life of our community going. To honor the resilience that duty demands, and because I love her, I dedicate this book to her.

Catastrophes do happen; but in the widespread myths of the flood, the ending always tells of the survivors preparing to offer sacrifice. Religion is basically optimistic.

~ Walter Burkert, *The Creation of the Sacred*

Introduction

Like the Darwinian struggle for survival, the effort to sustain a religious tradition over time is often imperceptible. Despite years of participating in such a project myself, I would never have taken note of it were it not for the backstage pass I received when my wife began her duties as a rabbi. One of her chief responsibilities is to insure that everything is in place for the religious performances of our community to proceed as they are supposed to, to make sure that the Torah scroll is rolled to the proper reading, that services begin on time, that the bulb in the eternal light has not burned out. Nothing about worship is easier to take for granted than the stage-managing required to make it possible; and yet without it, the seemingly self-perpetuating cycle of religious life would soon wind down—an observation true not just for my community, I imagine, but for any seeking to preserve what it has received from the past.

This book explores the struggle for cultural survival, the effort to keep things going, by focusing on a particular case study, the efforts of early Jews to preserve their religious traditions. Even in antiquity, the Jewish people was famous for its vigilant preservation of what it had inherited from the past, a trait that, according to the ancient Jewish historian Flavius Josephus (ca. 37–100 C.E.), was precisely what distinguished the Jews from all other peoples:

> In the eyes of the world at large there is something fine in breaking away from all inherited customs; those who have the temerity to defy them are credited with the possession of consummate ability. To us, on the other hand, the only wisdom, the only virtue, consists in refraining absolutely from every action, from every thought that is contrary to the laws originally laid down. . . . Practices which, under the name of mysteries and rites of initiation, other nations are unable to observe for but a few days, we maintain with delight and unflinching determination all our lives. (*Ag. Ap.* 2.182–2.183; 2.189)

The Jews as Josephus describes them shun any invention out of line with "inherited custom," in contrast with other peoples (especially the Greeks, the arch rivals of the Jews in *Against Apion*) who esteem innovation. Not only do Jews value tradition much more highly than others do; they are more skilled at maintaining it. Josephus was not alone in this view. A half-century earlier, Philo of Alexandria (ca. 20 B.C.E.–50 C.E.) acknowledged that while other peoples also guard their customs, the Jews "carry the likenesses of the commandments enshrined in their souls" (*Embassy* 210). Elsewhere, he anticipated Jewish ritual continuing forever:

> Moses is alone in this, that his laws, firm, unshaken, unmovable, stamped, as it were, with the seals of nature herself, remain secure from the day when they were first enacted to now, and we may hope that they will remain for all future ages as though immortal, so long as the sun and the moon and the whole heaven and universe exist. Thus, though the nation has undergone so many changes, both to increased prosperity and the reverse, nothing—not even the smallest part of the ordinances—has been disturbed. (*The Life of Moses* 2.14–2.15)

Even with all the religious innovations that would come to be associated with him, Jesus, too (or the Gospel author), could scarcely imagine the law that Jews had received from Moses undergoing even the smallest change: ". . . it is easier for heaven and earth to pass away, than for one stroke of a letter of the law to be dropped" (Luke 16:17). Such statements conceal the numerous changes that ancient Israel and its successor Jewish culture(s) underwent in antiquity. Of interest here, however, is not the historical accuracy of this image but what it reveals about the mindset and motivation of Jews in antiquity, their commitments and aspirations. Taking this self-image seriously, I seek to illumine the artfulness that it inspired—the effort, cunning, resourcefulness, and imagination early Jews invested in preserving what they had inherited from Moses.

Introducing the actors in this drama, those seeking to sustain Jewish culture in antiquity, is complicated by the fact that "Jew" and "Jewish" are themselves difficult to define, rendered all the more problematic by recent scholars who are wont to argue that, like all forms of social identity, the category of "Jew" in antiquity lacked fixed or stable characteristics.[1] Without denying the fluidity of Jewish identity, let me simply say that what I mean by the "Jews" in this study is the idealized self-image registered above, a people committed to preserving Mosaic law. This image may not correspond to how individual Jews actually behaved "on the ground," but this does not particularly disturb me because I regard the latter as beyond my reach anyway. It is difficult to get behind or beyond how this period is described by surviving texts, and seeing no way around this problem, I have opted to trace the struggle for Jewish cultural persistence as it plays out in and through literary representation. Within this domain, the category of "Jew" is remarkably stable, or rather is depicted as being so. The Jews in the texts we will be looking at consistently appear as a people steadfastly and successfully preserving their religious tradition down to its smallest detail. While arguably fictional constructions, they do personify a real struggle for cultural survival, I will be arguing—one we can detect not just because our sources describe it but because they often participated in it themselves.

The various components of the tradition at stake in this struggle did not fare equally well over the long run. The core of this tradition, the Temple cult itself, was remarkably resilient, in Josephus' reckoning lasting for 1,130 years, 7 months, and 15 days, but in the end it proved vulnerable, going extinct in 70 C.E. By contrast, other practices—circumcision, Sabbath observance, the Torah itself—persist to this day. It is tempting to invoke an evolutionary approach to account for why some of the practices prescribed by the Torah fared so much better than others, to argue as many scholars have, for instance, that the Temple did not survive because it was less mobile than other Jewish religious traditions (like the Bible itself). This sort of approach, recently revived by David Wilson, is not one that I embrace.[2] Cultural persistence is different from biological persistence in ways that make it very difficult to apply a Darwinian approach to the former. For one thing, one cannot trace it as one can follow the persistence or mark the extinction of an organism in the fossil record. There are Jews who believe to this day that a Temple still exists, albeit in a place where it cannot be seen, and this perception of continuity cannot be discounted as a genuine kind of survival since, as I will be arguing in different ways over the course of this study, the Temple was always an imaginary construct to some degree. The struggle for Jewish cultural survival is incomparable to the struggle for brute physical survival because it is not constrained by reality in the same way.

We also do not know enough about the environments in which the struggle for Jewish cultural survival unfolded. The present study focuses on the period between the destruction of the First Temple in 586 B.C.E. and the destruction of the Second Temple in 70 C.E., an age when Jews were ruled by a succession of foreign empires: Babylonian, Persian, Hellenistic, and Roman rule. There is much we can say about these empires—their organization, ruling strategies, their interests—but as is the case today, Jewish religious life was highly localized, developing in multiple and very specific historical and cultural environments within Palestine as well as in the various Diaspora communities around the Mediterranean and in Babylonia. We know something about some of these communities, especially Jerusalem and Alexandria, but others—Antioch, Rome, Babylonia—are much less accessible. As much as I might like to, I have been unable to reconstruct the struggle for cultural survival at this highly localized level.

What our evidence does reveal are the sorts of survival tactics that Jews employed, or considered employing, to sustain their ritual traditions. While I am skeptical of a Darwinian approach to cultural survival, biology does provide a useful analogy for identifying these tactics. In the struggle for biological survival, an organism impelled to persist must find ways to operate in a reality not fully under its control, to avoid or fend off stronger predators, and to make the most of whatever resources happen to be within reach. So too, Jews in the period covered by this book employed a variety of tactics—symbiosis, mimicry, playing dead—in their struggles to sustain their religious traditions. These tactics emerge most clearly in moments of crisis, episodes in which the existence of the Temple or Jewish ritual was threatened in some direct way: the destruction of Solomon's Temple by the Babylonians; the campaign to abolish Jewish religious practice initiated by the Hellenistic ruler Antiochus IV; the attempt by the infamous Roman emperor Caligula to install a statue in the Temple; and Rome's destruction of the Second Temple at the end of the Jewish Revolt. By no means were these empires consistently predatory; to the contrary, for most of the Second Temple Period, Jews appear to have existed more or less peacefully under foreign rule, direct conflict being more an exception than the rule. In certain periods, however, foreign rule did grow menacing, sometimes out of lust for the Temple treasure, sometimes to punish the Jews for disobedience, and sometimes for motives that remain unclear. These crises inscribed themselves deeply on Jewish memories in ways that other, more quotidian or more gradual threats to Jewish culture did not. Some of these memories survive in the form of narratives or other kinds of texts composed in this period, and it is through these that we can glimpse Jewish culture struggling to survive.

In focusing on foreign rule and the threat it posed to Jewish religious tradition, I do not mean to suggest that it was the only source of disruption or that Jewish culture would have persisted unchanged in its absence. In one of the most resonant episodes from the Second Temple period—Jesus' "cleansing" of the Temple—it is not a foreigner but a Jew who disrupts Jewish ritual performance. If I nonetheless ignore internal threats to Jewish cultural continuity, it is not because I discount their importance but because I see something paradigmatic about the threat that foreign rule posed. In theory at least, the Torah established a mechanism to prevent intrusions by troublesome Israelites: a priesthood descending from the line of Aaron, assisted by the larger tribe of Levi from which Aaron descended, charged with the authority of defending the sanctuary from unauthorized intruders.[3] In formulating that device, however, the biblical legislator does not seem to have envisioned the possibility that the priesthood might not have the power to stop the intruder, a problem that increasingly preoccupied Jews living in the Second Temple period under foreign rulers like the Persians, Greeks, and Romans. I have come to see these rulers as a symbol for the uncontrollability of things—the part of reality that is recalcitrant, hard to manage or constrain, indifferent, or even hostile to what it is that one is hoping to preserve.

The most likely point of collision between Jewish cultural tradition and this aspect of reality was the Jerusalem Temple. As conceptualized in the Second Temple period, the cult was a zone into which no foreigner was to enter (see Ezek. 44:6–9)[4]: In the first century C.E., a warning to this effect was posted around the perimeter of the sanctuary, in both Greek and Latin so that foreigners would be sure to get the message:

> No foreigner may encroach upon the forecourt and the balustrade around the sanctuary. Whoever is caught will have himself to blame for his subsequent death.[5]

The warning hints at grave consequences for those who dare trespass into the Temple (whether punishment was to be imposed by the Temple guardians or by God Himself is unclear), but when a foreign ruler resolved to enter the Temple there was little that Jews could do to stop him. They could try to use violence to defend the Temple, and sometimes succeeded, as the Maccabees did in their famous revolt, but often they avoid confrontation with foreign rule, recognizing the danger of challenging it directly. Witnessing what the Babylonians had done to Jerusalem and its Temple, their theft of its cultic vessels, Jeremiah counsels peaceful submission as the best way to survive for just this reason: "Bring your necks under the yoke of the kingdom of Babylon, and serve him and his people, and live" (Jer. 27:17). Many of the texts that survive from later periods urge a similar caution, most especially Josephus, our principle source for the Hellenistic-Roman period, who shapes his narratives of the Jewish past to illustrate the self-destructive folly of rebelling against the Roman Empire. Jews might count on God to intervene eventually, but in the meantime, they develop other survival tactics premised on their powerlessness. To survive under these circumstances required a certain kind of ingenuity, an ability to operate beyond the constraints imposed by powerlessness that I will be referring to henceforth as the arts of cultural persistence.

In developing this concept, I have relied on Michel de Certeau's notion of the "arts of the weak" introduced in his *The Practice of Everyday Life*, a study of how the weak create options for themselves in circumstances they do not control.[6] The actions that God Himself takes in defense of Jewish tradition qualify as what de Certeau describes in this work as a "strategy," calculated action undertaken by those who control the space in which they operate. Lacking such control as a people subject to foreign rule, Jews in the Second Temple period nonetheless had other options, ways of compensating for their lack of power—a kind of action de Certeau labels "the tactic" or the "art of the weak."[7] Since they do not fully control their environment, the weak must "make do" with what opportunities happen to present themselves, anticipating power's moves, exploiting its vulnerabilities, obstructing its field of vision or operating within its cracks. De Certeau recognizes the tactic as an "ageless art . . . preceding the frontiers of humanity," analogous to "the simulations, tricks and disguises that certain fishes and plants execute with extraordinary virtuosity."[8] Unable to control their destiny in the way that God does, Jews in the Second Temple period developed a variant of the arts of the weak, survival tactics by which they could operate within an environment controlled by foreign rulers in defense of their cultural traditions.

Greek and Roman military theorists, developing a science of strategy and tactics, identified a whole assortment of tricks or ruses by which a weaker army could overcome the advantages of a stronger foe—deception, ambush, and surprise attacks.[9] We will see that Jews developed analogous tactics to preserve their rituals, in some cases probably under the influence of Greek and Roman strategic thinking. (Actually, early Jews may have believed that the Greeks learned these tactics from them. According to the Christian author Clement of Alexandria, who might preserve an earlier Jewish tradition, the Greeks learned battle strategy from Moses, who was able to defeat the Egyptians and the Canaanites through what we are describing as the tactic—fleeing beyond their reach, anticipating the enemy's moves, using tricks, launching surprise attacks).[10] The tactics I have in mind were not always employed on the battlefield, however; they could be diplomatic, representational, and even magical. They are tactical in that they constitute ways of operating in the absence of power, expanding the options available to Jews in a world largely out of their control.

Most of these tactics can be sorted into one of the three following categories:

1. *Appeasement and Symbiosis.* Confronting empires too powerful to challenge directly, some Jews looked for ways to appease foreign rule and align Jewish tradition with its interests. This tactic, involving the arts of flattery, mimicry, and diplomacy, was used

to cast Jewish religious tradition as consistent with and even conducive to the foreigner's values and interests.

2. *Resistance.* Facing armies much larger and better equipped than their own, Jews developed ways to offset the enemy's military advantages. Some of these were tactical in a conventional sense, involving alliances with third parties (enlisting Rome against Antiochus IV, for instance) or using surprise attacks and other battle ruses, but others were employed to create options beyond the real through the use of "magical" practice.
3. *Flight, Concealment, Deflection.* Some Jews, unwilling to either align themselves with foreign rule or challenge its control directly, used another tactic to sustain their ritual life: fleeing to places beyond the reach of foreign power. Of course, the Temple could not run away in the way a fugitive slave or prisoner could, but there were other ways to conceal Jewish ritual practice, or misdirect foreign rule in its effort to monitor Jewish religious practice.

Classificatory schemes such as this one inevitably fail to capture the fluidity of the reality they are trying to pin down. Most of the chapters to follow will focus on tactical action that pivots between these options, using ambiguity, doublespeak, and other ways of doing more than one thing at a time. Ultimately, however, the basic options available to Jews were limited—one could ingratiate oneself with foreign rule, operate within its blind spots, or find a way to augment one's power and fight it off. What remains for us to explore is how early Jews made the most of so narrow a range of possibilities.

One thing many of these tactics share in common is a certain kind of opportunistic resourcefulness that de Certeau defines as the art of making do. Elsewhere, he refers to this skill with the French *manouvrier*, a term used in Diderot's *Encyclopedia* to designate arts that involve adapting existing materials.[11] Many of the tactics we will identify in this study "make do" in the sense that they draw on preexisting cultural material: biblical stories, Jewish ritual itself, and most interestingly, the discourse and practices of foreign rule. Even at their most imaginative, Jews were circumscribed by the boundaries of the real, confined in their struggle to survive to whatever resources happened to be available to them in their environment. We will see Jews making the most of these resources, especially in their use of their rulers' culture as a vehicle of Jewish cultural survival. Scholars have commonly interpreted Jewish adoption of foreign practices as evidence of assimilation, or adaptation to a non-Jewish environment. In some cases, however, what might look like assimilation to a foreign culture can be placed within an alternative narrative of cultural persistence, one in which Jews poach resources from the *other* for use in sustaining their own culture.

Another point of overlap between the various tactics we will identify is their use of the imagination. By imagination, I mean "the mental capacity to think of possibilities beyond the evidence of immediate sense perceptions."[12] Although the workings of the imagination often seem non-pragmatic, it has played a central role in human adaptation. "Without it," observes psychologist Ethel Spector, "there could be no picturing of mental alternatives to current discomfort or deprivation, no planning of a future course of action, no creative rethinking of the past to make it pertinent to the present and future."[13] There is nothing more forceful than the imagination, philosopher John Sallis has observed, because it makes the impossible possible, a potentially important tactical asset in an environment where very little is possible.[14] This study stresses the role of the imagination in the struggle for cultural survival as a capacity that allowed early Jews to reshape the past to accommodate present needs, to transcend the constraints of visible reality, and to conjure invisible allies. Each of the following chapters, though focused on a particular survival tactic, can in fact double as a study of a particular mode of imaginative activity—mythmaking, metaphor, magic, et cetera. One might be tempted to interpret these kinds of imaginative activity, disconnected from reality as we construct it, as the opposite of the sort of pragmatism required to survive. I will be arguing that they constituted a kind of practical action in their own right, sometimes less effective than direct forms of action but sometimes more so.

This focus on the imagination allows me to at least partially overcome the limits of the reality within which I operate as a scholar: the paucity of evidence from Jewish antiquity. Some traces of ancient Jewish religious practice do survive in the archaeological record, the flotsam and jetsam of ancient Jewish culture as it were: part of Herod's massive Temple complex; a dozen or so synagogues from the Second Temple period; some probable ritual baths; and a few phylacteries and *mezuzot* found in the Judean wilderness (the first, small black boxes containing scriptural passages, fastened to the head and arm during prayer; the latter, biblical texts affixed to doorposts).[15] In theory, it might be possible to reconstruct from such evidence the persistence of a ritual practice over time, but to do so would only speak to outcome, the survival of a particular practice or institution; it would not tell us of the struggle itself or how it was waged. We do better with the literary evidence. It is hard to think of an undertaking, apart from finding meaning in the biblical text, that engaged the skills of early Jewish authors as much as surviving the threat that foreign rule posed to their traditions. While all this gives us plenty of material to work with, it is not always clear what we should do with it. Many of the works we will encounter are better classified as myth or exegesis rather than history, describing events that never happened or reshaping them in light of fictional motifs. It has become increasingly clear that even those historical narratives that scholars customarily rely on for what "really" happened in the Second Temple period—the books of Ezra-Nehemiah, 1–2 *Maccabees*, and the writings of Philo and Josephus—thoroughly intertwine memory and fiction in ways that are hard to unravel.

Fortunately, the art of cultural persistence often lies somewhere in between the real and the imaginary. Where we cannot use a given source to learn about one, therefore, we can use it to learn about the other. Surviving accounts of how Jews salvaged something of the First Temple may not tell us much about what actually happened in that early period, a much-debated subject, but they do yield insights into the role of myth as an agent of cultural continuity. *Judith* cannot be connected in any direct way to history and may have fictional prototypes, but it does respond to reality indirectly, and in ways that may illumine the shifting of tactics required to sustain the Temple in the Hasmonean period. Josephus is a dubious source, clearly skewing his narratives to appease his Roman patrons, but how he does so may reveal something about the role of these narratives in his own efforts to sustain Jewish tradition. The fictiveness of our sources, a real constraint on our ability to reconstruct the struggle for Jewish cultural survival as it actually unfolded, is something we can turn to our advantage when it comes to understanding the role of the imagination in this struggle.

However energetic an organism may be in its struggle to survive, its fate is often determined by forces beyond its control, whether catastrophic collisions with external forces, an asteroid intercepting the earth, or more subtle environmental shifts, a slight increase in global temperature. Too much of their environment was beyond their control for early Jews to be able to guarantee the survival of their traditions by any tactic that they employed; indeed, a reasonable argument can be made that the fate of those traditions, especially the Temple, was determined as much by what the Romans did as it was by the Jews themselves. I do not seek to explain the outcome of the Jewish struggle for cultural survival (suffice it to say the results were mixed) but to illumine what Jews did to shape this outcome within the constraints imposed by foreign rule.

Such an undertaking affords us an opportunity to revisit a characteristic often ascribed to Jews, both ancient and modern. Early modern biblical scholars like Wilhelm de Wette and Julius Wellhausen identified the religious conservatism we are concerned with here—the efforts of early Jews to maintain the smallest details of biblical law—as signs of a spiritual petrification.[16] Their image of Jewish culture reflected a once common stereotype of Jews as an inert people resistant to change and incapable of creativity (Traces of this stereotype persist, as in a recent characterization of the modern state of Israel by the historian Tony Judt as "an anachronism" conserving an outmoded form of political organization).[17] Lacking the imagination to produce genuine art, or willfully shunning it as a religious taboo, Jews stifled the creative impulses at the heart of biblical spirituality through an obsessive project to maintain tradition in the minutest of detail. As is often the case with stereotypes, there is a bit of truth to this characterization. We have seen that early Jews themselves, Philo and Josephus, described their culture as a highly persistent one, preserving even the smallest details of Jewish law from change or corruption. This study takes this self-image seriously as a genuine motivation for Jewish cultural practice in antiquity. What it challenges is the view that associates the effort to preserve tradition with inertia, a lack of exertion or change. This study shows that the commitment to preserve Jewish religious tradition, far from retarding creativity, actually excited a considerable amount of it.

By a curious coincidence, a similar confusion of persistence with inertia has generated a blind spot in the scholarly understanding of ritual. Perpetuating practices from a remote past into the present, ritual practice can appear impervious to time, ancient, or even eternal. Many rituals are not nearly as old as they are thought to be, of course, but some are remarkably resilient, at least when compared with other modes of cultural activity, surviving for hundreds if not thousands of years (It has even been conjectured that one mode of ritual practice, sacrifice, is older than humanity itself).[18] Citing Judaism as a paradigmatic case, the ritual studies scholar Catherine Bell refers to this attribute of ritual practice as "traditionalism," the use of practices, speech, costumes, and other elements that seem "frozen in time" from an earlier age.[19] What she is describing has not been completely ignored in previous scholarship but it has received very little attention from a field much more engaged by historical change and the innovation of new practices. When scholars do address it, it is often only to reassert the conception of tradition that I wish to challenge here, one that associates persistence with inertia or reflexive self-reproduction.[20] Recent study of "invented tradition" has shown that much ritual tradition is actually quite innovative, but the concern in that case is the fabrication of new traditions passed off as old, not the preservation of "genuine" tradition.[21] What I hope to show is that the transmission of "uninvented tradition," though it may appear inertial, requires much inventiveness as well.

Although Jews such as Josephus saw the immutability of their culture as a distinctive characteristic, all societies seek to perpetuate themselves in one way or another, and so, I presume, develop their own arts of persistence. To date, so far as I know, no culture has actually achieved immutability—Judaism certainly has not—all, inevitably, succumb to change. Still, the urge to endure can be remarkably enterprising. For those who feel threatened by the perpetual undoing of things, as I do, there may be solace in tracing another culture's resilient struggle not to be undone.

~ 1

After Babel

In the wake of the Babylonian destruction in 586 B.C.E., little survived of Solomon's Temple for Jews to use in salvaging the tradition it represented. The army of Nebuchadnezzar had burned down the Temple itself, plundered the gold, silver, and bronze objects within it, and slaughtered the chief priests (2 Kings 25:9–21). That which remained of the Temple's vessels was carted off to Babylon and deposited in the temple of Nebuchadnezzar's gods, according to the Book of Ezra (1:7). According to this same text, however, less than a century elapsed before the Jews were back in Jerusalem, worshipping in a newly built Temple and celebrating the sacrifices mandated by Moses. They even managed to retrieve the vessels that Nebuchadnezzar had plundered.

How did the Temple cult survive such an experience? The Bible's explanation is preserved in the book of Ezra. It reports that when God sought to restore the cult, He appointed Cyrus, founder of the Achaemenid dynasty of Persia, to return the Temple vessels to the exiles of Judah. The exiles brought them back to Jerusalem and began to rebuild the Temple, completed in the days of King Darius. This version of events, though entrenched in the minds of biblical historians, has been called into question in recent decades.[1] While Ezra makes the Temple's restoration a Persian initiative, for example, some scholars place its rebuilding within the context of a revolt against Persia.[2] Still others, rejecting the Bible's portrait of Babylonian conquest as a profoundly disruptive event, argue that life in Judah actually continued more or less uninterrupted in this period, Israelite religious tradition preserved by those not taken off into exile.[3] Archaeology does little to help recover what happened in this period, much less confirm Ezra's account, revealing traces of Babylonian destruction and continued settlement in Jerusalem's environs but nothing related to the rebuilding of the Temple.[4]

It is fortunate that the history I want to recount here does not require us to reconstruct what "really" happened during this period. My focus is on the restoration of Solomon's Temple not as an historical event but as a storied one, a subject for Jewish mythmaking in the Persian, Hellenistic, and Roman periods. Regardless of what actually happened to the historical Temple, Jews in these later periods believed that some part of the Temple cult remained. The Babylonians may have destroyed the building, but according to the biblical account, some of its contents had survived.[5] This modest remnant of the First Temple was enough to revitalize religious tradition among later Jews—or at least to allow them to imagine its revitalization, inspiring various narratives about how the surviving contents of the Temple were used, or might be used, to restore the Israelite cult in full. As Peter Ackroyd recognized decades ago, such stories may not tell us much about the actual survival of cultic tradition, but they do bespeak an intense yearning for continuity.[6] What makes these stories valuable for our study despite their tenuous relationship to what really happened is the glimpse they offer of this yearning as it seeks out opportunities to assert itself.

In a work entitled *After Babel*, George Steiner speculates that "creative falsehood," or what I call "imagination" in the preceding chapter, has been instrumental in our species' survival because of the options it opens up in an otherwise intractable reality. "The semantically coded responses of the mind are constantly broader, freer, more inventive than the demands and stimulus of the material fact," he writes, allowing humans "to conceive of, to articulate possibilities beyond the treadmill of organic decay and death."[7] I want to suggest something similar for the stories that Jews told of the Temple's survival after its destruction by the Babylonians. In reality, the Jews' only viable option for restoring their Temple cult may have been to depend on the support of Persian rule, but storytelling identified alternative ways to salvage the Temple without surrendering one's fate to foreign rule. As little as they tell us about how the cult really survived the destruction of the First Temple, the narratives we will examine do reveal something of how later Jews *imagined* themselves surviving this crisis; that is to say, they can help us to understand the storytellers' struggle for cultural survival. Many of the tactics employed by Jews in the Hellenistic-Roman period reflect an ability to exploit opportunities beyond the constraints imposed by foreign rule. Storytelling played an important role in cultivating these opportunities by expanding what was possible in a world controlled by others.

Retrieving the Temple Vessels

The narratives that we will consider here all seek to repair Jewish religious tradition by asserting its persistence after the Temple's destruction. To do this, they work with what little survived. Babylonian conquest had left the Temple itself demolished and its contents, the Temple vessels, broken apart or carried off as loot. The latter were potentially recoverable as physical objects, but their significance as symbols of Israelite tradition was jeopardized, their having been wrested from their original setting and used by the Babylonians in their cult (in Dan. 5:1–4, they are used as drinking vessels in a banquet in honor of the Babylonian gods). Storytelling sustained the possibility of restoration by asserting that the Temple's contents had survived not just as objects in themselves but as a link to the tradition disrupted by foreign conquest.

Jews did not invent this kind of story or its role in sustaining tradition. They were preceded (and perhaps influenced) by the Babylonians themselves, who developed stories to assert the persistence of their own religious traditions in the wake of cultic disruption. Of particular concern was "godnapping," a common practice in Mesopotamian warfare—the capture, removal, and destruction of the statues that rendered the gods manifest and that were the focus of cultic practice.[8] The Hittites, the Assyrians, and others looted Babylon's cult statues, including that of its patron god Marduk, on a number of occasions. Such moments were profoundly disturbing for the Babylonians, constituting what sociologist Erving Goffman referred to as frame-breaking, a traumatic disruption of meaningful experience.[9] The experience of September 11 can help us to imagine the impact of such trauma. Part of what made the destruction of the Twin Towers so profoundly disorienting—apart from the horror of witnessing so many deaths—was that it shattered the frame in which we had been absorbed up until that morning, erasing a familiar landmark, disrupting the seemingly unshakeable rhythms of Wall Street and air travel, demolishing the illusion of American permanence and invulnerability. The capture of cult statues caused an analogous break in the even more fragile frame of Babylonian religious experience, disrupting not only cultic performance but, according to one text, the very structure of reality itself. "When I rise [from] my dwelling," the god Marduk says of the departure of his statue from Babylon, "the regulations [of heaven and earth] will disintegrate" (*Erra Epic* ll. 169–170).

For the Babylonians, storytelling played a central role in repairing the shattered frame of religious life, asserting that the god had survived his capture and that he remained in control of events. One example of such a text is known as the *Prophecy of Marduk* where the god describes the repeated capture of his statue as journeys that he himself initiated.[10] Another is the *Erra Epic*, the poem just cited, where Marduk, angry at being neglected by the Babylonians, abandons them in search of the materials he needs to repair himself. One might interpret the loss of the cult statue as evidence that the god it embodies was powerless or even lifeless, but Babylonian myth deflected such interpretations, acknowledging the loss of the statue but denying any loss of vitality. The removal of its image, far from signifying the powerlessness of the deity, was, these stories maintained, the deity exerting control over its image, choosing to go elsewhere. Mythmaking, in this case, represents an effort to suture the wound inflicted by enemy conquest, acknowledging the loss of the cult statue but interpreting it in a way that left the larger frame of Babylonian religious experience, the belief in the cult statue as a living manifestation of the divine, intact. It also laid the groundwork for a restoration of the statue, holding out the possibility of its return, or in case of its destruction, of the god reappearing in the form of a newly fashioned statue.

Even before the Babylonian conquest, ancient Judah, the culture that produced much of the Hebrew Bible, used similar kinds of stories to mitigate the loss of cult objects like the Ark of the Covenant, venerated as a footstool on which God rested.[11] According to 1 Samuel, the ark was once captured during Israel's war with the Philistines, a loss that was so devastating for the Israelites that some found it impossible to survive (see 1 Sam. 4:17–18). The story told of its conquest, preserved in 1–2 Samuel in a series of episodes that scholars refer to as the Ark Narrative (1 Sam. 4–6; 2 Sam. 6), closely resembles Babylonian myths of captured cult statues.[12] Similar stories were told about the "the vessels of the Lord's House"—the gold, silver, and bronze implements looted from Solomon's Temple by the Babylonians. The Babylonians first plundered these in 597 B.C.E. (2 Kings 24:13), and even at this early point before the Temple's destruction, the inhabitants of Jerusalem shaped their loss into a story of divine return. One such narrative is referred to in the book of Jeremiah, attributed to a prophet named Hananiah, who predicted that God would return the vessels within two years:

> Thus says the Lord of Hosts, the God of Israel: "I have broken the yoke of the king of Babylon. Within two years I will bring back to this place all the vessels of the Lord's house which Nebuchadnezzar of Babylon took away from this place and carried to Babylon." (Jer. 28:2–3)[13]

Though it describes events that have yet to happen, I refer to Hananiah's prediction as a narrative because of the way it orders experience into the same kind of story reflected in Babylonian myth (in fact, it specifically recalls the *Prophecy of Marduk*, which predicts the return of the god's statue to Babylon: "A king of Babylon will arise . . . He will lead me in procession to my city Babylon and bring me into eternal Ekursagila"). Hananiah's prophecy renders Babylonian rule a situation soon to be reversed, a temporary break in cultic tradition that would be repaired within a few years when God returned the vessels taken from the Temple. It was possible in this construction of reality to act independently of Babylonian rule; indeed, scholars suspect that Hananiah was emboldened by plans to do just that. In exactly this period, Nebuchadnezzar faced a revolt in Babylon, a moment of weakness that seems to have prompted Judah and neighboring kingdoms under Babylonian rule to plot rebellion. Hananiah's prophecy implies that God himself supported this venture as a step toward restoring the vessels.

For his part, Jeremiah rejected this prophecy—God would only return the vessels in the remote future, if at all, he countered—but the topos on which Hananiah drew lived on, surfacing in Ezra's account of the vessels' return. There, however, it has undergone significant adaptation, with God restoring the vessels through the agency of the Persian ruler Cyrus II, founder of the Achaemenid Empire that ruled Judah between 539/38 B.C.E. and its conquest by Alexander the Great. According to Ezra 1, God gave Cyrus his empire precisely so that he might rebuild the Temple in Jerusalem:

> In the first year of King Cyrus of Persia, in order that the word of the Lord by the mouth of Jeremiah might be accomplished, the Lord stirred up the spirit of King Cyrus of Persia so that he sent a herald throughout all his kingdom and also in a written edict declared: "Thus says King Cyrus of Persia: The Lord, the God of Heaven, has given me all the kingdoms of the earth, and he has charged me to build him a house at Jerusalem in Judah. Any of those among you who are of his people—may their God be with them—are now permitted to go up to Jerusalem in Judah, and rebuild the house of the Lord, the God of Israel—he is the God of Jerusalem; and let all survivors, in whatever place they reside, be assisted by the people of their place with silver and gold, with goods and with animals, beside freewill offerings for the house of God in Jerusalem. The heads of the families of Judah and Benjamin, and the priests and the Levites—everyone whose spirit God had stirred—got ready to go up and rebuild the house of the Lord in Jerusalem. All their neighbors aided them with silver vessels, with gold, with goods and animals, and with valuable gifts, besides all that was freely offered. King Cyrus himself brought out the vessels of the house of the Lord that Nebuchadnezzar had carried away from Jerusalem and placed in the house of his gods. King Cyrus had them released into the charge of Mithredath the treasurer, who counted them out to Sheshbezzar, the prince of Judah. And this was the inventory: gold basins, thirty; silver basins, one thousand; knives, twenty-nine; gold bowls, thirty; other silver bowls, four hundred ten; other vessels, one thousand; the total of the gold and silver vessels was five thousand four hundred. All these Sheshbezzar brought up, when the exiles were brought up from Babylonia to Jerusalem. (Ezra 1:1–11)

Ezra's account is suspect.[14] The only fact that can be verified is Cyrus's incorporation of the region encompassing Judah into his kingdom, and it is otherwise impossible to confirm or disprove Ezra's account. The authenticity of Cyrus's decree in Ezra 1:2–4 is in doubt largely because it contains "Judaizing" elements deemed out of place in an authentic Persian royal decree: It is written not in Aramaic, the official language of Persian royal administration, but in Hebrew; and it invokes the Israelite god, not a Persian deity, as one would expect a Persian king to do.[15] Another detail in Ezra 1:6—"all their neighbors aided them with silver vessels, with gold, with goods . . ." tacitly evokes the Exodus story (see Exod. 12:35–36), suggesting that the account as a whole has been patterned on biblical precedent.[16] This is not to say that Ezra's narrative is a complete fiction, but rather that whatever really happened has been framed by the narrative within a myth-like literary structure distantly related to earlier Israelite narratives of cultic restoration like the Ark Narrative and Hananiah's prophecy.

Though it inherits this topos from earlier literary tradition, however, Ezra introduces a striking adaptation, inserting Persia as the agent of restoration. Persia plays an analogous role in another text from the same period, the *Cyrus Cylinder*. The opening of this text is only partially preserved, but it seems to record sacrileges committed by Babylon's native king, Nabonidus, a disruption of worship that prompts the gods to abandon the city.[17] To restore things, Marduk appoints Cyrus to take over Babylon and return the gods to their shrines, a motif that obviously parallels Cyrus's role in Ezra 1. The second half of the text has Cyrus describe their return himself:

> The cult cen[ters acr]oss the Tigris whose (divine) dwellings had lain in ruins for a long time, I returned to their places the gods who dwelt in them and established (for them) an everlasting dwelling . . . and the gods of Sumer and Akkad . . . at the order of Marduk, the great lord, I had them installed in joy in their sanctuaries . . .[18]

Many scholars see behind this text a novel, empire-wide policy of religious toleration instituted by Cyrus, but Kuhrt has recently called the existence of such a policy into question.[19] He argues that the image of the Persian king as cultic restorer was a politically motivated and self-serving rhetorical construction, not an outright fabrication, but a highly manipulated portrait that seeks to disguise Persian domination of other cultures as the restoration of their native traditions.[20] This image was adapted to accommodate cultural differences. Here it is framed within the traditions of Babylon—emulating Babylonian royal building inscriptions, the text models Cyrus on the traditional behavior of the Babylonian king—but elsewhere it was adapted to other cultural traditions. A much-discussed example is an Egyptian inscription from a scribe-priest named Udjahorresnet who casts Cyrus's son Cambyses as a pious pharaoh helping to restore a defiled Egyptian temple.[21] In Ezra, we have a very similar kind of portrait, casting Cyrus as the divinely appointed agent of Jewish religious restoration.

For the construction of this image, Persia seems to have relied on native scribes—Babylonians, Egyptians, and Jews schooled in their respective traditions. Why would these locals play along in this way? We can only speculate about motives, of course, but there is a case to be made that such authors did in fact see Persia as an instrument of restoration. By mediating Persian rule, reconciling its power with indigenous traditions, native elites might advance not only their own personal interests but also those of the traditions to which they subscribed, enlisting Persian military power and resources in their defense. Upset at the presence of Persian soldiers in the temple precinct of Neith, for instance, Udjahorresnet had enough leverage with the king to persuade him to have them removed and the temple purified. Cooperation with Persia offered similar benefits to Jews seeking to preserve their traditions. Without the requisite funding, Jews may have been hard-put to cover the costs of rebuilding the Temple and maintaining its sacrifices. Neighboring communities, "the people of the land," were also a threat, seeking to interfere in the Temple's construction, according to Ezra's account (Ezra 4). Drawing on Persian support may have come at the cost of political autonomy, but it offered compensatory benefits for the Temple, the subsidizing of its cult and the legal authority to protect it from external interference.

Thanks to a sensational discovery made at the end of the nineteenth century, we have evidence of a smaller Jewish community in the Persian period that sought to establish this sort of symbiotic relationship with Persian rule. The community in question lived in Elephantine in southern Egypt in the fifth century B.C.E., serving as mercenaries for the Persian kingdom. The Elephantine community knew about the temple in Jerusalem, but it evidently did not regard it as the exclusive site of legitimate worship, cultivating its own altar, sacrifices, and priesthood. This cult was threatened in the way the Jerusalem Temple was, however, when the Egyptian priests of a nearby temple of the ram-god Khnum destroyed the Elephantine temple in 410 B.C.E. One of the Aramaic papyri found at the site records a petition from the Jewish leader Jedeniah and the priests of the temple of Yahu to the Persian governor Bagavahya, seeking his help in the reconstruction of this temple. At first the petitioners had appealed to the high priest Yohanan and a Jewish noble named Ostanes (probably in 407 B.C.E.) for help but had received no response. With this letter, they were turning to the Persian governor to intercede on their behalf: "May a letter from you be sent to them about the Temple in Elephantine of YHW the God to rebuild it in Elephantine."[22] The letter gives the governor two reasons to help them. First, it notes that the Temple had had Persian support in the past: Cambyses had implicitly endorsed their cult when he conquered Egypt, destroying all the temples of Egypt except theirs. Second, the governor had something personal to gain from helping them: in exchange for his intercession, the Jews would use their temple to reciprocate, interceding with their god on his behalf.

By such means, the Jews of Elephantine secured, or at least hoped to secure, cultic benefits not unlike those that Persian royalty conferred upon the Jewish community described by Ezra: the restoration of a destroyed temple in the face of hostile opposition. A similar exchange of religious capital for Persian patronage may lie somewhere behind the reconstruction of the Jerusalem Temple as depicted in Ezra. Because of interference from hostile neighbors, the rebuilding of the Temple as Ezra portrays the process proves to be a long and rocky process, suffering a delay from the time of Cyrus to the time of Darius some twenty years later. When the Jews finally resume construction, they do so without the express approval of Persian rule, and their efforts soon come under investigation by the governor Tattenai. In response to his inquiries, the Jews explain their actions in a speech forwarded to Darius by the governor in the form of an Aramaic letter cited by Ezra (5:6–17). The Jews here do not offer anything in return for Persia's assistance, making no promise to sacrifice or pray for the king, but Darius's response to the letter shows that he did expect such reciprocity:

> Whatever is needed—young bulls, rams or sheep for burnt offerings to the God of heaven, wheat, salt, wine or oil, as the priests in Jerusalem require—let that be given to them day by day without fail, so that they may offer pleasing sacrifices to the God of heaven, and pray for the life of the king and his children (Ezra 6:9–10)

Whether Ezra is an accurate account of the Temple's reconstruction or not, its author does seem to accurately understand what Persian rule required in return for its patronage—a public, ritualized acknowledgement from a cult dedicated to the welfare of the ruler and his successors. That Ezra reflects genuine practice is further corroborated by the *Cyrus Cylinder* where the king voices an expectation not unlike that of Darius: "May all the gods whom I have resettled in the sacred cities ask daily Bel (i.e., Marduk) and Nebo (his son) for a long life for me and may they recommend me."

Such expressions of gratitude and loyalty were of real value to a Persian empire that invested a tremendous amount of resources in gift-giving to maintain the loyalty and gratitude of its subjects (in Pierre Briant's terms, "the principle was simple: gifts were given by the king in return for services rendered").[23] Having subjects pray to their gods for the king's welfare was so important that, according to Herodotus, in Persian religion, worshippers were not allowed to pray for their own welfare, "but only for the king and for the general good of the community" (Hist. 1.132).[24] What the Elephantine letter allows us to glimpse, albeit at an administrative level lower than that of the king, is the kind of petitionary process Jews might use to initiate such a relationship. They need not wait for Persian largess, merely responding to what their rulers did as happens in Ezra, but could be proactive, sending letters of petition, making their case, tendering the gratitude and loyalty of their cult in advance.

A narrative like Ezra's may have had a role to play in facilitating such exchanges. The very elements in Ezra 1 that suggest its fictionality—emplotting Cyrus's rule within a story of divine restoration or modeling his return of the Jews on the Exodus—all represent ways of framing Persian rule within the framework of Jewish religious tradition. Other elements in the narrative resituate Jewish culture within the framework of Persian rule. This is a point that Ezra makes especially clear in chapters 4–6. There "the people of the land," non-Jewish residents of the land of Israel, are able to halt the Temple's construction by bribing officials and poisoning the king's perception of the Jews. When the Jews are finally able to resume construction, they are quickly interrupted again when the Persian governor Tattenai steps in to investigate. It is only when Darius finds a second decree of Cyrus in his archives, confirming that the Jews act with royal sanction, that they are able to finish the Temple. In the world as described by Ezra, there is no operating outside of Persian control: it can detect what the Jews do within its territory and has the power to obstruct their restorative efforts if so inclined.

Storytelling thus plays an important role in mediating between Jewish culture and foreign rule, keeping their perspectives and interests aligned. It plays this role *within* the narrative of Ezra in fact. What allows the Jews to overcome Persia's suspicions of it—the mistaken impression that the Jews were trying to build the Temple without its permission—is an act of narration, a report that their elders make to Tattenai, who then passes it on to Darius. As it happens, this narrative rehearses the very story with which Ezra 1 begins—Cyrus's edict and his return of the Temple vessels:

> We are the servants of the God of heaven and earth, and we are rebuilding the house that was built many years ago, which a great king of Israel built and finished . . . King Cyrus of Babylon, in the first year of his reign, made a decree that this house of God should be rebuilt. Moreover, the gold and silver vessels of the house of God, which Nebuchadnezzar had taken out of the temple in Jerusalem and had brought into the temple of Babylon, these Cyrus took out of the temple of Babylon, and they were delivered to a man named Sheshbezzar. He said to him, "Take these vessels; go and put them in the temple of Jerusalem, and let the house of Jerusalem be rebuilt on its site." Then this Sheshbezzar came and laid out the foundation of the house of God in Jerusalem . . . . (5:11–16)

The story as it appears here, transmitted through Tattenai to King Darius, is used to represent the Jews to Persian rule, reassuring the king that the Jewish temple was properly authorized (I speak now of the role of the story narrated within Ezra 6, not the role of Ezra 6 itself). The version in Ezra 1, recounted in Hebrew, is addressed internally, resembling the *Cyrus Cylinder* in its effort to legitimize Persian rule as a continuation of indigenous religious tradition. Despite their different functions and intended audiences, however, what the two tellings share in common is their use of this narrative to bridge the perspectives of Jews and their Persian rulers—to render the behavior of one in terms that the other would find consistent with its own aspirations.

Although the details of Ezra's description may or may not correspond to what really happened in history, its premise that Persia played an instrumental role in the restoration of the Temple cult is not implausible, especially when one calls to mind how the Elephantine community turned to Persian rule for help in its efforts to restore its temple. What I am suggesting here is that the narrative of Ezra itself played a role in sustaining this symbiotic relationship. For a Jew viewing reality as filtered through its account, Persian rule was what reconnected Jews with their cultic tradition, literally transferring to them the last physical vestiges of the Temple. It also had the potential to disrupt this tradition, to be recruited by enemies. The best way to survive in an environment conceptualized in this way was to cultivate an alliance with Persian rule, to enter into the economy of ritualized patronage and reciprocity that bound the Persian king and his subjects to one another in a relationship of mutual (if unexpressed) self-interest. Ezra's narrative helps sustain this relationship by fostering the perception of God and Persia as allies serving each other's interests.

If texts like Jeremiah and Ezra are any indication, foreign rule severely restricted the ability of Jews to sustain their religious tradition, sapping them of the physical power needed to defend it from violence and despoliation. Even so, they did have options—they could attempt a revolt or seek to recruit foreign rule as an ally by offering its loyalty in exchange for its cultic patronage. Narrative not only asserted the restorability of tradition; it could help Jews make the most of these opportunities. Hananiah's prophecy renders rebellion a feasible tactic by imagining a reality in which Babylonian rule is on the verge of ending. Ezra facilitates a symbiotic relationship with foreign rule by aligning it with Jewish tradition. In different ways, each narrative opens up opportunities within the "space of the other" by identifying sources of renewed mobility and empowerment, either imagining an outside to foreign rule, a space and time beyond its control, or turning foreign rule itself into a resource.

Readings of the Lost Ark

Although Ezra was eventually accepted into the biblical canon, Jews in later periods believed that it did not tell the whole story of the Temple's survival. Telling the rest of that story offered an opportunity to identify options beyond those presented in the Bible itself, articulating alternatives to both rebellion and submission. The rest of this chapter focuses on two of these narratives, each rehearsing yet another survival tactic.

Some time in the Hellenistic period, Jews began to notice that one cult object was missing from the list of Temple vessels returned in the days of Cyrus: the ark of the covenant. What happened to it is a matter of speculation to this day. It may have been taken by the Babylonians or even by some earlier conqueror—the Egyptian king Shishak, perhaps, who attacked Jerusalem in the time of Solomon's son Rehoboam, the tenth century B.C.E., and removed "the treasures of the house of the Lord" (1 Kings 14:25–26)—but the Bible itself never provides an answer, leaving later Jews to imagine its fate.[25] One instance of this appears in the preface to a work known as *2 Maccabees:*[26]

> It was also in the same document that the prophet (Jeremiah), having received an oracle, ordered that the tent and the ark should follow with him, and that he went up to the mountain where Moses had gone up and had seen the inheritance of God. Jeremiah came and found a cave dwelling, and he brought there the tent and the ark and the altar of incense; then he sealed up the entrance. Some of those who followed him came up intending to mark the way, but could not find it. When Jeremiah learned of it, he rebuked them and declared: "The place shall remain unknown until God gathers his people together again and shows his mercy. Then the Lord will disclose these things, and the glory of the Lord and the cloud will appear, as they were shown in the case of Moses (when he established the Tabernacle cult), and as Solomon asked that the place should be specially consecrated. (2:4–8)

We saw that Ezra's vision of cultic restoration is premised on submission to more powerful others; the community it describes loses custody over the Temple's contents when these are seized by Nebuchadnezzar, and the Jews are only able to save their cultic traditions by acknowledging the power of a foreign ruler. The hidden ark legend, in which the core of the Temple cult is hidden from the enemy, envisions Jewish ritual surviving without an intervening period of dislocation. In this version of things, Babylon never captures the ark, and it is a native, not a foreigner, who serves as the agent of restoration.

Here, as in later versions of the hidden ark story, supernatural ability is required to hide the ark. Jeremiah only knows to hide the vessels because he has received an oracle instructing him to do so, and God himself seems to intervene to prevent other people from finding its location. In a later form of the story, a version from the Roman period preserved in the apocalyptic text known as *Syriac Baruch*, an angel does the hiding:[27]

> He (an angel) descended into the Holy of Holies and . . . took from there the veil, the holy ephod, the mercy seat, the two tablets, the holy raiment of the priests, the altar of incense, the forty-eight precious stones with which the priests were clothed, and all the holy vessels of the Tabernacle. And he said to the earth with a loud voice, "Earth, earth, earth, hear the word of the mighty God, and receive the things which I commit to you and guard them until the last times so that you may restore them when you are ordered, so that strangers may not get possession of them. For the time has arrived when Jerusalem shall be delivered up for a time, until the moment that it will be said that it will be restored forever." And the earth opened its mouth and swallowed them up. (6:7–9)[28]

If Ezra falls somewhere between history and myth, the hidden ark story clearly falls into the latter category. In fact, a reading of the biblical text may have inspired the tradition. In the earliest extant form of the myth, Jeremiah is the one who hides the ark, a role perhaps suggested by Jeremiah 3:16: "In those days," says the Lord, "they shall no longer say 'the ark of the covenant of the Lord.' It shall not come to mind, or be remembered, or missed; nor shall another one be made." The

Hebrew of this passage can be read not as a prophecy but as a command to Jeremiah: "Let the ark not come to mind, or be remembered or sought out." This verse is not cited in *2 Maccabees*, but it may refer to it obliquely: "the prophet, *having received an oracle*, ordered that the tent and the ark should follow with him" (*2 Macc.* 2:4). The passage in Jeremiah seeks to reconcile its audience to life without the ark, to render it expendable and even replaceable. The author of the hidden ark story understands it very differently: the ark is not gone for good but hidden in a place from which it might one day be retrieved.

Even if built of legend and exegesis, however, the story's vision of cultural survival is not completely far-fetched, for concealment was employed by other ancient communities trying to save statues or temple treasures from the enemy. The priests of the famous temple of Delphi considered hiding its cult treasures when it came under attack from the Persians (*Hist.* 8.36), for instance. A similar tactic may have been employed in Syria-Palestine itself during the Late Bronze and Early Iron Ages. Archaeologists have uncovered statues buried in the ground at sites in Syria and Canaan from this period, perhaps hidden there by devotees hoping to conceal their gods from the enemy (though other explanations are possible).[29] This is not to suggest that the ark really was hidden from Babylon, only that the story of its concealment registers a practicable survival tactic, one that early Jewish imaginations could plausibly imagine being employed to save the ark.

In Chapter 5, we will see evidence that at least one Jew may have tried to put this tactic into practice after the destruction of the Second Temple in an effort to preserve some of its contents. Our focus here, however, is not the tactic itself, but the story of its employment and what that story did to enhance the prospects of cultural survival. The telling of such a story created yet another opening in reality, imagining it in a way that makes the hiding of the ark *a possibility.* Ezra, conceding control over the world to the Persians, does not leave any room for such a possibility; the moment that Persia suspects that the Jews might be building the Temple without its permission, it intervenes to stop the construction. In the hidden ark myth, a part of reality—the cave where Jeremiah hides the ark or the earth in which it is concealed by an angel—is outside, or underneath, the territory controlled by foreign rule, an unseen locale in which the core of the Temple cult can persist impervious to external surveillance and interference. It does not make much of a difference that this hidden core is a figment of Jewish imaginations, the ark permanently lost with the Temple's destruction if not at some earlier point. From the perspective of Jews who believe in this story, the Temple's contents survive, intact, inviolate, and potentially recoverable. In revealing their hiddenness (what is disclosed in these narratives is not the ark's whereabouts but only the act of its concealment), the hidden ark story establishes yet another option for cultural survival, saving the Temple by keeping the knowledge of its continued existence a secret until the end of foreign rule creates an opportunity to recover it.

Survival of the Wittiest

Ezra imagines the biblical cult surviving through collaboration with foreign rule. The legend of the hidden ark preserves it by hiding it from the enemy. Between these two tactical extremes, there were still other options that I want to illustrate by looking at one final narrative of cultic restoration, *1 Esdras.* Also probably written in the Hellenistic period, *1 Esdras* offers yet another account of how the Jews retrieved the Temple vessels, adapting material from the biblical sources 2 Chronicles and Ezra-Nehemiah, but adding some material of its own.[30] One of its additions to the canonical narrative purports to explain how the Persian king was persuaded to return the vessels, a narrative known as the story of the three guards (chapters 3–4). Like Ezra, *1 Esdras* assigns a central role to foreign rule as an agent of cultic restoration, but like the hidden ark legend, it also exposes something obscured behind Ezra's account—not the concealment of cult objects but the cunning initiative of a Jewish courtier.

The Jew in question is Zerubbabel, a figure mentioned briefly in Ezra as a Jewish leader in charge at the time when the Second Temple's foundations were laid. Identified as one of Darius's three bodyguards, the Zerubbabel of *1 Esdras* agrees to a contest with the other guards to see who can best answer the question "What is the strongest thing?" Darius himself is to judge the results. The first guard proposes the answer "wine is the strongest," supporting his case with various examples of wine's ability to overcome even the most powerful rulers (3:17–24). The second guard, perhaps hoping to flatter his royal audience, answers "the king," a figure able to command complete obedience (4:1–12). It is then that Zerubbabel speaks, curiously proposing two answers to the question. First, he identifies women as stronger even than the king: Men owe their lives to women and are ready to make fools of themselves because of them (13–32). Then, as if revising his answer, he identifies Truth as the strongest of all (33–40). Darius is so impressed with this second answer that he offers Zerubbabel whatever he wishes even beyond what he has already promised. Rather than asking for riches, Zerubbabel reminds the king of his vow to return the vessels and rebuild the Temple.

The story of the three bodyguards appears to have been adapted from some earlier folktale, and its integration into its present narrative setting is not seamless.[31] By placing the return of the vessels in the time of Darius, the editor contradicts the account in Ezra 1, paraphrased earlier in *1 Esdras*, where the vessels are returned in the time of Cyrus. The fact that Zerubbabel gives two answers—women and truth—is also puzzling, probably the result of the second answer having been added belatedly.[32] Why did Ezra's version of events not suffice as an explanation for the Temple's restoration?

The difference between *1 Esdras* and Ezra may reveal something about the motive for the interpolation. In Ezra, Jewish leaders do little more than serve as passive recipients for the king's generosity. In *1 Esdras*, by contrast, the Persian king plays a passive role—he is not even conscious as the story begins, having fallen asleep so deeply that the bodyguards are able to hide their answers under his pillow without waking him (3:3–12). What saves Jewish tradition in this version of things is not just the benevolence of Persian rule but also the "wisdom" of a Jewish courtier, his ability to discern how the world works. As *1 Esdras* portrays it, wisdom is willing to speak "truth" to power, literally, even to the point of angering the king. To demonstrate the power of women, for example, Zerubbabel confronts Darius with an image of himself humiliated by his concubine, surely a risky way to demonstrate his thesis:

> Is not the king great in his power? Do not all lands fear to touch him? Yet I have seen him with Apame, the king's concubine, the daughter of the illustrious Bartacus; she would sit at the king's right hand and take the crown from the king's head and put it on her own, and slap the king with her left hand. At this the king

> would gaze at her with mough agape. If she smiles, he laughs; if she loses her temper with him, he flatters her, so that she may be reconciled to him. (4:28–31).

The second speech in praise of truth also ventures some thinly veiled criticism by implying a contrast between truth and royal power: "With (truth) there is no partiality or preference, but it does what is righteous instead of anything that is unrighteous or wicked" (in implicit contrast to what kings typically do). Such statements lead Gruen to conclude that *1 Esdras* is poking fun at foreign rule, entertaining its Jewish audience with a story of how a Jew gets away with mocking the king.[33] This is a reading I embrace but would like to further nuance. Zerubbabel's "wisdom" allows him to mock the king but it also wins his favor in the end, just as the concubine, Apame, is able to both slap the king and dazzle him at the same time. In the world as *1 Esdras* imagines it, it is possible to act independently of foreign rule, even to make fun of it, but this does not preclude securing its favor. Wisdom allows the Jews to accomplish both at once.

A closer reading of Zerubbabel's answer confirms that it is doing more than one thing at once, mocking the king, but subtly flattering him as well. As the Greeks describe them, the Persians had a reputation as lovers of the truth.[34] In Xenophon's *Cyropedia*, for example, Cyrus warns another king to tell the truth and not to commit the offense that is hated more than any other by lying (3.1.9). The king's commitment to the truth, *arta* in Persian, may reflect how Persian kings actually represented themselves. In the famous Behistun Inscription, Darius himself advises his successors: "King, whoever you are, who may arise after me, guard yourself from great lies" (l. 55).[35] In this inscription, lying is the arch-vice—and a political one at that, Pierre Briant has observed, planting the seeds of rebellion against legitimate power.[36] In identifying the "Truth" as the strongest thing of all, then, Zerubabbel is doing more than simply telling the unvarnished truth; his answer also reaffirms the value system of foreign rule, its sense of how things should be. The content of Zerubbabel's speech may risk offending the king, but its very candor, its assumption that the king will tolerate painful truths about himself, is itself an implicit appeal to the king's self-image as a ruler aligned with the truth—as Zerubbabel describes it, the source of all enduring power.

Another trait essential to the Temple's recovery according to *1 Esdras* is what we might describe as Zerubbabel's opportunism. There is no hint in the narrative that Zerubbabel set out to restore the Temple; he is simply doing his job as the king's guard when he sees the chance to gain the king's favor, a contest held the day after a royal banquet. In the Persian court, as it is portrayed in other early Jewish texts, the royal banquet offers courtiers an opportunity for self-advancement, granting access to the king at a time when he is in a good mood. Esther's success in saving the Jewish people depends on her ability to make the most of such banquets and the generosity they inspire in the king (see Esther 5, 7). Public competitions are another such occasion, as when King Ahasuerus sponsors a beauty contest to find a wife for himself (Esther 2)—a chance to stand out from the crowd, outdo rivals, and show one's loyalty and utility to the king. Like Esther and Mordechai, Zerubbabel knows how to make the most of these occasions. His ambitions are different from that of his fellow guards—not to win gifts and status but to safeguard his traditions—but his behavior is otherwise typical of royal courtiers, at least as such figures were represented in early Jewish literature.

Like the hidden ark story, then, *1 Esdras* uses storytelling to identify an opportunity for cultural survival beyond what seems possible in Ezra. It does so, however, not by extending the imagination beyond the spatial-temporal limits of foreign rule but by interpolating foreign rule, inserting into it opportunities for initiative and independent action. As in Ezra, serving the king and sustaining tradition are utterly compatible in *1 Esdras*. Here, however, they are reconciled not through passive acquiescence to foreign rule, the passive acceptance of its patronage, but rather through the courtier's arts of flattery and manipulation, his ability to say what the king wants to hear while acting independently of his power at the same time.

While *1 Esdras* tells us nothing about the actual struggle for cultural persistence in the aftermath of the First Temple's destruction, it does reflect this struggle *as a later Jew imagined it*. The author's perception of palace life, probably conditioned by fictionalized stories of court Jews like Esther and Mordechai as much as by any real experience in a royal court, suggested options for restoring tradition beyond what was visible in the world as described in Ezra. *1 Esdras* does not actualize these options in any practical sense but the story it tells can be seen as a kind of a dry run—a mind running through a scenario, testing out its options for cultural survival. If the solution it comes up with seems more playful than serious, it is worth remembering the role of playfulness within the world described by *1 Esdras.* The playfulness of the king's concubine Apame, her flirtatiousness, makes her stronger than the king, enabling her to belittle the king without risking her position or life. Zerubbabel's playfulness—his ability to play games, play to his royal audience, and play it safe at the same time—gives him a similar control over his environment, allowing him to impress the king, to mock him, and to retrieve the Temple vessels all at once. Reading such a story opens up possibilities not evident from Ezra alone, if only by modeling how playfulness—mastering the rules of the game, mimicking and manipulating language, moving freely within prescribed limits—can work to sustain Jewish tradition under foreign rule.

Storytelling As a Way of Keeping One's Options Open

What evidence we have suggests that the cultic tradition of preexilic Judah only survived Babylonian conquest to the extent that later Jews imagined it surviving. Narratives like Ezra, the hidden ark story, and *1 Esdras* show us that imagination at work, if not reflecting reality, then reshaping it in ways that enhanced the Temple's chances of survival. The challenge of cultural survival in the Second Temple period was the challenge of operating in a world controlled by others. By means of narrative, Jews could maneuver in ways this world made difficult or even denied, facilitating alliance with foreign rule or rendering such alliance unnecessary by placing tradition beyond its reach. Storytelling did not act directly on the world, but it did help Jews to develop certain options and to keep them open, describing the world in ways that made it seem possible to shake off the yoke of foreign rule, or evade its notice, or manipulate the king's power to one's own advantage. Later chapters will explore efforts to employ these tactics in the real world, examining historical instances of cultic symbiosis, concealment or revolt. Part of what sustained these tactics as viable options, I am suggesting, was the kind of stories that Jews told about the destruction of the First Temple, stories that showed them working effectively in the imagined past.

We now face the challenge of moving beyond Jewish imaginations into the world in which they had to operate. It was not nearly as easy to reshape this world as it was to maneuver within the fictive realms generated through narrative. As it played out in history, the struggle for cultural survival required considerable flexibility, an ability to switch from one tactic to another. One particular moment in this struggle, the Maccabean war defending Jewish religious tradition against the Hellenistic ruler Antiochus IV, presents us with an opportunity to explore this shifting between tactics, what I call the art of the pivot, and the role of the imagination in making it possible.

~ 2

Maccabean Maneuvers

In the early 160s b.c.e., the Temple faced a threat so dire that some twenty-two centuries later its survival is still celebrated as a miracle on the holiday of Hanukkah. In 169 b.c.e., Antiochus IV, ruler of the Seleucid kingdom of which Palestine was then a part, attacked Jerusalem, massacred its inhabitants, and even dared enter the sanctuary itself, stripping it of all its sacred vessels and ornaments. In contrast to the Babylonian conquest of Jerusalem, however, this time there was more than just the Temple at stake. As Antiochus sought to compel the Jews to forsake their ancestral laws, Judaism as a distinct way of life came under threat of extinction. Antiochus ordered books of the law destroyed, and anyone found with a copy was to be executed (*1 Macc.* 1:56–57). The same penalty was imposed on those who practiced circumcision. In one horrifying case, two women who circumcised their children were paraded through the streets with their babies hanging from their necks and thrown from a wall (*1 Macc.* 1.60–61; *2 Macc.* 6:10). Antiochus did more than threaten the Temple, the sources claim; he sought to expunge *any* expression of Jewish tradition.

These same sources depict Jews responding to this threat in a number of ways. Some willingly adapt to the changes Antiochus imposed, abandoning their native practices: "many even from Israel gladly adopted his religion; they sacrificed to idols and profaned the Sabbath" (*1 Macc.* 1:43). Others try to escape the king by seeking out hiding places like the Judean wilderness (1:53; 2:29). According to *1 Maccabees*, neither tactic is viable. The Jews who abandon the law are described as doing evil in the land, while those who seek to hide are hunted down and slaughtered. (2:29–38). From its perspective, there is only one option left, the course taken by the heroes of *1 Maccabees*, the priest Mattathias and his sons the Maccabees. When a Seleucid officer orders them to offer a sacrifice as the king has commanded, Mattathias brazenly refuses:

> Even if all the nations that live under the rule of the king obey him, and have chosen to obey his commandments, everyone of them abandoning the religion of their ancestors, I and my sons will continue to live by the covenant of our ancestors. Far be it from us to desert the law and the ordinances. We will not obey the king's words by turning aside from our religion to the right hand or to the left. (19–22)

Just as he finishes this speech, another Jew steps forward to offer a sacrifice, a sight that so angers Mattathias that he slays both the Jew and the officer presiding over the sacrifice (23–24). This scene is clearly a strike against those who would align Jewish religious practice to the dictates of foreign rule. Mattathias and his sons run for the hills to escape arrest (28), but they come to reject this option as well when they learn about the slaughter of other Jews who tried to hide: "let us not all die as our kindred died in their hiding places" (2:41). By the end of its second chapter, *1 Maccabees* has shut down the very tactical possibilities articulated by Ezra and the hidden ark story—cooperation with foreign rule or taking refuge from it—and opened up another: rebellion.

Exemplifying the successful deployment of this tactic is Mattathias' third son: Judah the Maccabee. Beginning his campaign against the Seleucids with only a few hundred men, Judah is nonetheless able to score a number of unexpected victories, eventually reconquering Jerusalem and reconsecrating the Temple. *1–2 Maccabees* attribute these victories to divine intervention, with angels sometimes directly intervening in the battle, but they also suggest that Judah was a cunning guerrilla warrior, using ambush and other unconventional tactics to offset the superior military might of his Seleucid foes. He is so effective in this regard that the mere sight of him is enough to send the enemy into retreat (see *1 Macc.* 5:34).

As *1 Maccabees* continues its narrative, however, Judah and his brothers Jonathan and Simon also show a tactical flexibility. To offset the superior strength of the Seleucids, for example, they cultivate an alliance with other foreign powers, the Romans and the Spartans.[1] As *1 Maccabees* 8 explains, Judah turned to the former because of their military strength—among their victories was the defeat of Antiochus IV's predecessor Antiochus III in 189 B.C.E.—and also because they could be counted on to keep their commitments to those to whom they pledged friendship. More than friendship connected the Jews to the Spartans. In his overture to them, Jonathan cites evidence of a family connection, a letter sent to the high priest Onias I by the Spartan ruler Arius I which claims that the two peoples share an ancestor in Abraham—probably an "invented tradition" fabricated by Jews to facilitate an alliance with the Spartans.[2] The Maccabees, such evidence suggests, were able to shift quickly from warfare to diplomacy when it served their interests. To do so, they apparently recruited the help of experienced diplomats, such as Eupolemus, descended from a man who had himself been an emissary to Antiochus III (*1 Macc.* 8:17; cf. *2 Macc.* 4:11).

The Maccabees were even prepared to reach out to their archenemy, the Seleucid kingdom. When the Seleucid ruler Antiochus III had conquered Palestine in 200 B.C.E., he quickly established a cordial relationship with the Jews, offering to subsidize the Temple cult and declaring it unlawful for foreigners to enter the part of Temple from which they were forbidden (*Ant.* 12.138–46).[3] Both *1* and *2 Maccabees* attest to an effort to revive this relationship during the Maccabean period, citing various documents that, if authentic, testify to ongoing negotiations between the Seleucids and the Maccabees.[4] *1 Maccabees* cites a letter from Demetrius I, a pretender to the Seleucid throne, promising to declare Jerusalem "holy and free from tax" and to subsidize the rebuilding of the Temple in exchange for the allegiance of Jonathan and the Jews (*1 Macc.* 10:31). *2 Maccabees* 11 records three conciliatory letters from the Seleucids—including one that may have come from Antiochus IV himself—allowing the Jews to practice their customs (27–33). The Maccabees' reputation as warriors notwithstanding, the polite letters recorded in the sources suggest an elite keeping the diplomatic channels open.[5]

The Maccabees' openness to diplomacy afforded them the opportunity to partake in a new form of foreign protection that emerged in this period. In Greek thought, a temple, or any object or person in contact with it, was considered to be under the protection of the god, a status referred to as "sacred and inviolable."[6] Sometime in the second century B.C.E., the Seleucid kingdom established itself as the ultimate arbiter of inviolability in Syria-Palestine, granting this status to various cities and temples. The king was bound by custom to respect the inviolability of sacred places, but it was he who determined which places were sacred in the first place, formally expressing his acknowledgement in royal edicts or memoranda.[7] A city or temple that secured such a decree would proudly declare its inviolability in coinage and inscriptions, evidence which suggests that this status did not exist in Syria-Palestine prior to 145 B.C.E. but spread quickly after that in the period between the 140s and the 70s. The first city in the area that laid claim to the title of "sacred and inviolable" was Tyre, in 141/140 B.C.E., followed in succeeding decades by Sidon, Beirut, Antioch, Baetocaece, Damascus, Byblos, Ashkalon, Gaza, Sepphoris, and other cities.[8]

What exactly the recognition of a city's inviolability signified is unclear. Some scholars read it as a concrete promise of military protection from warfare and theft, but others, noting that in reality such grants did not offer much real protection, counter that they were probably more honorific than real, a marker of status and dignity.[9] Whatever its effect, the rise of the inviolability grant in the late second and early first centuries C.E. brought with it a new threat to the Temple but new opportunities as well. It rendered the Jerusalem Temple even more vulnerable than it was before—in the absence of official recognition, there was no reason (from a Seleucid perspective) not to violate its sanctity—but it also represented a way to sustain that sanctity. If Jews could persuade the king to recognize the Temple's inviolability, *his* authority would protect it from sacrilege.

2 Maccabees registers the impact of Hellenistic inviolability, employing the term "sacred and inviolable" at one point (*2 Macc.* 3:12), but it imagines the Jews protecting the Temple's inviolability without Seleucid consent. The high priest Onias employs the formula when petitioning the Seleucid official Heliodorus not to plunder the Temple, hoping to persuade him to respect its sanctity, but the official ignores him, proceeding to attack. It is at this moment that God himself intervenes, sending an angelic horseman accompanied by two glorious young men, to flog Heliodorus until he falls prostrate. Later, when Antiochus IV violates the Temple, God intervenes again, sending the Maccabees to restore its purity. The stress that both *1* and *2 Maccabees* place on protecting the sanctity of Jerusalem and its temple reflects the emerging importance of inviolability in Seleucid Syria-Palestine as a marker of civic status, but both texts maintain that the Maccabees achieved that status independently of Seleucid rule, relying on God's power, not that of the Seleucid king, to protect the Temple's sanctity.

If the royal documents cited in *1–2 Maccabees* are any indication, however, the Maccabees did not completely forgo the option of negotiating with the Seleucids, if not winning a full-fledged inviolability grant, then achieving something comparable. The letter that Demetrius I sends to the Jews bears a particularly close resemblance to Seleucid inviolability decrees, including among the privileges it grants a promise to declare Jerusalem "holy and free from tax" (*1 Macc.* 10:31). This is not quite the formula "sacred and inviolable," but it was close enough for Josephus to have rendered it in this way in his paraphrase of the letter in Ant. 13.51 (in fact, being declared "free" or "autonomous" was an even greater privilege than being declared "sacred and inviolable").[10] As it happens, Jonathan and his followers reject the offer, but only because they mistrust Demetrius, not because they are disinterested in what he has to offer. Also similar to an inviolability decree is the letter sent to Simon by Antiochus VII that grants "freedom to Jerusalem and its sanctuary" (15:1–9), and this time Simon seems to accept it, sending two thousand troops and a large amount of military equipment to support the king in a military campaign (15:26).

If Demetrius had in fact offered to declare Jerusalem sacred and inviolable (doing so in 151 B.C.E. if our understanding of the chronology of this period is correct), and had the Jews accepted, the city would have been the first in all Syria-Palestine to achieve this status, beating out greater cities like Tyre, declared sacred and inviolable in the late 140s. That is hard to believe. The testimony of Hasmonean coins, or rather their silence, deepen one's suspicions, for they fail to identify Jerusalem or its temple as "sacred and inviolable" as one might expect.[11] On other grounds, some scholars have concluded that the royal documents in *1 Maccabees* are later fictions composed in the late second century B.C.E. when *1* and *2 Maccabees* are believed to have been composed and when inviolability was already in vogue.[12] Even if these letters are forged, however, it is telling that Jews felt moved to reproduce them, suggesting that they felt the same impulse that led so many cities to mint coins and post inscriptions boasting the status of "sacred and inviolable"—a desire to demonstrate, with written documentation, that the sanctity of one's city and temple had been recognized by Seleucid rule.

It is not hard to understand why the Maccabees might be open to allying themselves with the Seleucid kingdom. Going to war against it was highly risky because of its superior size and resources, an anxiety registered by *1 Maccabees* even as it describes the heroics of the Maccabees (*1 Macc.* 3:17). Indeed, it is worth remembering that Judah dies in the act of challenging it in battle. What is harder to understand is why the Maccabees do not stick to this tactic, why they so often revert to confrontation and violence. The sacrileges of Antiochus IV obviously soured relations, but it was not the only factor. Part of the problem may have been the Seleucid's reputation for treachery. Seleucid rule as portrayed in *1 Maccabees* is extremely duplicitous, using diplomatic overtures to trick the Jews or simply reversing itself later on (1:30; 6:55–62; 7:8–18, 26–30; 11:53; 12:39–48; 13:12–19; 15:26–27). To the extent that Jews shared *1 Maccabees*' suspicions, any alliance with Seleucid rule would appear highly unreliable. Many Jews might also have had religious reasons for resisting an alliance. During the reign of John Hyrcanus, son of Simon, Antiochus VII offered a truce on the condition that the Jews lay down their arms, pay compensation for cities taken from the Seleucids, and allow a garrison in Jerusalem (Ant. 13.245–48). The Jews accepted the first two conditions, but the third was unacceptable to them because it threatened the boundary between Jews and Gentiles. Jewish religious scruples did not make an alliance with the Seleucids impossible, but this episode suggests that they did restrict the room for diplomatic maneuvering, taking certain concessions off the table if they appeared to threaten traditions to which Jews were committed.

Moreover, for the Maccabees and their successors (known as the Hasmoneans), the advantages of a Seleucid alliance would always have to be balanced against the risk of appearing to betray the very foundation of their rule, their reputation as zealous warriors who saved Jewish tradition by going to war against Seleucid rule. The Hasmonean line was in fact always struggling to maintain its legitimacy, its authority among Jews having been generated by what Max Weber would have described as their charisma, the extraordinary power bestowed on them by God and their own heroics during the Maccabean Revolt.[13] That legitimacy seems to have grown especially fragile after Simon, the last in the line to be directly involved in the revolt. From the reign of Hyrcanus on, the Hasmoneans faced mounting opposition from Jews who protested their religious authority, and who sometimes defected to competing charismatic movements like the Pharisees and the Qumran sect.[14] While the Hasmoneans laid claim to traditional authority as well, assuming the role of high priest, that claim was questionable because the Hasmoneans did not inherit this office in a traditional way, usurping it from the family through whom this office had been transmitted prior to the revolt. Their claim to power ultimately depended on their role in that revolt, and its memory, inextricably interwoven with the memory of what the Seleucids had done to harm the Jews and their traditions, presumably made it difficult for them to justify an alliance with them.

On the other hand, the Hasmoneans were not exempt from the political and military pressures that induced so many other elites in the region to ally with Seleucid rule. The challenge of political survival under these circumstances was not unlike that facing certain contemporary Middle Eastern rulers who depend on America's support but jeopardize the support of their subjects if they get too close to the Great Satan. Similarly pulled in different directions, having much at stake in cultivating an alliance with Seleucid rule but constrained by the demands of Jewish religious tradition and their own image as defenders of that tradition, the Hasmoneans could not simply choose between the tactics of rebellion or submission; *they had to be ready to pivot between them.*

A possible reflection of the Hasmoneans trying to play both roles at once has been preserved in the form of coins minted under rulers like Hyrcanus. On one side appear symbols suggesting their abiding commitment to Jewish tradition—a pomegranate with its connection to the high priesthood, and the use of paleo-Hebrew, evocative of Israel's ancient past. Turn the coin around, however, and one finds symbols that mirror those of the Seleucid monarch, anchors for instance, suggesting an elite wishing to identify with or be associated with the Seleucids.[15] The Hasmoneans seem capable of flipping roles just like the coins, at one moment playing the role of pious traditionalist, the next, aligning with Hellenistic rule. They did so, I am suggesting, as a matter of survival. Their own legitimacy among fellow Jews depended on their willingness to resist and fight Seleucid rule, but there were also powerful pressures pushing them into an alliance with it. To persist under these circumstances required an ability to shape-shift, to switch abruptly from one role to the other.

It is not a coincidence, I believe, that narratives written (or at least thought to have been written) in this period ascribe a similar flexibility to heroes able to move successfully from the role of zealous warrior to that of loyal vassal—or vice versa—while remaining true to the defense of tradition. In turning to these stories now, I am interested in them as models not of particular survival tactics but in what they tell us about the art of the pivot, how a Jew might switch from warfare to détente without compromising his or her identity as a zealous warrior or forgoing the option of reverting back to violence if necessary.

Recruiting the Enemy

Hyrcanus's dealings with Antiochus VII suggest that a Maccabean/Hasmonean would embrace Seleucid rule provided that the latter respected Jewish tradition. This Antiochus VII proved willing to do, establishing a truce with the Jews that allowed them to celebrate the festival of Tabernacles and sending a magnificent sacrifice to the Temple (*Ant.* 13.242–43). Antiochus later confirmed his piety when, joined by Hyrcanus in his invasion of Parthia, he stopped for two days so that the latter could observe a festival (*Ant.* 13.251–2). Alliance with the enemy was apparently palatable for a Hasmonean so long as the Seleucids worked within the framework of Jewish religious tradition, confining any demands for support within the constraints of Jewish custom.

Threatening this tactic was the kind of suspicion of Seleucid rule evinced in *1 Maccabees* where the Seleucids often approach the Jews with friendly offers of support only to change their minds later on. In this account, Antiochus VII himself breaks the agreements he established with Hyrcanus's father Simon (15:26–27). Why should Jews not regard his conciliatory behavior in Hyrcanus's day as another ruse, a pose temporarily adopted to lower the Jews' guard? *2 Maccabees* suggests how storytelling may work to mitigate these suspicions. As it happens, its author may have actually been a diplomat. The present form of *2 Maccabees* is an abridgement of a five-volume work attributed to a Jason of Cyrene, who has been identified with the Jason sent as an emissary to Rome (*1 Macc.* 8:17).[16] Whether there is anything to that connection, the story that *2 Maccabees* tells can be read as an attempt to rehabilitate diplomacy as a credible alternative to combat, something to which a Maccabee could resort without compromising either Jewish tradition or his reputation as a zealous warrior.

How it does this comes into focus when *2 Maccabees* is contrasted with *1 Maccabees.*[17] In the latter work, Seleucid rule is a threat from its very inception. Its founder, Alexander the Great, grows arrogant after his conquests, an example emulated by his successors and most especially Antiochus IV. *2 Maccabees* presents Antiochus's persecution against a different backdrop. The first sacrilege that it reports, Heliodorus's attempted temple robbery, disrupts a status quo of Seleucid respect for Jewish custom: "the kings themselves honored the place and glorified the temple with the finest presents, even to the extent that King Seleucus of Asia (predecessor of Antiochus IV) defrayed from his own revenues all the expenses connected with the service of the sacrifices" (*2 Macc.* 3:1–3). Heliodorus's sacrilege thus appears as a marked disruption of the normal relations between the Jews and their rulers, and that relationship is restored after God beats the offender into submission—an experience that does more than deter Heliodorus but converts him into a supporter of the Temple (3: 35–40).

A similar contrast involves the Seleucid general Nicanor, an arch-villain in both *1 Maccabees* and *2 Maccabees* who threatens to destroy the Temple. While the two accounts agree in many details, *2 Maccabees*' portrait of Nicanor is far more sympathetic. In *1 Maccabees*, Nicanor is yet another blasphemous Seleucid official defeated by the Maccabees, a portrait consistent with *1 Maccabees*' overall depiction of non-Jews as ineluctably hostile to the Jews.[18] When the general establishes a cease-fire with Judah, he does so with characteristic treachery, secretly intending to violate it all along (*1 Macc.* 7:26–30). In *2 Maccabees*, though Judah suspects treachery, the narrative goes on to establish Nicanor as honorable. He becomes Judah's friend, and even advises him to get married and settle down (*2 Macc.* 14:22–25). When he does turn against Judah, it is because he has been compelled to by the king, and he does so with regret, "grieved that he had to annul their agreement when the man had done no wrong" (26–28). In the end, Nicanor proves an enemy, and his defeat is celebrated as a great victory to be commemorated on the day before the festival celebrating Mordechai (see *2 Macc.* 15:36). Still, the Nicanor of *2 Maccabees* is partially rehabilitated, displaying qualities that might have made him a lasting friend had circumstances allowed it.

Even Antiochus himself is not completely evil in *2 Maccabees*' account of things. In *1 Maccabees*, Antiochus, stunned by the Maccabean victory, comes to realize that he is being punished for his sins against the Jews. In *2 Maccabees*, Antiochus undergoes a similar change after God afflicts him with pain, but he goes much further in restoring the damage he has done, vowing to liberate Jerusalem, adorn its temple, and even become a Jew himself:

> Then the abominable fellow made a vow to the Lord, who would no longer have mercy on him, stating that the holy city, which he was hurrying to level to the ground and to make a cemetery, he was now declaring to be free . . . and the holy sanctuary, which he had formerly plundered, he would adorn with the finest offerings; and all the holy vessels he would give back, many times over; and the expenses incurred for the sacrifices he would provide with his own revenues; and in addition to all this he also would become a Jew and would visit every inhabited place to proclaim the power of God. (9:13–14, 16–17)

Doron Mendels has argued that Antiochus's illness and repentance as portrayed here reflect an established literary tradition, educing as a precedent a story about the impious Babylonian king Nabonidus partially preserved in an Aramaic text from Qumran now known as "The Prayer of Nabonidus."[19] *2 Maccabees*, in drawing on this topos, adds an ironic twist to Antiochus's end—the king who had inflicted so much suffering on the Jews to force them to disavow their religion is not only tortured himself but dies vowing to become a Jew—but it does more than simply register the divine comeuppance of the king. Going beyond anything in the parallel account of Antiochus' death in *1 Maccabees* 6, *2 Maccabees* puts the king on record as giving his support to the Temple cult, assimilating his character to a pattern manifest in its portraits of Heliodorus, Nicanor, and other Seleucids. In reality as

2 Maccabees depicts it, even the most arrogant of Seleucid kings is capable of showing respect to the Temple cult.

One one level, such portraits seek to reverse the power imbalance with Seleucid rule, asserting the power of God: "It is right to be subject to God," Antiochus admits, "mortals should not think that they are the equal to God" (*2 Macc.* 9:12). At another level, however, they also acknowledge the importance of securing Seleucid recognition; indeed, it seems important to the author of *2 Maccabees* to get Seleucid rule on record *declaring* its respect in a public way. Thus, after his flogging, Heliodorus is said to "bear testimony to all concerning the deeds of the supreme God, which he had seen with his own eyes" (3:36); a defeated Nicanor runs away to Antiochus where he "proclaimed that the Jews had a Defender" (8:36), and a chastened Antiochus IV resolves to "visit every inhabited place to proclaim the power of God" (9:17). Each of these characters is moved by his experience of God's power to tell others of that power and to discourage them from attacking the Jews. A happy ending for *2 Maccabees* is not the end of Seleucid rule but a kingdom ready to recognize the Temple's sanctity.

This is a very different image of Seleucid rule than the one constructed in *1 Maccabees*. The kingdom it describes occasionally seeks a settlement with the Jews, even offering to support the Temple as we have noted, but it almost invariably reverses itself, breaking its treaties or abandoning them when a new king comes to power. Thus, Antiochus V "broke the oath that he swore" to the Jews (*1 Macc.* 6:62); Nicanor's offer of peace is treacherous (7:27; 30); King Demetrius "broke his word about all that had been promised; he became estranged from Jonathan" (11:53); and Antiochus VII "broke all the agreements he formerly had made with Simon" (15:27). The only remaining option left under these circumstances is to operate outside the realm of Seleucid power. In the Seleucid kingdom that *2 Maccabees* describes, by contrast, détente is a viable option. Prior to Heliodorus, Seleucid kings had respected the Temple's sanctity, and Judah remains open to such a relationship, rebelling when necessary but switching to a diplomatic track when Seleucid rule makes the requisite overtures (11:15; 14:25). Without compromising his zeal, *2 Maccabees* reshapes him into a model of flexibility, a hero prepared to fight for the law but also willing to lay down his arms when the enemy shows respect for his tradition.

As paradoxical as it may seem, in fact, *2 Maccabees* presents the Maccabean revolt as an effort to preserve the option of détente. In its description of Antiochus' pillage of the Temple, it notes an offense not mentioned by *1 Maccabees:* the king swept aside "the votive offerings that other kings had made to enhance the glory and honor of the place" (*2 Macc.* 5:16). Antiochus's plunder of the Temple, this detail suggests, is not just an assault against its sanctity; it also disrupts the Temple's role as a medium of peaceful exchange between the Seleucids and the Jews through which the former showed their respect for Jewish tradition. In restoring the Temple, therefore, Judah also restores the possibility of peaceful coexistence. Much of the violence in *2 Maccabees* has a similar effect, softening the hostility of the Seleucids, garnering their admiration and respect, laying the groundwork for improved relations. Thus, God's flogging turns Heliodorus around to warn the king against defiling the Temple; God's blows against Antiochus IV compel him to repent of his offenses against the Jews; and after his defeat by Judah, the general Lysias "realized that the Hebrews were invincible because the mighty God fought on their side, so he sent to them and persuaded them to settle everything on just terms" (11:13–14). Violence in these episodes is not the opposite of détente; it restores it as an option by teaching Seleucid rule to respect Jewish tradition.

We know too little about when *2 Maccabees* was written to pinpoint its composition on the zig-zagging trajectory of Hasmonean-Seleucid relations.[20] *2 Maccabees* may help us to understand what made this zig-zagging possible, however. The leeway of a Hasmonean ruler like John Hyrcanus to terminate his war with the Seleucids and to become an ally was constrained by the apparent contradictions between vassalage and Jewish tradition. To accept a Seleucid garrison in Jerusalem for example—one of the terms required of Hyrcanus by Antiochus VII—was unacceptable to Jews precisely because it threatened a religious boundary that the Maccabees had risked their lives to defend. The story that *2 Maccabees* tells mitigates the appearance of contradiction. To befriend Seleucid rule is not to abandon the Maccabean cause, it implies, but to return to the peaceful relationship that had once been the norm.

As *2 Maccabees* depicts things, effecting this kind of change in Seleucid policy depends on supernatural intervention, a deity willing to make his power manifest. That may seem unrealistic, but what we know about Seleucid rule from other sources indicates a willingness to acknowledge such power, and to respect and support the religious claims of its subjects. In Hellenized contexts, this meant respecting the sacred inviolability of temples; in Babylon, the Seleucid king was prepared to act piously according to that tradition's religious norms.[21] With some notable exceptions, the Seleucids maintained the same policy in its relationship with the Jews, offering support and protection for their Temple from the moment Judea was conquered by Antiochus III. The continuation of this relationship was made difficult for Jews by what happened under Antiochus IV, but the memory of this experience was malleable, and it could be shaped in ways that either discredited or revived the possibility of détente. *1 Maccabees* diminishes this possibility by emphasizing the Seleucids as inflexibly hostile and treacherous. In contrast, *2 Maccabees* opens it up by imagining a Seleucid rule capable of pious self-restraint and genuine repentance. If rulers like Hyrcanus felt they could abandon warfare in favor of an alliance with Seleucid rule without appearing to stray from the cause of the Maccabean Revolt, it was perhaps because narratives like *2 Maccabees* had helped to legitimized such a switch, asserting a religiously elastic Seleucid kingdom and a tactically flexible Judah the Maccabee who, though sometimes at dangerous odds with one another as in the days of Antiochus IV, could each pivot toward a more conciliatory relationship.

Double-Agency

If Josephus's account is to be believed, John Hyrcanus would make yet another about-face in his relationship with Seleucid rule, seizing on a period of weakness to revert from his friendship with the Seleucid king back to revolt. The switch happened at the death of Antiochus VII, slain during his invasion of Parthia, when Hyrcanus realized that the cities of Syria were undefended, and when the new Seleucid king was distracted by a struggle for control over the throne. The power vacuum in Syria-Palestine allowed Hyrcanus to initiate a military campaign that resembled that of his Maccabean ancestors in its effort to drive the Gentile presence from the land of Israel. Especially redolent of the Maccabees was Hyrcanus's destruction of the Samaritan temple at Gerizim and the forced circumcision of the Idumeans, a neighboring Gentile people (Ant. 13.256–258)—acts that emulated the violence of Mattathias, Judah's father, as he fought to reclaim the land of Israel: "Mattathias and his friends went around and tore down the altars; they forcibly circumcised all the uncircumcised boys that they found within the borders of Israel" (*1 Macc.* 2:45–46). Hyrcanus' alliance with the Seleucids lasted only as long as he had reason to fear them. At the moment that Seleucid power recedes, he embraces the role of a Maccabean warrior.

Even so, there are signs that the Hasmoneans' dealings with the Seleucids had had a lasting effect on their reputation, discrediting them in ways that surface indirectly, in rumors about their background. According to a story that Josephus relates in Ant. 13.288–92, the sect known as the Pharisees was especially hostile to Hyrcanus. During a banquet, a quarrelsome Pharisee named Eleazar told Hyrcanus that he should give up the priesthood. When Hyrcanus asked him why, he replied "Because we have heard from our elders that your mother was a captive in the reign of Antiochus Epiphanes." The story struck at the very core of Hasmonean legitimacy, calling into question their claim to the high priesthood (according to Lev. 21:14, a priest who descends from a defiled woman is considered profaned) and their reputation as valiant warriors who had been able to defeat Antiochus IV. The story was false according to Josephus—in his description in J. W. 1.57–60, Hyrcanus's mother remains true to the Maccabees' legacy of heroic defiance, bravely enduring death rather than betray herself and her son.[22] True or not, however, the other story about Hyrcanus's mother persisted, dogging the Hasmoneans into the reign of Hyrcanus's successor Alexander Janneus where it moved a crowd to denounce him during the festival of Tabernacles (Ant. 13.372). Reflected in this story is a counterimage of the Hasmoneans that undercuts the image of defiant warrior that Hyrcanus was asserting at the time, one that exposes something compromised in the Hasmonean's background, a lingering residue of humiliation and defilement at the hands of the Seleucids.

How did the Hasmoneans ally themselves with the Seleucids without appearing to substantiate those suspicions? How did they manage the behaviors required of vassals—submitting to foreign rule, acting the part of loyal friend, serving its interests—without eroding their reputation as zealous warriors? We cannot answer these questions directly; but we can point to evidence that they were engaged during the Hasmonean period itself, in a Jewish story about a zealous warrior who defends the Temple by playing the role of a war captive.

The book of *Judith* tells the story of how the Temple was saved from destruction through the exploits of a widow named Judith. Angry that the peoples of Cilicia, Damascus, and Syria, including Jerusalem, have refused to submit, Nebuchadnezzar (here an Assyrian king) vows revenge, sending his general Holofernes to force them to surrender, and one by one, they do. Hearing of these events, the Israelites place their trust in God, preparing to defend themselves, but after a prolonged siege, with their supplies running out and no possibility of escape, their faith begins to waver and they implore their leaders to surrender too: "It would be better for us to be captured by them. We shall indeed become slaves, but our lives will be spared" (*Jth.* 7:27–28).

It is at this moment that the title character appears, the beautiful and pious widow of an Israelite named Manasseh. She urges her people to refuse to surrender, arguing that it will not save them in the end: "our slavery will not bring us into favor (neither with God nor with the slave-owner), but the Lord our God will turn it into dishonor" (8:23). The high priest asks her to pray for them, but Judith promises something better—deliverance from the enemy. Removing her widow's garments, she bathes, perfumes herself, and puts on festival attire, tiara, and jewelry "to entice the eyes of all the men who might see her" (*Jth.* 10:4). Making her way to the enemy's camp, she gains entrance by posing as a fugitive who has come with intelligence that will help the Assyrians defeat the Israelites. Holofernes is intrigued by that intelligence but is entranced by Judith's beauty—so much so that a few days later, he invites her into his tent to seduce her. Before he can do so, however, he gets drunk and falls asleep—the moment that Judith has been waiting for. Springing into action, she takes the sword hanging from Holofernes' bedpost and cuts off his head. By this point in the story, Judith has already established a custom of leaving the Assyrian camp, ostensibly to appeal to God for help in defeating her countrymen (*Jth* 11:17; 12:6–7). This gives her the opening she needs to make her escape, and she returns to her people with Holofernes' head hidden in a bag. Meanwhile, in the enemy's camp, the Assyrians discover their general's headless body, a sight that panics them into fleeing. And so the Israelites are delivered, just as Judith promised.

Although *Judith* is set during the reign of Nebuchadnezzar, many scholars believe it was written, or at least revised, in the Maccabean/Hasmonean period because its plotline shares so many elements in common with the Maccabean Revolt (parallels so pronounced that some medieval retellings of the story identify Judith as a sister of the Maccabees).[23] Nebuchadnezzar's threat against the Temple and demand that he be worshipped as a god (*Jth.* 3:8) resemble the sacrileges of Antiochus IV; Judith's name bears a striking resemblance to Judah; and her defeat of Holofernes seems partially modeled on Judah's defeat of the Seleucid general Nicanor (both are beheaded, for example). This does not mean that *Judith* was written during the Maccabean Revolt; it might come from a later period of Hasmonean rule. That the story is set in Samaritan territory, under Jewish control only during Hyrcanus' reign (Ant. 13.275–83), suggests that *Judith* was composed at this time.[24] The conversion of the Ammonite Achior at the end of the story—he is so impressed by Judith's victory that he agrees to be circumcised—recalls Hyrcanus' campaign to circumcise Gentiles living on Judea's periphery. While it is not possible to prove a Hasmonean provenance for *Judith*, there is enough evidence to justify trying to read it in this historical context.

When appreciated as a product of the Hasmonean age, *Judith*'s engagement with the problem of how to switch from one tactic to another comes into sharp relief. Its narrative suggests that the shift from rebellion to détente need not be the inconsistent about-face that it appears to be. Rather, a posture of vassalage can function as a maneuver, a ruse, in a covert struggle against the enemy. Until the moment that she cuts off Holofernes's head, Judith appears to play the role of a loyal slave. She speaks with the requisite self-abasement and servility, bowing to Holofernes when she first sees him and referring to herself as his slave (e.g., *Jth.* 11:5 "Accept the words of your slave, and let your servant speak"). She strokes his ego: "We have heard of your wisdom and skill, and it is reported throughout the whole world that you alone are the best in the whole kingdom, the most informed, and the most astounding in military strategy" (11:8). She offers to help him, promising to provide intelligence that will insure the Israelites' defeat (11:17–18). And she makes herself extremely enticing to him, acting happy to accommodate his desires: "Who am I to refuse my Lord? Whatever pleases him I will do, and it will be a joy to me until the day of my death" (12:14). Judith's performance is so convincing that to the enemy, she appears "like one of the Assyrian women who serve in the palace of Nebuchadnezzar" (12:13), but it is all a trick. Judith's real intent, as she reveals in a prayer before setting off on her mission, is to "bring wound and bruise on those who have planned cruel things against your covenant" (9:13).

To accomplish her mission, Judith acts as a double agent, appearing to serve one master while really serving another. Even as she professes loyalty to the enemy, Judith's nods and winks to her Jewish audience reassure her readers that she remains loyal to their cause. So long as she is in Holofernes's camp, her very speech is double-dealing, communicating one message to the Assyrians and another to Jews listening in, as in the following two statements, each ambiguous enough to be read as an expression of fealty either to Holofernes or to God:[25]

> If you follow out the words of your servant, God will accomplish something through you, and my lord will not fail to achieve his purposes (*Jth.* 11:6)

> Who am I to refuse my Lord? Whatever pleases him I will do at once, and it will be a joy to me until the day of my death (12:14)

In the first statement, Judith sounds like she is promising success to Holofernes—and that is how he interprets her—but the reader who knows Judith is being deceitful detects another meaning: if Holofernes believes her, God will indeed accomplish something through him, not the victory for which he hopes but the destruction of his army. In the second, Judith seems to yield to the general while secretly affirming her commitment to God. One cannot prove that this second, covert significance is really there—certainly the Assyrians do not pick up on it—but the carefully sustained ambiguity of Judith's speech allows her to insinuate its presence without blowing her cover. It is precisely this ambiguity, the ability to pivot between meanings without being pinned down to one or the other, that allows Judith to curry favor with Holofernes and to play the role of a compliant servant without betraying her allegiance to God and Jewish tradition.

Like the hidden ark legend and *1 Esdras*, *Judith* cannot serve as a historical source for the struggle for Jewish cultural survival. Its author may have believed his story really happened, but in telling it, he draws on conventional motifs and plot elements found in earlier stories of guileful women. Recently, it has been suggested that *Judith* was modeled on a story set against the backdrop of Alexander the Great's defeat of the Sogdian noble Spitamenes.[26] What made it possible for Alexander to defeat Spitamenes according to this story (known in two versions: one in the *History of Alexander* by Quintus Curtius Rufus, the other in the *Metz Epitome*) was Spitamenes's beautiful wife who, when the general got drunk at a banquet, seized on the opportunity to behead him, and then escaped to Alexander's camp. *Judith* emulates biblical models as well, most famously the story of Jael and Sisera in Judges 4–5 where a heroine welcomes an enemy general into her tent, only to drive a peg through his head.[27] The female characters in these stories—deceitful seductresses who use the promise of sex to lure foolish men to their destruction—embody a stock image found in both Greek and biblical literature, drawn in works like the Book of Proverbs to illustrate the danger of being misled by one's sexual desires: "With much seductive speech she persuades him; with her smooth talk she compels him. Right away he follows her and goes like an ox to the slaughter" (Prov 7:21–22). *Judith* works hard to distinguish its heroine from such figures, stressing her piety and sexual control, but her literary pedigree is recognizable nonetheless. The resemblance is so close that in medieval versions of the story, Judith returns from her mission only to have the guards mistake her for a prostitute.[28]

That *Judith* has fictional prototypes does not preclude its potential as a model for Jewish cultural survival in the Hasmonean period, however. As a woman (and as a fictional character), Judith could maneuver in ways that John Hyrcanus could not, but there is evidence hinting at a similar duplicity in the latter's actual dealings with Seleucid rule. Brought before Holofernes, Judith insists on keeping her ancestral customs, asking permission to leave the camp each day in order to pray. At work in this request is the same kind of duplicity reflected in Judith's use of doublespeak—an ability to disguise a subversive act as something less threatening—for she has another motive for wishing to pray every day that becomes clear only after Holofernes' death: it provides her with a plausible pretext to leave the camp and thus make her escape (*Jth.* 13:10). In his dealings with Antiochus VII, Hyrcanus demurs when the king demands to install a garrison in Jerusalem in exchange for a truce—a commitment to tradition as tactical as Judith's, for while the reason that Hyrcanus gives for refusing the garrison—that the Jews are not allowed to come into contact with foreigners—may be true, one also notices that this supplies a convenient pretext for keeping the Seleucid army out of Jerusalem. There is nothing in Josephus's report to confirm the suspicion of an ulterior motive, but as with Judith, Hyrcanus's piety creates an opportunity to evade the enemy's surveillance.

While we cannot draw a direct connection between the composition of *Judith* and Hasmonean rule, the heroine's story offers an alternative way to understand the latter's zig-zagging relationship with Seleucid rule, putting a different spin on it than *2 Maccabees* does. At no point in her story does Judith betray her resolve to defend her people and her tradition with the sword, and yet even as she pursues this mission, she is able to slip into and out of a posture of loyal submission to foreign rule. What allows for this possibility are the sorts of tactics that women used, or were imagined as using, to maneuver within a male-dominated world—tactics that overcome the greater physical power of men by appearing to yield to it. In employing these tactics, Judith may come close to compromising her identity as a pious Jew committed to the defense of Jewish tradition, but she sustains her true allegiance through an artful use of ambiguity. In a similar way, it is possible to understand Hyrcanus's willingness to ally with Antiochus VII not as a sincere response to a Seleucid change of heart but as the same kind of deceit that Judith engages in, the Hasmonean feigning submissiveness until the moment that violence becomes a viable option (as it does after Antiochus VII dies). In this construction, vassalage is not a relaxing of hostility but a way to maneuver into a better position from which to strike.

In a certain sense, *Judith* licenses the same kind of behavior that *2 Maccabees* does, imagining a scenario in which it is acceptable for a Jew to come to terms with foreign rule. Of course, our heroine is only pretending to play such a role, never for a moment abandoning her intention to strike at the enemy. Until the moment when she is alone with Holofernes, however, Judith keeps that intention a secret, and there is nothing in her outward appearance or demeanor to distinguish her from an Assyrian concubine. *Judith* thus establishes another rationale for Hasmonean détente with Seleucid rule. Submission to foreign rule need not involve a relaxation of one's commitment to defend Jewish tradition. To the contrary, it can allow one to maneuver covertly when it is not safe to do so in the open. At some point zeal needs to manifest itself as violence, but in the meantime, it protects itself by simulating a posture of servility.

The difference between this and genuine subservience is so hard to pin down that, in the end, we cannot be certain what a ruler like Hyrcanus was really up to. By imagining a Seleucid kingdom that can truly reverse itself, *2 Maccabees* allows the Jews the option of reversing themselves in turn and accepting Seleucid domination sincerely. Whether Hyrcanus's friendship with Antiochus VII represents such a response or is actually a Judith-like trick cannot be determined from the sources we have available and may not have even been clear at the time. While there were moments when the Hasmoneans committed to a particular tactic, making an alliance or launching a revolt, for much of their rule, their best option may have been to keep their options open through equivocation and doublespeak, leaving it unclear whether in their dealings with Seleucid rule they were actually submitting to it, or merely pretending to do so.

The Art of the Pivot

Side-switching and double-dealing were common enough in the treacherous world of Hellenistic politics, characterizing Seleucid rule itself according to *1 Maccabees*.[29] In this, the Hasmoneans were characteristically opportunistic. If what I have argued here is correct, however, sustaining that opportunism required more than pragmatism or adaptability; it also required imagination, an ability to reconceptualize a sacrilegious enemy as a pious supporter or present oneself as a double-agent. Tactic switching seems to have placed a strain on the Hasmoneans' public persona by pulling it in different directions. One sign of this strain is the conflicting stories told of Hyrcanus's mother—for some a Maccabean-like hero; for others a compromised captive. In a story like *Judith*, it is possible to play both of these roles at once, resisting the enemy by pretending to be a captive. Not only did fiction present more options than there are in reality; it offered more ways of moving between those options.

Whatever options were available to the Hasmoneans, however, they were shut down soon after the Romans, friends from the time of Judah the Maccabee, conquered Judea in 63 B.C.E. By this point, two scions of the Hasmonean dynasty, Hyrcanus II and Aristobolus II, were locked in a power struggle, a conflict resolved only when the Roman general Pompey intervened and carried Aristobolus off to Rome in chains. Hyrcanus ruled as high priest for several more years and was succeeded by Aristobolus's son Antigonus, but Herod finished the Hasmoneans off when he executed his wife Mariamne, granddaughter of Aristobolus and Hyrcanus, and her sons. The Hasmonean line had survived all the twists and turns of Seleucid rule—defeating it in battle, escaping its ruses and betrayals, siding with this Seleucid ruler against that one—only to go extinct after only a few decades of Roman rule.

Despite the menace that Roman rule posed, however, Jewish culture did manage to survive. How it did so is my subject in the remainder of this book. More fully in control of things than the Seleucid kingdom was, Roman rule made it difficult to employ survival tactics that had worked in the past, but it also introduced new resources that Jews appropriated and re-purposed as they sought to develop options for themselves. Their use of these resources will be our focus in much of what follows, beginning with Jewish efforts to recruit the Roman emperor himself as an ally in the struggle for Jewish cultural persistence.

~ 3

Friends In High Places

As SACRILEGIOUS AS THE SELEUCID kingdom could be, the Roman Empire posed an even graver threat. From the moment it conquered Jerusalem in 63 B.C.E., Rome displayed a devastating obliviousness to Jewish religious sensibilities, a victorious Pompey daring even to enter the Holy of Holies, which was off-limits to all but the high priest. Over the next century, Roman rulers repeatedly violated Jewish tradition. Pompey's co-consul Marcus Licinius Crassus accepted a bribe from a priest not to loot the Temple and then robbed it anyway, taking treasure that Pompey had left behind (see *J. W.* 1.179; *Ant.* 14.105–9). In 4 B.C.E., soldiers of the procurator Sabinus set fire to the porticoes of the Temple and looted it again (*J. W.* 2.49–50; *Ant.* 17.257–64). Pontius Pilate, the procurator infamous for his role in Jesus' death, was notorious in his day for breaking Jewish law, installing effigies of Caesar in Jerusalem and appropriating sacred funds for the construction of an aqueduct (*J. W.* 2.169–77; *Ant.* 18.55–62). Caligula attempted to install a statue of himself in the Temple, and during his reign, the Greek population of Alexandria attacked the synagogues of the city in an effort to ingratiate themselves with the emperor. Jews employed a number of survival tactics to evade, deflect, or repel imperial rule, as we will see, but in the end, when the Romans resolved to destroy the Temple, nothing that its defenders did could prevent the sacrilege.

Despite the dangers of Roman rule, however, some Jews also recognized its power as a potential resource. As a friend and ally, the Roman Empire could hold itself back from impiety; it could even use its resources and strength to defend the other's tradition. Both Philo and Josephus described the Romans as pious defenders of Jewish tradition:

> The Romans never overstepped the limit fixed for the profane, never violated one of our sacred usages, but beheld with awe from afar the walls that enclose our sanctuary . . . Indeed, if one must nicely fit the phrase to the fact, it is the Romans who may well be found to have been the upholders of our laws. (*J. W.* 4.182–4)

Elsewhere Josephus lists a whole series of public edicts from important Romans showing their respect for the Jews (*Ant.* 14.186–267). Some documents affirm the status of the high priest in Jerusalem; others give the Jews of various Diaspora communities the right to live in accordance with their ancestral customs—to practice the Sabbath and other festivals, to gather at the synagogue, or to send sacred monies to Jerusalem. Whether or not each and every individual document is authentic (a much-debated question), the collection as a whole suggests a Roman government willing to protect and honor Jewish tradition.[1] Decades earlier, Philo registered a similarly positive view of Roman rule, recalling that Augustus and other members of the imperial family had honored the Temple with various gifts, admired its beauty, and respected Jewish law, including its prohibition of images (*Embassy* 294–320).[2] Roman power imperiled Jewish tradition in new ways, but it also offered new opportunities to insure its continuity.

One of those opportunities was imperial rule itself as personified in the image and person of the emperor. Especially after the reign of the emperor Caligula (37–41 C.E.), who created a mass panic among Jews when he ordered a statue of Jupiter installed in the Temple, Jews were well aware of how dangerous emperors could be. Like other imperial subjects, however, they could also look to the emperor as an ally. Clifford Ando has emphasized the emperor's role and image as a protector, someone to whom provincials could appeal even against abusive Roman officials ruling on the emperor's behalf.[3] The emperor came to be known as "common benefactor," "the savior of the entire human race," and other epithets that cast him as a benefactor who extended his generosity and protective power to all his subjects regardless of their ethnic identity.[4] Mirroring this language in their own descriptions of the emperor (Philo refers to Augustus as "the first and the greatest and the common benefactor," for example), Jews attempted to enlist him as a supporter and protector. They looked to the emperor and his family to play the role of cultic patron, subsidizing the Temple sacrifices, and they appealed for his help against intrusive local officials like Pilate, and also against hostile non-Jewish neighbors like the non-Jewish population of Alexandria.

One way in which Jews recruited the emperor as an ally was to literally befriend him. Friendship in the early Roman Empire was both a pragmatic and an affective relationship, overlapping with the client-patron relationship but rooted in personal affection and respect rather than a quid pro quo exchange of services between people of different status.[5] Transcending kinship or birthplace, friendship could be formed across the cultural and religious differences between Jews and Romans. Herod formed such a relationship with Augustus—only Marcus Agrippa was a dearer friend to the emperor according to Josephus (J. W. 1.400; Ant. 15.199–201)—and Herod's grandson and successor Agrippa I (10 B.C.E.–44 C.E.) was a friend to both Caligula and Claudius, laying claim to the title "Great king, Friend of Caesar, Pious and Friend of the Romans." The role of friend was a formalized status at this level of political interaction, masking Machiavellian considerations on both sides of the relationship, but it is a conceit that we must take seriously if we are to understand the language and tactics that Jewish leaders employed to cultivate the emperor as a defender of their traditions.

The bond of friendship, as opposed to that between a patron and a client, connoted equality of status, or if not equality, a like-mindedness that transcended differences in status. The texture of friendship is captured in Cicero's observation that one who looks into the face of a friend will find "a copy of himself," someone in perfect agreement about matters human and divine (*On Friendship* 1.6–7). In their efforts to recruit imperial support, Jews sought to portray themselves as something like a copy of imperial rule, a nation of friends animated by a deep affection for the emperor and sharing his interests and values. Constructing such a portrait required Jews to accentuate their resemblance to the emperor despite the differences imposed by Jewish and Roman custom, and to explain how their behavior, even when different from that of the emperor, served his interests as much as their own. It was also necessary to differentiate themselves from that slippery figure notorious for disguising himself as a friend, the flatterer, who imitated the qualities of friendship in order to undo the powerful. Meeting these challenges required a certain kind of artfulness that we will seek to reconstruct in this chapter, a delicate tightrope walk between like-mindedness and imposture, truth-telling and flattery that I refer to as the art of mimicry.

A Friend in Need

Our chief informant in this investigation is Philo of Alexandria (20 B.C.E.?–50 C.E.?), a figure superbly positioned to serve as an intermediary between the Jews and the emperor. Alexandria had been under Roman control since 30 B.C.E., and at the uppermost echelons of the Alexandrian Jewish community, Philo's family came to enjoy an influential position within its administration, as well as a personal relationship with the emperor himself. Philo's brother Alexander was an *alabarch*, apparently an office responsible for the collection of taxes. Alexander's sons bore Roman names, Marcus and Tiberius, and the latter held a succession of offices under the Roman empire: procurator in Judea in 46–48 C.E.; prefect of Egypt between 66–70 C.E; and chief of staff for Titus, future emperor, in the final year of the Jewish Revolt (69–70 C.E.). Philo's family connections suggest why he was sent to Rome to represent the Jews before the emperor Caligula in 40 C.E. Two years earlier, in 38 C.E., tensions between the Greek and Jewish communities of Alexandria, inflamed by the malfeasance of the Roman governor Flaccus, had erupted in an anti-Jewish riot. Both the Greeks and the Jews sent delegations to the emperor to win his support, an experience in which Philo was personally involved as the head of the Jewish delegation and which he describes in a work entitled *The Embassy to Gaius*. Philo's account in that work is as close as we could hope to come to an eyewitness description of how Jews in this period approached the emperor, what they said to him, and how they tried to befriend him.

One of the central themes of the *Embassy* is the emperor's role as a generous and impartial protector, willing to help all his subjects regardless of whether they are Greeks or foreigners. The model in this regard was the first emperor, Augustus, who in Philo's description transcends all ethnic difference:

> This is the Caesar who calmed the torrential storms on every side, who healed the pestilences common to Greeks and barbarians, pestilences which descending from the south and the east coursed to the west and the north sowing the seeds of calamity over the places and waters which lay between. This is he who not only loosed but also broke the chains, which had shackled and pressed so hard the habitable world. This is he who exterminated wars both of the open kind and the covert which are brought about by the raids of brigands. This is he who cleared the sea of pirate ships and filled it with merchant vessels. This is he who reclaimed every state to liberty, who led disorder into order and brought gentle manners and harmony to all unsociable and brutish nations . . . He was also the first and the greatest and the common benefactor in that he displaced the rule of the many and committed the ship of the commonwealth to be steered by a single pilot, that is himself, a marvelous master of the science of government. (*Embassy* 145–149)[6]

Augustus's treatment of the Jews was in accord with his role as a "common benefactor," allowing the Jews of Rome to worship in synagogues and collect monies to send to their temple in Jerusalem, sending gifts to the Temple himself, and subsidizing the continuous sacrifice of whole burnt offerings (*Embassy* 155–157). His respect for Jewish tradition set a precedent that was emulated by his successors down into the reign of Caligula himself. When the procurator Pilate infringed on Jewish tradition by dedicating some shields in Herod's palace, the Jews sent letters to Tiberius appealing to him to intervene. Although the emperor was not easily moved to anger, the report of Pilate's sacrilege enraged him as a "audacious violation of precedent" and without a moment's hesitation, he dashed off a letter to Pilate ordering the removal of the shields (298–305). Imperial rule could sometimes grow hostile, as it would during Caligula's reign, but by and large, Jewish tradition could best survive the sacrileges of its enemies, Philo believed, by relying on the emperor's justice and piety.

In response to the emperor's benevolence, Philo stresses in this work, the Jews loved Caesar, taking every opportunity to show their affection and gratitude. They expressed their love through the medium of ritual, much as other imperial subjects did, but with a difference. Non-Jewish subjects of the emperor paid him honor through what has come to be known as the imperial cult, a system of ritual practices that included venerating the emperor's image, offering sacrifices to him or in his honor, and addressing him as god.[7] Jewish tradition, with its laws against worshipping other gods or bowing down to statues, placed many of these practices off-limits, but Jews found other ways to express their feelings for the emperor:

> For in all matters in which piety is enjoined and permitted under the laws (the Jewish People) stood not a whit behind any other either in Asia or in Europe, in its prayers, its erection of votive offerings, its numbers of sacrifices, not only those offered at general national feasts but in the perpetual and daily rites through which is declared their piety, not so much with mouth and tongue as in intentions formed in the secrecy of the soul by those who do not tell you that they love their Caesar but love him in very truth. (280)

It is true, Philo admits, that the Jews do not express their love of Caesar in the way that the Greeks do, but they do feel it nonetheless, channeling it through their own tradition. Thus, in the Temple cult, Jews made special sacrifices to honor the accession of an emperor and also made ongoing sacrifices, offered twice daily, in honor of the emperor and the Roman people (*Embassy* 356). Jews also used the synagogue for this purpose. The synagogue had emerged some time in the Hellenistic period not as the substitute Temple it was later understood to be, but as a place where Jews could study Mosaic law and offer prayer to God.[8] By Philo's day, the synagogue also served Jews as a "means of showing reverence to their benefactors" (*Flaccus* 48), Jews dedicating offerings and posting inscriptions to honor benefactors.[9] They used the synagogue to honor the emperor as well, a role that Philo emphasizes: "everywhere in the habitable world the religious veneration of the Jews for the Augustan house has its basis as all may see in the meeting-houses, and if we have these destroyed no place, no method is left to us for paying this homage" (*Flaccus* 49).[10]

At the time that Philo was expressing these views, or rather shortly before, the friendship between the emperor and the Jews was in jeopardy, threatened by Greek attacks against the Jewish population of Alexandria and elsewhere, and by Caligula's plan to install an imperial statue in the Temple. Part of what had precipitated this crisis was the nefarious influence of Alexandrian flatterers who were all too ready to accommodate Caligula's delusions of divinity (cf. *Embassy* 166–173; 203–206; 355). Through fawning words of praise for the emperor and subtly clever slanders against the Jews, they had misled the emperor into believing that the Jews' ritual practices did not express love and appreciation but ingratitude and disrespect. Caligula's effort to install a statue of himself in the Temple was an effort to conform its cult to the norms of imperial veneration, as was the violence targeted at the Jews of Alexandria in 38 C.E.:

> They collected great bodies of men to attack the meeting-houses, of which there are many in each section of the city. Some they ravaged, others they demolished with the foundations as well, others they set fire to . . . I say nothing of the tributes to the emperors which were pulled down or burnt at the same time, the shields and gilded crowns and the slabs and the inscriptions, consideration for which should have made them spare the rest. But they were emboldened by having no fear of the vengeance of Gaius. They knew well that he had an indescribable hatred of the Jews, and so they surmised that nothing anyone could do would gratify him more than the infliction on the nation of every kind of ill-treatment. And as they wished to ingratiate themselves with him by further novelties in flattering and so secure complete immunity for their maltreatment of us, what do you suppose they did? The meeting-houses which they could not raze or burn out of existence, because so many Jews live massed together in the neighborhood, they outraged in another way, thereby overthrowing our laws and customs. For they set up images of Gaius in them all and in the largest and most notable a bronze statue of a man mounted on a chariot . . . they had extravagant hopes of getting praise and reaping greater and more splendid benefits for turning our meeting-houses into new and additional precincts consecrated to him. (*Embassy* 132–137).[11]

Philo explicitly describes the riot as an attempt to flatter Caligula, the rioters seeking to win the emperor's favor by installing statues of him in the imageless synagogues of the Jews and turning them into shrines of imperial veneration. In fact, the rioters were being disrespectful to the emperor, Philo alleges, destroying the synagogues without regard for the imperial tributes within, but Caligula failed to recognize the true nature of the act, deceived by the sycophants in his court that the violence was a sincere attempt to honor him (165). If their traditions and institutions were to survive, Jews would have to find some way to counter the poisonous effects of flattery, and convince the emperor that it was they, not the sycophantic Greeks, who were his true friends.

The initial response to this threat as the *Embassy* depicts it is paralysis. Philo reports that he and his fellow delegates were simply petrified when they learned of the emperor's plans (*Embassy* 189), and seeing no way to stop him, they could only place their hope in God (196). When the leaders of the Jewish community in Judea learned of the order from the governor Petronius, they responded in the same way: "they stood riveted to the ground, incapable of speech" (223). Hearing that the governor's forces were already arrayed against them, there was nothing for them to do except offer themselves up to slaughter (229–236). Despite their apparent powerlessness, however, they did try one last option, making a direct appeal to the emperor himself (239–241). The rest of the *Embassy* is a chronicle of that effort. Won over by the Jews, Petronius sends a letter in an effort to stall the emperor, providing an elaborate excuse for why his order need be delayed (248–253). Despairing for their traditions, the Jews would burn down their crops, he warns, making it impossible to accommodate the emperor when he passed through Palestine on his way to Alexandria, as he was planning to do. Caligula sees through this ruse, however, secretly plotting to punish Petronius at the first opportunity (255–260). At this point the Jewish king Agrippa makes an appearance at the imperial court, and learning of the situation, he too sends a petitionary letter. His status as the emperor's "friend" compels him to be more open and candid than Petronius, a risky posture to assume but one presenting opportunities as well.

According to a number of Greek and Roman authors, true friends are those who think the same thoughts and share all things in common, overlapping in their mental life as if they are two bodies sharing a single soul.[12] Despite his fear of Caligula, Agrippa seems to enjoy just such a relationship with the emperor who, in fact, refers to him explicitly as "my dearest and most familiar friend" (*Embassy* 268). This, presumably, is what makes it possible for the two of them to know each other's inner thoughts by reading the other's eyes or face (261–263). In his letter to the emperor, Agrippa seeks to construct a similar affinity between the Jews and imperial rule, not merely asserting his people's love for Caesar but depicting them as a people motivated by the same values and interests. Precisely because true friends "think the same thing," the letter argues, Caligula can understand the Jews by understanding his own impulses and feelings.

Agrippa appeals to this commonality at the very beginning of his letter, in fact, asserting a kinship between his own commitment to Jewish tradition, alien though it might seem to the emperor, and the emperor's commitment to *his* tradition:

> All men, my emperor, have planted in them a passionate love of their native land and a high esteem for their own laws; and on this there is no need to instruct you, who love your native city as ardently as you honor your own customs. Every people is convinced of the excellence of its own institutions, even if they are not really excellent, for they judge them not so much by their reasoning as by the affection which they feel for them. (*Embassy* 277)

Implicit in this statement is an acknowledgement that Jewish ritual may not be defensible on rational grounds, Agrippa appearing to concede that the Jews judge their laws worth keeping not because these are "really excellent" or rationally defensible but because of the Jews' emotional connection to them (Agrippa does not commit himself to this position—he will argue the opposite, in fact—but his phrasing allows Caligula to think what he likes of Jewish ritual for the moment). Far from marking the difference between the Jews and others, however, the Jews' commitment to their traditions is something that actually connects them with others, including the emperor himself who makes Agrippa's case precisely through the love he feels for his own tradition. Over the course of the ensuing letter, Agrippa turns again and again to the emperor's own tradition as a reason for him to respect Jewish tradition, alien though it might be.

The passage cited above, where Philo stresses Jewish ritual as the venue through which Jews publicize their affection for the emperor (*Embassy* 280), illustrates this effort to establish an affinity between the Jews and imperial rule. Jewish ritual may differ from Roman ritual but beneath this difference, inhabiting the innermost self of the Jews, is exactly the same sentiment that animates the imperial cult: a love of Caesar; in fact, Jewish ritual is more attuned with the emperor than the more familiar but less sincere cultic gestures of the Greeks. Jewish ritual accords with Roman values in other ways as well. Agrippa paraphrases a letter allegedly written by Augustus to the governors of Asia when he learned of an effort to interfere in their synagogue assemblies. He orders that the Jews be allowed to assemble in their synagogues, explaining that these "were not based on drunkenness and carousing to promote conspiracy and so to do grave injury to the cause of peace, but were schools of temperance and justice" (312). The passage accords with Philo's description of Augustus himself earlier in the treatise as "the guardian of peace" seeking to lead disorder into order (147). What prompted Augustus to leave the synagogue alone, Agrippa suggests by echoing this portrait, was his recognition that it reflects the very goals he was trying to achieve through the Roman Empire.

Augustus appears in the letter as one of several imperial ancestors who embody for Agrippa a "pattern of a gentler line of treatment." Also noted are Caligula's great-grandmother Julia Augusta who adorned the Temple despite its lack of images; his grandfather Marcus Agrippa who grew so enamored of the Temple that he felt moved to visit it repeatedly; and Tiberius who intervened to protect the law from Pilate. This part of Agrippa's argument, stretching for nearly half of the letter (294–322), uses the emperor's own family to argue that a violation of Jewish tradition would also be a violation of Roman tradition. In Roman religion, the dead ancestors, the *di parentes*, were regarded as vital protective spirits whose presence was rendered visible in ceremonial processions by actors who wore masks to simulate their features and even mimicked their voices.[13] Agrippa's review of Caligula's ancestors simulates this custom, staging a literary procession of Caligula's ancestors that culminates with them speaking to the emperor, an effect Agrippa achieves by donning the verbal equivalent to a mask, a device known as *prosopopoiia*, from the Greek for "mask":[14]

> The cause of the laws is pleaded by emperors to emperor, by Augusti to an Augustus, by grandparents and ancestors to their descendants, by several to one, and you may almost hear them say, "Do not destroy the institutions which under the shelter of our wills was safeguarded to this day, for even if no sinister result were encountered through their overthrow, still the uncertainty of the future cannot entirely fail to strike fear into the most courageous unless he holds things divine in contempt." (*Embassy* 322).

Through *prosopopoiia* the Roman orator Quintilian observed, a writer or speaker could "bring down the gods from heaven *and raise the dead*" (*Institutions* 9.2.31), and the latter is what Agrippa does in a sense, not *quite* impersonating Caligula's ancestors (he inserts the qualifier "You can almost hear them say"), but asking the emperor to imagine himself hearing their speech. Summoned from the dead, they act in their customary role of protective spirit, warning the emperor of the potential consequences of his sacrilege. Agrippa here renders himself familiar in the most literal of senses, assuming the guise of the emperor's own family members in an effort to convince the emperor that it is not just Jewish tradition that he threatens to disrupt, but his own as well.

This part of Agrippa's argument allows us to appreciate Agrippa's mimicry as more than a mere imitation of Roman rule; it entails a highly manipulative appropriation of imperial tradition. For one thing, Agrippa must suppress memories that undercut his portrait of imperial rule. In describing Tiberius, for example, he plays down the emperor's expulsion of the Jews from Rome in 19 C.E., an incident obviously at odds with his portrait of the emperor as respectful of Jewish tradition. Speaking in his own voice in *Embassy* (159–160), Philo notes that there were troubles during Tiberius's reign, but he blames them on the emperor's advisor Sejanus.[15] Agrippa does not even mention these troubles, focusing his description of Tiberius on the latter's treatment of the Temple (299–305). Agrippa's description acknowledges that Pilate invoked the emperor as authority for his action ("Do not take Tiberius as your pretext for outraging the nation," the Jews complain to the procurator), but as he presents things, the emperor knew nothing of what the procurator was doing in his name. Agrippa manages not only to minimize his culpability, but also to transform the episode into an exemplum of imperial piety, a precedent that Agrippa urges Caligula to emulate.

Agrippa's portrait of imperial rule is not an act of pure invention; some of it resourcefully appropriates what the Romans themselves said about the emperor. This seems to be the case, for example, in Agrippa's description of Augustus:

> This great ruler, this philosopher second to none, reasoned in his mind that within the precincts of the earth there must needs be a special place assigned as sacred to the invisible God which would contain no visible image. (*Embassy* 318)

At first glance, this description might seem far-fetched, contradicting the emperor's use of statues to make his power manifest. What may underlie this description, however, is a Roman tradition associating Augustus with the rejection of statues, reflected, for example, in Suetonius's report that Augustus melted down silver statues set up in his honor (*Augustus* 52). Agrippa's suggestion that Augustus had achieved the same religious insight that led the Jews to reject images, that an invisible God ought not to be worshipped in a visible form, is probably a projection, the real emperor probably motivated in his iconoclasm by an impulse specific to Roman culture. The republican tradition of treating rulers as citizens was difficult for Romans like Augustus to reconcile with the Hellenistic norm of divinizing rulers, a tension that the emperor resolved by publicly refusing divine honors offered to him.[16] That the parallel with Jewish aniconism was accidental did not make it any less useful for Agrippa's efforts to accentuate the like-mindedness of the Jews and the emperor, however. Hovering somewhere in the background of Agrippa's letter, Augustus's destruction of images would have rendered his alleged sympathy for Jewish aniconism all the more plausible for the emperor, giving it a resonance within his own cultural tradition.

It is not Agrippa's goal in any of this to collapse the difference between Jewish and Roman tradition—to the contrary, he wants Caligula to respect his distinctive customs even though they are different from his own—but he seeks to create under the surface of that difference an internal alignment: the Romans feel the same respect for tradition that animates the Jews; Romans and Jews are united in their commitment to temperance, justice, and peace; aniconism may seem subversive, a pretext for not venerating the emperor's image, but it was something that the first emperor realized was necessary once he joined the Jews in recognizing the existence of an invisible god. In another treatise, Philo suggests that this convergence of perspectives can create a virtual "tie of kinship" that transcends the differences between nations (*Spec. Laws* 2.73). The label that a Roman might have applied to this shared internal life was friendship.

Agrippa's efforts to foster this resemblance calls to mind a tactic often employed by flatterers according to an ancient expert on the subject, the biographer and moralist Plutarch (born around 46 C.E.). The resemblance between a flatterer and a friend were so close, in fact, that Plutarch (and others) felt it necessary to publish advice on how to distinguish between them—his treatise *How to Tell a Flatterer from a Friend* where the flatterer appears as a chameleon-like creature emulating the qualities of a true friend in an effort to deceive and destroy the powerful. Chief among these qualities is imitativeness, which Plutarch portrays as absorption of the other's properties:

> (the flatterer) acts as though the man were some animal running at large in a pasture, and by affecting the same pursuits, the same avocations, interests and manner of life, he gradually gets close to him, and rubs up against him so as to take on his coloring, until his victim gives him some hold and becomes docile and accustomed to his touch. (*How to Tell a Flatterer* 51)[17]

Friends also resemble their companions as we have noted, which is one reason it is so hard to distinguish them from flatterers. This is why Plutarch recommends careful attention to the particular nature of the resemblance: A friend resembles his companion, *selectively*, only imitating his virtues: "The true friend is neither an imitator of everything nor ready to commend everything, but only the best things" (*How to Tell a Flatterer* 53). A flatterer imitates without discrimination, copying every quality except his virtues: "For (just as) the chameleon can make himself like to every color except white, the flatterer, being utterly incapable of making himself like to another in any quality that is really worthwhile, leaves no shameful thing unimitated" (53).

As Philo portrays him, Caligula himself falls into the latter category. As emperor, his only superiors were the gods, and these he endeavored to imitate in every attribute except their virtues (this Philo demonstrates at length. See *Embassy* 77–113). He was also surrounded with such figures as we have noted, the Alexandrians whom Philo describes as "adepts at flattery and imposture and hypocrisy, ready enough with fawning words but causing universal disaster with their loose and unbridled lips" (*Embassy* 162). Given the impersonation involved, it may not be a coincidence that many of these were professional performers, the tragic actor Apelles (203–204) or the jester Helicon, "scorpion in the form of a slave" (166–173; 205–206). Philo distinguishes Agrippa from such courtiers, but in light of what we have seen here, it can be argued that his rhetorical tactics are not completely dissimilar from those of the flatterer, especially in the ways that they endow Jewish tradition with an imperial coloring.

If Agrippa were here to speak for himself, he would no doubt take deep offense at the association with flattery. He is adamant about his absolute dedication to the emperor—"I am in loyalty . . . second to none, I might almost say the first," he insists (*Embassy* 286)—and the same is true of his people, who not only adore Caesar but were the first to announce his succession to the throne (288). One of the behaviors that can give a flatterer away, Plutarch observes, is their mutability. The tastes of a true friend are uniform and permanent—he always takes delight in the same things; commends the same things, and lives his life according to a single pattern—whereas the flatterer is constantly fluctuating in his attitudes, shifting to reflect those of his audience (*How To Tell a Flatterer* 52). By this measure, Agrippa proves himself a true friend, for he remains unwavering in his commitment to Jewish tradition:

> I exchange all for one thing only, that the ancestral institutions be not disturbed. For what would be my reputation among either my compatriots or all other men? Either I must seem a traitor to my people or no longer counted your friend as I have been . . . If your mind harbour any hostility to me, do not imprison me as Tiberius did, rather do away with any idea of future imprisonment and at the same time bid me to take myself out of the way forthwith. For of what value would life be to me whose one hope of salvation lay in your goodwill? (327–329)

If he were a flatterer, Agrippa would never own up to his own feelings or convictions, and would certainly never risk alienating Caligula, but would only say what he thought the emperor wanted him to say. That he is prepared to abandon his friendship with Caligula and even to risk death to avoid betraying his people is proof, therefore, that what he is arguing is completely sincere. He is so convincing in this regard that while Caligula is annoyed by Agrippa's stubborn adherence to his traditions, he admires him "for disguising and concealing nothing of his real self" (332).

For a flatterer of sufficient skill, however, even sincerity could be simulated:

> The most unprincipled trick of all that (the flatterer) has is this: perceiving that frankness of speech, by common report and belief, is the language of friendship especially (as an animal has its peculiar cry), and, on the other hand, that lack of frankness is unfriendly and ignoble, he does not allow even this to escape imitation. (*How to Tell a Flatterer* 51)

By the end of the first century C.E., orators had perfected the imitation of frankness, developing what classicist Shadi Bartsch refers as "the art of sincerity."[18] By this point, praise of the emperor had become so common, its ulterior motives so transparent, that Roman audiences had come to presume its insincerity, often sensing some hidden, subversive meaning concealed within its adulation. To forestall being read in this way, writers developed rhetorical techniques designed to show that they were not merely feigning affection or admiration but really meant it, that their public declarations and true thoughts were one and the same. Knowing that flatterers only utter praise, a writer might recall a past incident where he had refused to do so at great personal risk, thus proving the unwavering truthfulness of his character: "There is no fear that I may ever be thought guilty of flattering you," the orator Dio Chrysostom declares when praising the emperor of his day, "since I did not flatter the hateful tyrant (Domitian) or utter a single ignoble or servile word, at a time when many were glad to save their lives by any deed or word at all" (*Oration* 3.12-13). The remark seems to establish Dio as one who remains true no matter what the risk. Then again, Dio had a stake in *seeming* sincere, in proving that his praise was different from flattery even though it might sound the same. Whatever peril there was in calling an earlier emperor a tyrant (and the risk was minimal since Dio was not applying such a label to the current emperor but rather distinguishing him from Domitian as someone to whom subjects could speak the truth unafraid), Dio's truthfulness was tactical, an effort to avoid the risk of appearing insincere. It is even possible, Bartsch suspects, that Dio exaggerated his earlier integrity to sharpen the opposition between his own praise and that offered to the earlier emperor, simulating sincerity lest he too be suspected of flattering the emperor simply to save his life.

Even when Agrippa appears most sincere, then—declaring himself ready to give up his friendship with Caligula and abandon all concern for himself—he may be merely imitating sincerity, adopting an established rhetorical device to create the impression that he is hiding nothing of his true self. Philo's description makes very clear how frightened he was of Caligula. When the emperor told him of his plan to desecrate the Temple, Agrippa was overcome with trembling, nearly fainting in the emperor's presence. For days afterward, he remained in a coma and even after he resolved to petition the emperor, he could not bear to do so face-to-face but sent a letter instead. It is precisely in such circumstances, as Philo suggests elsewhere in his writings, that telling the truth is a bad idea. In his treatise *On Dreams* (2.78–92), Philo observes that those who openly oppose a tyrant are lunatics who bring death upon themselves and their loved ones. "Untimely free-speaking" as he refers to this reckless candor, is as foolish as seeing a storm coming and setting sail anyway, or provoking a savage beast: "[W]ould anyone who has seen a bear or a lion or a wild boar sweeping along to attack him, instead of soothing and calming them as he should, provoke them to savagery just to offer himself as a banquet to satisfy the cruel appetites of the carnivorous brutes?" (85, 87). It is far better to wait for fair weather, to try to soothe the beast, as Abraham illustrates in Genesis 23:7 when he chooses to bow down to the more powerful Hittites:

> It was not out of any feeling of respect for those who by nature, race, and custom were the enemies of reason (that Abraham bowed down) . . . Rather, it was because he feared their power at the time and their formidable strength and took care to give no provocation. (90)

Philo draws from Abraham's example a lesson about how to speak truth to power. "The safe course is to keep quiet, and if we wish to gain any help from [the powerful], the fitting course is to soften and tame them" (92). In this very passage, Philo may be adhering to his own rhetorical advice. When he suggests that one might use such speech to tame "the stinging scorpions and asps of Egypt," for instance, he is almost certainly referring to Alexandrian opponents like Helicon, whom he elsewhere describes as a scorpion—but he stops short of identifying them directly, as that kind of truth-telling would be reckless. That Agrippa's letter is so clearly designed to soften and tame its audience makes one wonder whether it is really showing as much of its author's true self as Caligula thinks or whether it might rather reflect the kind of speech that Philo talks about in *On Dreams*, a discourse shaped by discretion.

In the end, of course, there is little point in speculating about whether Agrippa was a flatterer or a friend, because he is himself a rhetorical device. His letter is another example of *prosopopoiia*, Philo impersonating the voice of the Jewish leader in the best position to influence imperial policy (that influence was even greater after the death of Caligula; Agrippa had been brought up in the imperial court with Claudius and helped him to come to power after Caligula's assassination). Most of the arguments that Agrippa makes have parallels elsewhere in the *Embassy*, in the appeal made to Petronius, the governor of Syria, in an effort to dissuade him from following the emperor's order (229–242), and in the efforts of Philo's delegation to reason with Caligula (349–367). These similarities suggest that Agrippa's letter is not authentic but a fictional vehicle through which Philo expresses his views.[19] According to E. R. Goodenough, Philo probably intended the *Embassy* to be read by Caligula's successor, Claudius, in the hope of winning his support for the Jews.[20] Perhaps, then, the issue we should be struggling with is whether Philo himself ought to be identified as a friend or a flatterer of imperial rule, expressing real like-mindedness or feigning it.

According to Goodenough, he was closer to a flatterer than a friend. Noting what Philo wrote about "untimely free-speaking," Goodenough argues that Philo's praise of Rome was tactical, concealing a resentment of Rome that would occasionally slip out in his allegorical writings.[21] There is something to be said for this interpretation, for under Caligula's rule, truth-telling, a defining trait of true friendship, was extremely dangerous. Caligula's advisor Macro had proven his loyalty to Caligula long before he was emperor. Wishing to protect his charge from the corruption of courtly life, he "gave his admonitions frankly and without disguise." "You ought not to be like those around you or anyone else at all," he once cautioned the emperor, fearful that Caligula was becoming too like the entertainers he was enjoying (43–51). This angered the emperor, who from that point forward began plotting Macro's destruction (32–61). Another friend was Caligula's father-in-law, M. Silanus, who "concealed nothing which might tend to improve and benefit Gaius' character, conduct and government." Taking those chastisements as an insult, Caligula had him murdered (62–65). Macro and M. Silanus embodied the virtue of frank criticism—precisely the kind of open, uncensored criticism that distinguishes a true friend from a flatterer—and their honesty proved fatal.[22] Given the peril of truth-telling in Caligula's court, and the success that flatterers enjoyed, it would not be implausible to conclude, as Goodenough does, that Philo resorted to flattery, including its imitation of sincerity, to secure the emperor's favor.

I am not sure this is what Philo understood himself to be doing, however. He presents himself as a truth-teller willing to risk everything to save his traditions: "Well so be it, we will die and be no more," he declares when initially considering whether he should petition Caligula for the Temple, "for the truly glorious death, met in defense of laws, might be called life" (*Embassy* 192). This might be a pose but given his professed commitment to the law of Moses, a sage "who loves and teaches the truth which he desires to engrave and stamp on all his disciples" (*Special Laws* 1.50), it may reflect Philo's genuine self-understanding. In fact, Jewish tradition as Philo presents it in other, seemingly apolitical writings demands openness and candor. Sinners seek "holes and corners of the earth and profound darkness" to keep their deeds "veiled out of the sight of all." Not so the disciples of Moses who let the sunlight shine on their lives by employing a "freedom of speech" that conceals nothing (1.319–322). Assuming that Philo means what he says, to conceal one's true self, as Goodenough accuses him of doing, would have been to violate the very tradition he claimed to be defending.

It would also have meant risking exposure as a flatterer, for the emperor was not without the ability to detect hidden meanings. One reason that Agrippa seems to have feared approaching Caligula directly was that the latter was "skilled in discerning a man's secret wishes and feelings from his open countenance" (263).[23] This was how he was able to read between the lines of Petronius's appeal, recognizing that the governor was merely trying to stall him. Flaccus, the prefect of Egypt at the time, was similarly adept "at understanding what was left unspoken better even than what was said" (*Flaccus* 2). Even when it could escape detection, flattery's benefits were only short-lived. Sycophants like Apelles and Helicon enjoy the emperor's favor, but only for a while. In a rare moment of prolepsis, Philo notes that Apelles was eventually thrown into irons, and that Helicon was executed by Claudius (*Embassy* 206). Truth-telling may have been dangerous, but over the long run, flattery was too.

Given the dangers of both frankness and flattery, there were two options left—both described in *On Dreams.* The first was simply to keep quiet, an option to which Philo and his fellow delegates resort when they see that their arguments are having no effect on Caligula: "Silence too may in a way serve as a defense, particularly to us, who could not answer any of the points which (Caligula) was investigating and wished to press, because our customs and laws muzzled the tongue and closed and stitched up the mouth." (360). The second option was to "soften and tame" the enemy. Philo does not elaborate on what he means by this, but by opposing it to "untimely frankness," he seems to have in mind a certain kind of discourse—not insincere speech that misrepresents one's true feelings but a "timely" or opportune frankness, a discourse that navigates between silence and the frank criticism that did in Macro and M. Silanus. Agrippa's letter allows us to glimpse what this discourse might look like. Everything that Agrippa writes to the emperor is sincerely intended (as confirmed by Caligula himself), but it is a filtered truth, avoiding frank criticism while seizing on truths likely to appeal to the emperor. Flattery may know how to mimic frank speech, and that may be what the historical Philo was doing in composing Agrippa's letter, but *On Dreams* suggest that he is instead pursuing another tactic just as effective but less risky: frank speech that mimics flattery by adjusting itself to soften and tame the powerful.

Proving that this is what Philo understood himself to be doing—that he was not merely imitating sincerity but being sincere in an opportune way—is impossible since, unlike Caligula, we are unable to discern his secret thoughts and wishes. While Goodenough thought that he had detected the real Philo in passages that seem critical of Roman rule, these comments likely fall within the parameters of what was considered "safe criticism" in this period, criticism that was safe to express to the emperor because, while it might rebuke local officials or even bad emperors from the past, did not criticize the present emperor (Claudius) or challenge the fundamental legitimacy of imperial rule.[24] In an environment in which straightforward truth-telling was often fatal, and where the emperor was on the lookout for hidden meanings, we must assume that what we have in Philo's writing, even when it seems to criticize Roman rule, was formulated with the wariness Philo recommends in *On Dreams*.

While *we* may be unable to distinguish flattery from frankness, however, Philo insists that it was possible for the emperor to tell the difference, and the key to distinguishing between them was precisely the commitment of the Jews to preserving their customs. Although other nations also suffered under Caligula, these tended to flatter him out of all proportion to his merits, even to the point of betraying their own traditions, as happened in Italy, for example: "Some even introduced into Italy the barbarian practice of prostrating themselves, a degradation of the high tradition of Roman freedom" (*Embassy* 116). Not so the Jews, who alone of all the nations remained steadfast in their allegiance to their traditions, risking death to do so (115–118; 209–212; 308). That commitment prevented them from demonstrating their love for Caesar in the ways that Caligula expected them to, by addressing him as god or by venerating his statue. Far from showing their disloyalty, however, this refusal to be fully adulatory was actually what proved the sincerity of the adulation they did offer. In Philo's construction of reality, the imperial cult of the Greeks is the ritual equivalent to flattery—meaningless in its conformity and hypocrisy—whereas Jewish sacrifices on the emperor's behalf, precisely because they did not fully conform to imperial vanity, prove that the Jews *really* mean what they say when they say they love Caesar.

Philo's argument as we have reconstructed it is, to paraphrase Homi Bhabha's famous description of mimicry, that the Jews are almost the same as the emperor but not quite.[25] The "not quite" that complicates this equation is Jewish tradition—aniconism, the synagogue, and other practices that make it difficult for the emperor to recognize in the Jews a "reformed, recognizable Other" (to mimic Bhabha once again). The *Embassy to Gaius* seeks to preserve that difference even as it asserts an underlying affinity between Jewish tradition and imperial rule. What makes this argument all the more effective—and paradoxical—is its use of this "not quite" not just to qualify but to confirm the affinity it establishes between Jewish culture and imperial rule. Within the Roman imagination that Philo was addressing, friendship was marked by like-mindedness but it also required difference, the true friend proving his affection by only partially imitating his companion. By emphasizing his people's refusal to imitate everything about the emperor, Philo resists the imperial desire for a recognizable Other even as he accommodates it, his model in this endeavor, the true friend who proves his love by being almost the same but not quite.

A Friend Indeed?

One of the factors that allowed the Jews to sustain their traditions under Caligula's rule was having friends in the right places. Caligula was no friend of the Jews, but he was soon assassinated, replaced by Claudius, a much more sympathetic emperor. We have three edicts issued by the new emperor in 41 C.E., each allowing the Jews to practice their ancestral customs (Two are recorded by Josephus, one sent to Alexandria and Syria, the other to the rest of the world. Their authenticity is in question, but a third edict, almost certainly authentic, has been transmitted independently in a papyrus).[26] In the second of the two edicts transcribed by Josephus, Claudius makes it clear that friendship played a central role in his support of the Jews:

> King Agrippa and Herod, my dearest friends, having petitioned me to permit the same privileges to be maintained for the Jews throughout the empire under the Romans as those in Alexandria enjoy, I very gladly consented, not merely in order to please those who petitioned me, but also because in my opinion the Jews deserve to obtain their request on account of their loyalty and friendship to the Romans" (Ant. 19.288–89).

Claudius's preference for the Jews in their conflict with the Alexandrians is tied up with personal fondness for Agrippa and his brother Herod.

Their friendship is corroborated, or at least illustrated, by a text known as the "Acts of Isidore," included in the so-called *Acts of the Alexandrian Martyrs*, a collection of quasi-historical stories from the perspective of the Alexandrian Greeks.[27] The surviving fragments of "Acts of Isidore" record a trial that pits Agrippa against Isidore and Lampo (we know Isidore as a Greek "sycophant" who slanders the Jews during Philo's interview with Caligula in *Embassy* 355). Claudius is present, and his sympathies are clear, warning the Greeks not to attack his "friend" Agrippa. The text is almost certainly referring to Agrippa I who grew up with Claudius in the imperial court, and played a central role in resolving his conflict with the Senate after Caligula's death (Ant. 19.265–66).[28] Claudius was so fond of Agrippa I that he expanded his dominion, delivered a panegyric on the king, and celebrated a treaty with him in the Forum (19.274–75). That same affection seems to explain the emperor's responsiveness to Agrippa and Herod, described here, not implausibly given Agrippa's role in Claudius's rise to power, as his "dearest friends."

Apart from wanting to please those friends, however, another consideration is said to motivate Claudius, his opinion that "the Jews deserve to obtain their request on account of their loyalty and friendship to the Romans." What ties the Romans and the Jews together is the same kind of affection that binds Claudius and Agrippa, a friendship that leads Claudius to gladly confer privileges on them. Claudius speaks as if he had reached this opinion on his own, but what we have seen here suggests that he was probably conditioned in his views by how Jews presented themselves, a process that, as we have reconstructed it here, required more than simply demonstrating one's loyalty and like-mindedness but also distinguishing oneself from a flatterer disguised as a friend. If Philo is to be believed, Agrippa I seems to have been especially effective at depicting the Jews in this way, momentarily convincing Caligula to refrain from violating the Temple (*Embassy* 333). That same skill, very possibly practiced by the same Agrippa, may lie behind Claudius' subsequent embrace of the Jews as his friends.

Despite this friendship, relations with the Romans would deteriorate rather quickly, culminating with the Jewish Revolt and the Temple's destruction. Why Jewish-Roman relations take this course is a complicated question that far exceeds the limits of our sources and the ambitions of this book, but at least part of the problem can be glimpsed in the encounter between Gessius Florus, the procurator of Judea on the eve of the Jewish Revolt, and the Jews. Florus did a number of things to provoke the Jews; according to Josephus, "he stripped whole cities, ruined entire populations, and almost went the length of proclaiming throughout the whole country that all were at liberty to practice brigandage on condition that he received his share of the spoils" (*J. W.* 2.278). Matters reached a crisis level when Florus extracted seventeen talents from the Temple. Jews rushed to the Temple to protest the outrage, calling on the emperor to liberate them from Florus's tyranny, a demonstration that prompted Florus to send his army to suppress the uprising. Seeking to avoid a confrontation, the citizens of Jerusalem went out to greet the procurator with an "obsequious reception" (2.297), but he dismissed the gesture. Dismayed by his contempt, the Jews dispersed, and Florus attacked the city. He is said to have killed 3,600 people, helping to launch the Jewish Revolt.

The personal connections, institutions, and practices that had tied Jews to the Roman Empire all seem to fail in this episode. The Herodian line continued through the person of Agrippa II, son of Agrippa I, but he happened to be away in Alexandria at the time of Florus's attack. His sister Berenice was present and tried to petition Florus, but the procurator not only ignored her, but had captives executed before her eyes and would have killed her too had she not fled to her palace (*J.W.* 2.309–314). In an earlier phase of the crisis, the Jews had tried to bribe Florus, but though he accepted their money, he had done nothing in return (2.288). Gestures of servility did nothing to win him over either, the procurator dismissing the obsequiousness of the Jews as a "show of cordiality" (2.299). The Jews had not forgotten that the emperor might intervene to protect them, and when Agrippa II returned to Jerusalem, they pressed him to send an embassy to Nero to denounce Florus. The king was reluctant to do this, however, and his effort to talk the Jews into putting up with Florus so exasperated the populace that they formally banished him from the city (2.342–407). For their part, a Jewish faction had decided to halt the sacrifices offered in the Temple on behalf of the Romans and the emperor (2.408–9), a move that terminated the Jews' personal bond with the emperor by disrupting the offerings through which they expressed their love and gratitude to him. Administrative mismanagement and mutual resentment quickly overwhelmed all the mechanisms that had sustained Jewish friendship with Rome: Herodian mediation, formal delegations to the emperor, and the use of the Temple as a virtual imperial cult.

Before we consider how Jewish tradition endeavored to survive this crisis, however, we must consider another art of cultural persistence used to sustain the Temple under Roman rule, one that was artful in the conventional sense of the term.

~ 4

Optical Elusions

In 1981 the U.S. Department of Energy established a task force to address the very problem that preoccupies this book—how to sustain something over time. The task force was commissioned to develop a plan for protecting nuclear waste repositories from what the government referred to as "the human interference factor"—the possibility that people living 100, 1,000, or 10,000 years from now, having forgotten the dangers of getting too close to radioactive waste, might try to gain access to the sites and their contents. The Human Interference Task Force, as this commission was called, did not have to figure out how to build containers that would last that long or where to place them—these were problems for engineers to solve (though they still have not done so to this day). Its job was to develop a warning system that could alert people 300 generations from now about the dangers of radioactivity without relying on English or on linguistic and social conventions bound to change between now and 12000 C.E. The challenge facing the task force was how to institute a self-perpetuating, fail-safe tradition protected from future intruders regardless of how different their inclinations or psychologies may be from our own.

To come up with a solution, the task force commissioned Thomas Sebeok, the famous semiotician from Indiana University. Sebeok reasoned that since we cannot know how people 10,000 years in the future will communicate or what they will understand, whether they will know how to read or not and which physical senses they will rely on for information, it was best to send the warning repeatedly and through every imaginable channel: posting numerous signs of course, but also developing ways to inculcate a habit of avoidance, creating myths of supernatural retaliation and curses like those which guarded the tombs of the pharaohs, establishing a self-perpetuating "atomic priesthood" to make sure would-be intruders stayed away; even investing the place with a really bad smell in case people in the future only rely on their noses.[1]

The ancient Temple in Jerusalem was also vulnerable to the "human interference factor," with imagined consequences of intrusion no less lethal than radioactivity. To defend against such incursions, the Bible establishes defense mechanisms not unlike those devised by Sebeok: taboos restricting entrance into the Temple; stories warning of divine punishment for encroachers, and a self-perpetuating priesthood charged with protecting the Temple. Jewish efforts to enforce this taboo created a danger of its own, however, one that Sebeok's plan does not address. In the famous myth of Pandora's box, the proscription against opening the box (in the original myth, a vase) is precisely what tempts Pandora to open it, the restriction engendering in her what psychoanalysts refer to as scoptophilia, the urge to see forbidden objects.[2] The Pandora myth helps expose a potentially fatal flaw in Sebeok and the Bible's effort to construct a fail-safe taboo: any attempt to forbid humans from entering a space might actually increase the chance of intrusion by exciting the impulse to see what is forbidden.

This is the predicament in which Jews found themselves in the Greco-Roman period, their efforts to keep intruders out of the Holy of Holies actually creating in some foreigners the compulsion to see what was hidden behind the Temple curtain. In an incident described by *3 Maccabees*, the Hellenistic ruler Ptolemy IV Philopator was impressed when he saw the Temple's "excellence and beauty" and wanted to see more (1:9), threatening to enter that part of the Temple restricted to foreigners. The Jews did everything they could to discourage him from going any deeper into the Temple's interior, explaining that only the High Priest was allowed into the inner sanctuary and he only once a year. Their efforts to keep him out only increased the king's resolve to go in, however, "Why should not I at least enter, whether they wish it or not?" (1:15) The Romans were also gripped by scoptophilia, which proved irresistible for some. When Pompey forced his way into the Temple in 63 B.C.E., he was impelled to enter the sanctuary not to plunder it but simply to behold its secrets—the candelabrum and lamps, the table, the vessels for libation, and other sacred treasures (*J. W.* 1.152; *Ant.* 14.71–72). The Romans who helped Herod to capture Jerusalem were so eager for "a view of the temple and the holy things in the sanctuary" that Herod had to hold them back with threats (see *Ant.*14.482–3, *J. W.* 1.354). Decades later when Titus conquered the Temple, he was overcome by this impulse as well, drawn into the Temple's interior where he "beheld the holy place of the sanctuary and all that it contained—things far exceeding the reports current among foreigners" (*J. W.* 6. 260).

Josephus's description of the Romans is consistent with what we know about their addiction to visual stimulation, an addiction that as Carlin Barton has noted, the Romans themselves described as a cannabalistic hunger of the eyes.[3] In the first century, these eyes were constantly feeding on a steady diet of elaborately staged spectacles supplied to them by their rulers and patrons—gladiator games, circuses, chariot races, aquatic shows, and "fatal charades," public executions staged as a retelling of an historical event or mythological tale.[4] The Romans were also hungry for exotic sights, and the emperor did his best to supply those as well, appropriating the statues of foreign gods, obelisks, and other curiosities from Egypt, Greece, and other conquered territories for public display in Rome. All this had a highly disruptive effect on the cultures from which these marvels were plundered, including, as Josephus's narrative makes clear, Jewish culture where Roman curiosity about what lay inside the Temple led to its violation. The anxiety this threat provoked in Jews may be registered in *3 Maccabees*, thought by some to have been composed in the Roman period.[5] There the king's threatened penetration of the Temple's interior is associated with the exposure of everything that is traditionally hidden in Jewish culture of the time. When the unmarried maidens learn of what the king plans to do, they rush out from the chambers in which they are normally closeted; and newlyweds, heedless of their nakedness, leap from their beds and run about the city. The scene is fictional, but it registers a worry that was very real, the fear of losing control over all the secrets of one's culture under a regime insatiably curious about what it cannot see. The fact that the core of Jewish culture, the interior of the Temple, was visually off-limits to foreigners threatened to exacerbate Roman intrusive instincts by courting scoptophila, rendering the Temple a mysterious Pandora's box begging to be pried open.

Within a century and a half of conquering Jerusalem, Roman eyes did finally pry into the Temple's hidden interior. The culmination of that process was the triumphal parade orchestrated by Vespasian and Titus after the Revolt, a spectacle described in vivid detail by Josephus (*J. W.* 7.131–62). One of the main purposes of the triumph was to share the sights of battle with the citizens of Rome, and included in this particular parade was a series of painted panels that pictured the various stages of the war so realistically the spectators felt they "were happening before their eyes."[6] The parade also featured the exhibition of captured booty, the most conspicuous of which were the objects that Titus had removed from the sanctuary—the golden table of the showbread, the famous seven-branched menorah, and a copy of the Jewish law (7.148–150). In the end, the Roman appetite for exotic sights overwhelmed the defense mechanisms that Jews had developed to protect the Temple from incursion, not only breaking into the forbidden Holy of Holies for a look but also exposing its contents to public display.

And yet, for roughly 130 years prior to the Temple's destruction, Jews had managed to sustain the Temple under the Roman gaze, keeping the Temple intact even though they could not keep Roman curiosity at bay. One of the ways they accomplished this was simply by threatening those who tried to penetrate the Temple, as Herod did by brandishing a sword to keep the Romans from seeing anything they were not allowed to see (*Ant.* 14.483). Obstructing the Roman gaze was a risky undertaking, however, as the guardians of the Temple once discovered when they inadvertently blocked the Romans' view of things. This had not been their intention; the eyes they had intended to repel were those of the Jewish king Agrippa II who had constructed a tower overlooking the Temple where he could view the Temple proceedings while dining. Believing it "contrary to tradition for proceedings in the Temple—and in particular the sacrifices—to be spied upon," Temple officials built a wall obstructing Agrippa's view. In the process of doing so, they also blocked the view of the Roman guard stationed in the Temple, enraging the Roman procurator Festus who demanded that the wall be taken down. The conflict was eventually resolved when Nero ruled that the wall could remain, but his decision came at a cost, for the emperor also detained the Temple treasurer and high priest as hostages (*Ant.* 20.191–6). To avoid the costs of direct confrontation with Rome, I wish to argue, Jews developed an alternative to physical obstruction, a way to satisfy Roman eyes without allowing them to violate the Temple.

Something like this tactic is reflected in a story told by the third century Roman author and teacher of rhetoric Claudius Aelianus (fragment. 47). According to Aelianus, the mythical king Battos of Cyrene sought to indulge his "greedy eyes" by seeing the mysteries of the goddess Demeter, secrets not to be spoken about, much less seen by the uninitiated.[7] In the end, Battos got his just deserts when those guarding the mysteries ambushed him, but it is the initial effort to deter the king from even trying to enter the temple that has relevance for us. In a preemptive ruse, the Temple priestess tried to distract Battos's attention by engaging him with other sights that he could view without violating the sanctity of the mysteries. In what follows I wish to propose that Jews attempted to keep the Romans out of the Temple through an analogous tactic, not deflecting them in so direct a way but doing so indirectly through descriptions of the Temple designed to tempt the eyes away from its interior. At first glance, these descriptions, the best examples of which are preserved in Philo and Josephus (the latter writing after the Temple's destruction but probably reflecting in his descriptions of the Temple representational conventions crystallized earlier in the Roman period),[8] read like eyewitness accounts, and that is how they are read by scholars who use them to reconstruct what the Temple looked like. A closer look exposes them as an effort to manipulate the act of seeing—to shape what the viewer sees of the Temple, or wants to see. My argument is that these descriptions are an attempt to counter Roman scoptophilia—not to directly thwart Roman eyes because that may only whet their appetite more, but to lure them away from the Temple's forbidden interior, to distract them and keep them satisfied with sights they could safely feast on without violating the prohibition against foreigners in the Temple.

The tactics that Jews used in constructing these descriptions of the Temple were not of their own making but were drawn from the stock of techniques that Greek and Roman authors used to convey the visual experience of seeing a spectacle or a great work of art in writing, a rhetorical mode known as *ekphrasis.* Although these descriptions appear to be quite conventional, to characterize them as slavish imitations of Greco-Roman rhetoric would obscure their creative negotiation between the desire to see and the constraint imposed on seeing by the Temple's sanctity. To appreciate how these descriptions served the struggle for Jewish cultural persistence, we must think of Greco-Roman literary convention not as an influence that Jews absorbed passively but as a representational toolkit that they drew on selectively. Philo and Josephus are particularly helpful in this regard, since they allow us to observe texts switching these techniques on and off as they guide the reader through the Temple.

While we have no way of measuring the effect of these literary descriptions or their role in deflecting Roman intrusiveness, there is one indication of the kind of effect they might have had. Josephus tells us that after gaining control over the Temple, Titus convened a meeting of his generals to decide what to do with it. Some urged that the Temple be destroyed since the Jews would never surrender otherwise; others argued that the Temple should be saved if the Jews surrendered. Titus rejected both proposals, deciding that he would not "under any circumstances burn down so magnificent a work; for the loss would affect the Romans, inasmuch *as it would be an ornament for the empire if it stood*" (*J. W.* 6.236–242, italics mine). The Temple was ultimately destroyed of course, but for a moment, Titus contemplated saving it so as not to deprive the empire of something marvelous to look at. I am arguing that imperial rule did not come to see the Temple in this way on its own but was conditioned in its response by Jewish efforts to use literature to mediate what foreigners saw of the Temple and how they saw it.

Pandora's Box Inside Out

At first glance, the descriptions of Philo and Josephus do not seem to deflect the viewer's gaze but rather to draw it close by accentuating the visual delights that the Temple offered. According to Philo, the Temple's monumental dimensions attracts the eye to it, especially that of foreign visitors who are mesmerized by what they see:

> The huge size and height of the sanctuary make it in spite of its comparatively low situation as prominent as any of the highest

> mountains. In fact, so vast are the buildings that they are seen conspicuously and strike the eye with admiration, especially in the case of foreign visitors, who compare them with the architecture of their own public edifices and are amazed both at their beauty and magnificence. (*Spec. Laws* 1.73)

So astounding a spectacle was bound to attract Roman eyes, and that indeed is its effect according to a story that Philo tells about Marcus Agrippa, grandfather of Caligula:

> When he surveyed the temple and the rich array of the priests and the worship paid by the native population he was filled with wonder, thinking that he had seen something to be profoundly reverenced, something greater than words could describe. His discourse to those of his friends who were there with him consisted of nothing else but praise of the sanctuary and all that pertained to it. Thus throughout the days which he spent in the city out of courtesy to Herod he resorted to the precinct, delighting himself with the spectacle both of the ornate structure and of the sacrifices and the ritual observed in the services and the majestic aspect of the high priest when arrayed in the sacred vestments and conducting the holy rites. (*Embassy* 295–296)

The spectacle of the Temple so mesmerizes Agrippa that he cannot stop talking about it to his friends and feels impelled to return again and again for the delight of seeing it. One might think that this was exactly the kind of attention that the Temple would want to avoid. It was the Temple's impressive exterior that tempted Ptolemy Philopator's to try to enter its forbidden inner sanctuary, causing panic among Jews, and Caligula's discovery "that of all the temples anywhere (the Temple) is the most beautiful" (*Embassy* 198) is what tempts him to appropriate it. This is not what happened when Marcus Agrippa visited the Temple, however. Its marvelous appearance did draw him to it, but he never transgressed its sanctity and even became a benefactor (297).

Marcus Agrippa's reverence for the Temple, though it manifests itself in what seems like religious devotion, was inspired not by religious belief but by artistic delight, the aesthetic wonder triggered by the Temple's size and beauty. Even as Jewish efforts to stress the Temple's eye-catching qualities posed a risk to the extent that they attracted Rome's attention, that attention was held in check by the reverence that a great work of art could inspire. The Romans recognized that art required oversight, preservation, and protection.[9] In fact, some artwork was kept in Temples like the Temple of Peace, where Vespasian deposited the golden vessels of the Temple after their triumphal procession, a kind of Temple-museum embellished "with ancient masterpieces of painting and sculpture" (*J. W.* 7.160). To the degree that Jewish representations of the Temple could induce the Romans to view it as a work of art, they enhanced the Temple's chances of survival by casting the Romans in the role of curators motivated to safeguard the Temple not because they had a stake in maintaining Jewish tradition per se but because anything of great aesthetic value deserved preservation. As we have noted, this is how Titus did respond to the Temple according to Josephus, deeming it worth saving because of its ornamental value.

Facilitating the transition of the Temple into an aesthetic experience was Herod's redesign of the Temple complex, a building project beginning in 20/19 B.C.E. and lasting at least nine and a half years (according to John 2:20, building was still ongoing in Jesus' day). The basic parameters of the Temple itself were constrained by biblical law and ancestral custom, but Jewish tradition did not dictate the design and decoration of the larger complex in which Herod embedded the Temple when he reconstructed it, and Herod was clearly motivated by a desire to make it beautiful as well as religiously acceptable. This at least is Herod's stated goal according to a speech reported in *Ant.* 15.385 in which he declares that "the enterprise which I now propose to undertake is the most pious and beautiful one of our time." With the Temple platform expanded to 172,000 square yards, there was plenty of room to make it beautiful in fact—to inspire awe by the sheer size of the Temple complex and its buildings, and to engage and delight by means of intricately designed and highly ornate gates, porticoes, columns, and arches.[10] The degree of direct Roman influence on the Herodian Temple design still awaits investigation, but Herod does seem to have had his Roman benefactors in mind when building it, as he did with other cities and buildings he dedicated to them, including his renovation of the tower adjoining the Temple renamed "the Antonia" by Herod in honor of his friend Mark Antony.[11]

In addition to its role in defending the Temple, in fact, the Antonia may have provided Romans like Marcus Agrippa with the vantage point they needed to take in the spectacle of the Temple cult in all its majesty.

The Temple's transformation into an aesthetic object was not realized through architecture alone, however; it also depended on literary mediation—intervention by texts that called attention to the Temple's artistic attributes and modeled how to respond to them. By the first century C.E., Greco-Roman representation of aesthetic experience, *ekphrasis*, was governed by long-established conventions, many of which we can illustrate with help from Josephus's description of Vespasian's triumph. He begins by calling attention to his inability to convey in words what was seen on that day—"It is impossible adequately to describe the multitude of those spectacles and their magnificence" (*J. W.* 7.132)—as if to distance what then follows in the text, a description of the pageant, from an experience mediated through words. Josephus then turns to what scholars of *ekphrasis* refer to as "pathetic optics," the focalization of the scene through the perceptions and emotions of spectators within the narrative.[12] In describing the *pegmata* featured in Vespasian's triumph (moving stages on which were depicted various scenes from the war), he emphasizes their effect on onlookers: "the art and magnificent workmanship of these structures now portrayed the incidents to those who had not witnessed them, as though they were happening before their very eyes" (146). Through such devices, the text conveys a sense of what it was like to experience the scene directly, an effect that the Greeks referred to as *enargeia:* "the expression of things in words in such a way that an affair seems to be taking place and the subject to be present before the eyes." (Not coincidentally, this is the effect that the *pegmata* within Josephus's narrative have on those viewing the triumphal procession, their lifelike images portraying events "as though they were happening before their very eyes," a *mise en abyme* which helps to further attenuate the distinction between direct and mediated experience).[13] The effect of unmediated perception is an illusion, however, concealing the narratives efforts to mold and model the reader's response.

There is evidence that Jews already employed such devices in the Hellenistic period. Both of the techniques described above are found in the Letter of Aristeas, a text from the Hellenistic period which uses them to convey the amazing beauty of cult objects: 1) focalizing the reader's perceptions through the eyes of eyewitnesses ("those who approached to view it were unable to tear themselves away from the brilliance and delight in what they saw . . . As people looked at the actual furnishing in gold, a certain fascination ensued, coupled with awed amazement. . ." (77–78); and 2) emphasizing the limits of verbal description ("every man who comes near the spectacle I have described will experience astonishment and amazement beyond words" (99). Jews continued to use both techniques in the Roman period, Philo in the *The Special Laws* ascribing to the Temple "a beauty baffling description" (1.72) and describing its buildings from the perspective of foreign visitors "who compare them with the architecture of their own public edifices and are amazed both at their beauty and magnificence" (1.73). A second look at Philo's story of Marcus Agrippa reveals that this scene alone employs both of these devices within a single sentence, using the Roman himself as the spectator through whom it focalize its description, even as it calls attention to the limits of description: "he was filled with wonder, thinking that he had seen something to be profoundly reverenced, something greater than words could describe" *(Embassy* 295*).*

This last example suggests that such descriptions could serve a tactical role in the struggle for Jewish cultural persistence. It is drawn from the letter that the Jewish king Agrippa I sends to Caligula in his attempt to dissuade the emperor from installing an imperial statue in the Temple (see the last chapter). In the letter, the reader will recall, Agrippa conjures a procession of imperial ancestors, seeking to demonstrate to Caligula that his family had an established history of supporting the Temple despite its lack of imperial images. The case of Marcus Agrippa does more than simply provide another precedent, however. Using the sort of literary motifs that Homer used to describe the shield of Achilles, and Virgil deployed to depict the artwork of Daedalus—ascribing to the Temple the same power to elicit wonder, even as it resists description—Agrippa aims to turn the Temple into an aesthetic experience that transcends cultural differences between Jews and Romans. The intended effect can be compared to the "taxonomic shift" imposed on African and Indian religious objects when they were installed in European museums to be viewed alongside of, and in analogy with, European art. In this case, though, one committed to the preservation of his own indigenous culture, the Jewish Agrippa (or the author Philo), actively encourages the reclassification of the Temple as fine art in an effort to forestall the far more disruptive taxonomic shift threatened by Roman rule: the Temple's transformation into a pagan shrine.[14] *Enargeia,* the power that Greek and Roman imaginations ascribed to words that made it possible for them to make an object appear before the eyes, presented an opportunity for Jews seeking to sustain the Temple. Through descriptions designed to simulate visual experience, Jewish authors intervened in how the Temple was seen by Roman rulers, accentuating its aesthetic qualities, and modeling a reverential response to seeing it.

Turning the Temple into an aesthetic object could not stop Roman eyes from wanting to see too much, however. To the contrary, as *3 Maccabees* illustrates, a foreigner entranced by the Temple's beauty might not be content with viewing it from the outside in and might try to see more than Jews were allowed to reveal. To address this challenge, when Jewish authors turned their attention from the Temple's exterior to its forbidden interior, they shifted discursive tactics, practicing what one might describe as the opposite of *enargeia:* the description of an experience in such a way that there appears to be nothing for the eyes to see, or to get excited about seeing. After praising the Temple for its magnificence, for example, Philo goes on to say of the Holy of Holies:

> For all inside is unseen except by the high priest alone, and indeed he, though charged with the duty of entering once a year, gets no view of anything. For he takes with him a brazier full of lighted coals and incense, and the great quantity of vapour which this naturally gives forth covers everything around it, beclouds the eyesight and prevents it from being able to penetrate to any distance. (*Spec. Laws* 1.72)

When the High Priest enters the inner sanctum once a year on the Day of Atonement, it is not to glimpse some mystery, Philo explains; to the contrary, the priest cannot see anything at all because of the vapor coming from his incense burner. In a move that inverts the technique of pathetic optics, Philo describes things from the perspective of the high priest as he enters the sanctuary, and the experience he conveys is the negation of perception, an eye unable to penetrate the scene. This is in marked contrast with how Philo describes the Temple's outer courts which, in his account, are designed to be maximally accessible to the eye, the law prohibiting all groves and thickets around the Temple on the principle that "broad spaces and openness and absence of restriction on every side where there is nothing to hinder the sight are most suitable to a temple, to enable those who enter and spend their time there to have an accurate view" (1.75). The Holy of Holies seems an exception to this principle—there sight is hindered—but Philo's inversion of pathetic optics evacuates it of alluring mystery: there is really no point to wanting to peek into it since not even those allowed to enter can see anything inside.

When Josephus's narrative turns the reader's attention to the Holy of Holies, it does not merely fog things up; it claims that there was nothing there to be seen at all, depicting the Holy of Holies as a black hole completely devoid of matter and light:

> The innermost recess measured twenty cubits, and was screened in like manner from the outer portion by a veil. In this stood nothing whatever: unapproachable, inviolable, invisible to all . . . (*J. W.* 5.219)

In the *Jewish War*, we are given some information about the interior of the Temple building, its measurements and what it contained (*J. W.* 5.215–218), only the Holy of Holies is rendered "invisible." In the *Antiquities*, all that lies within the Temple building is completely occluded. Instead, the reader is told that King Herod was not allowed into the priestly courts where the Temple stood since he was not a priest (Ant. 15.420).

The Holy of Holies as depicted by both Philo and Josephus is marked by its nullification of spectacle, the voiding of anything that might fascinate, delight, or astound. Reinforcing this impression is a carefully timed deployment of the conventions of *ekphrasis*. Especially instructive in this regard are Josephus's descriptions, probably based (as I have noted) on sources composed before the Temple's destruction. These offer an elaborate description of the Temple complex, like Philo using pathetic optics to convey the emotional impact of seeing it with one's own eyes. Describing the ornate interior of the porticos, for example, Josephus remarks in the *Antiquities* that these "seemed incredible to those who had not seen them and were beheld with amazement by those who had set eyes on them" (Ant. 15.416). Especially in that work, however, he only applies ekphrastic convention to those parts of the Temple complex that may be entered by a foreigner or that may be seen from where foreigners were allowed to stand in the complex. Beyond that limit—clearly marked by the inscriptions forbidding entrance to foreigners (417)—there are no more references to the response of onlookers, and barely any description of the Temple's interior (391–417). That Josephus stops using ekphrastic technique might reflect the fact that there really was much less in this part of the Temple to impress spectators, but the historian's earlier description of the Temple complex in the *Jewish War* shows that there was more to be described than he chooses to disclose in the *Antiquities*. I think it more likely, then, that the abandonment of *ekphrasis* is deliberate, that, in contrast to his description of the Temple's outward parts, Josephus's goal in describing the Temple's interior is precisely *not* to draw readers in, *not* to make them feel present, *not* to engage their emotions.

While the Temple's interior was already considered visually off-limits to non-priests in the biblical period, there was nothing inherent in this taboo to prevent an author from disclosing its contents through words, as happens in Ezekiel (chapters 42–43) and in apocalyptic descriptions of the Heavenly Temple.[15] The few descriptions of the Temple that we have from the Hellenistic period that use the techniques of *ekphrasis* afford a relatively unimpeded view of the sanctuary and its contents. The *Letter of Aristeas* allows its title character, an ambassador from Egypt, to take in "the entire scene" of the Temple and its cult: the design and decoration of the altar and the movements of the priests as they performed their services. Viewing things from a nearby citadel, Aristeas has such a clear line of sight that he can even make out the tiny flowered tassels decorating the high priest's vestments (96). Similarly, the author known as Hecataeus, ostensibly a Greek from the fourth century B.C.E. but perhaps really a Hellenistic Jew writing under a pseudonym in the second century B.C.E., has his readers enter the Temple and view its contents without mentioning any limit on what the eye can see (a passage cited by Josephus in *Against Apion* 1.197–99). In these earlier descriptions, there is no shifting of rhetorical gears, no switch from *ekphrasis* to anti-*ekphrasis*, as there is in descriptions of the Temple from the Roman period.

It is in the Roman period, moreover, that we have evidence of other authors seeking to negate vision in the same way that Philo and Josephus do. One such author is the Greek geographer Pausanias (ca. 150 C.E.) who used a very similar technique to protect the cultic secrets of Greece. A kind of literary tour-guide of Roman Greece, Pausanias's account points out numerous features about its landscape and history that might be of interest to a Roman sightseer, but it becomes notably uncommunicative when describing temples and cults, clouding things up with what John Elsner calls a "rhetoric of absence."[16] Thus (to cite an example we shall return to in Chapter 5) when Pausanias describes the sacred mysteries venerated by the Messenians, he says only that it was a "secret thing" and never tells us exactly what it was or what it looked like. When turning to the sanctuary of Eleusis, he even suggests that the gods themselves intervened to prevent him from revealing any details: "My dream forbade the description of the things within the wall of the sanctuary, and the uninitiated are of course not permitted to learn that which they are prevented from seeing" (*Description of Greece* 1.38.7).[17] Pausanias generally accommodates his reader's curiosity about the monuments and marvels of Greece.[18] When he comes to its temples, however, he reverses course, translating the taboo against physical access to the sacred into a representational taboo that denies the reader access as well; as Elsner writes, "the reader who travels through Greece with Pausanias, in his order, at his pace, along his roads, is left outside the sacred wall."[19] According to Elsner, this rhetorical move was an attempt to preserve the cultic and mythological traditions of Greece outside the domain of Roman rule, safely impenetrable to all outsiders including Pausanias's Roman readers.

The similarity to what is observed in Philo and Josephus suggests that the rhetorical devices deployed by these authors to describe the Temple—*ekphrasis* and its negation—were both taken from Greco-Roman literary practice. What strikes me as especially resourceful—and opportune—about the Jewish use of these devices to describe the Temple is the way it combines them. *Ekphrasis* invests the reader in the Temple as an aesthetic delight worthy of preservation, but in switching to a "rhetoric of absence" just as the reader's imagination enters the inner sanctuary, Jewish authors direct attention away from the Temple's interior, and toward the shimmering surface that could be viewed by an outsider without transgression. The resulting impression of the Temple turns it into an inverted Pandora's box, with an awe-inspiring outside designed to attract and engage the eye, and an interior that generates no temptation despite being off limits, because it offers nothing to see or that is worth seeing.

What prompted Jews to develop this way of describing the Temple, I would argue, was the challenge of surviving under a scoptophilic Rome. The Temple stood a greater chance of being left intact if it was perceived by the Romans as an aesthetic treasure, as an ornament for their empire. Jews encouraged this perception by drawing on the conventions of *ekphrasis* to emphasize the Temple's artistic qualities. That tactic also posed risks, however, drawing Roman eyes to the Temple in a way that could easily prove dangerous if they were tempted to see more of the Temple than Jewish tradition allowed. It was to protect against this threat that Jews sought to render the Temple's interior unenticing through a "rhetoric of absence" that offered nothing for eyes prone to penetrate the forbidden. The descriptions from this period that scholars rely on for their knowledge of the Herodian Temple's appearance, however accurate the measurements and other details they provide, are the product of these tactics operating in tandem, working to excite wonder at the sight of the Temple's exterior while dampening curiosity about its hidden interior. They may or may not allow us to see what the Temple *actually* looked like, but they do allow us to see what their authors *wanted* the Temple to look like, at a time when its chances of survival would go up if it could manage to appear both mesmerizing and unalluring simultaneously.

Lethal Exposure

Jewish use of *ekphrasis* may have deflected Roman eyes for a time, but the sights it offered were illusory, relying on various rhetorical gimmicks to pass verbal descriptions off as direct visual experience. In the end, the hunger of Roman eyes could only be satisfied by direct visual experience, the kind that Titus achieved when he broke into the Temple to see for himself what lay inside and then shared with others by parading the Temple's hidden contents through the streets of Rome. The Greek historian Polybius observed an analogy between *ekphrasis* and the sort of triumphal pageant in which the Temple's contents were displayed: both shared visual experience with those not present to see it directly, only instead of relying on words to transport its audience to the scene, the triumph brought the scene to the audience in a form it could actually see with its own eyes.[20] Taking a detour before the theatres of Rome "in order to give the crowds an easier view," the triumph celebrating the Roman victory over the Jews was designed to do just this. The *pegmata*, depicting various scenes from the war, allowed spectators to view its highlights "as though they were happening before their eyes," an effect heightened by the stationing of captives on the moving stages, posed in the attitude in which they were taken (*J. W.* 7.146–147). In a similar way, the display of the golden menorah and other cult vessels captured from the Temple allowed the citizens of Rome to see for themselves what Titus had seen in the sanctuary, an experience unconstrained by the limits of verbal description.

Thanks to the so-called Arch of Titus, we can glimpse this procession with our own eyes. Probably built in his honor by his brother Domitian after Titus's death in 81 C.E., the arch's inner side features the famous relief depicting the contents of the sanctuary—the seven branched menorah, the table of showbread, the priestly trumpets—carried aloft in Titus's triumphal procession.[21] The scene is most lifelike, the attendants appearing to move away from the viewer toward an arch in the distance, but a closer look reveals that this realism is the result of what art historians have come to refer to as "Flavian illusionism."[22] What appears to be an unmediated glimpse of the vessels is anything but, the panel directing the eye's movements by foregrounding parts of the scene and obscuring others in darkness. In a cruel twist, the scene projects the negative image of the Temple as portrayed by Jews, thrusting its unseen contents into the illuminated foreground while erasing its visible exterior from view.

Still, something of the Temple survived. Noting the survival of the golden menorah and of other cultic objects looted from the sanctuary, Josephus himself may have believed it possible to retrieve them from Rome, thus allowing the cult to be resuscitated just as the Temple had been restored in the days of King Cyrus. In the *Antiquities*, Josephus notes many earlier instances when benevolent foreign rulers—Cyrus, Darius, Ptolemy Philadelphus, Antiochus III—had opted to return plundered cult vessels, make a gift of new vessels, or help to rebuild the Temple, often citing royal decrees to document their generosity (*Ant.* 11.12–18; 123–30; 12.40–84; 13.138–44). The most recent of these was a decree issued in 45 C.E. by Claudius that returned to the Jews the holy vestments and crown of the high-priest kept under Roman control (20.10–14). On the basis of these precedents, Josephus may have hoped that the Flavian dynasty might restore what it had taken. Titus even seems to have made a promising start, making a gift of sacred books to Josephus himself (*Vita* 418).

If Josephus had had expectations for a full-fledged restoration of the Temple, however, he was disappointed, Rome refusing to allow such a thing, at least in the historian's lifetime (see Chapter 8). The cult still might not have gone entirely extinct, however. While much of the Temple's contents languished in Vespasian's Temple of Peace never to be retrieved, some vessels may have escaped the Romans' grasp, perhaps enough to have restored the cult. There may even have been ways to salvage the cult without such objects. Even if we had far more evidence from this period than we do, detecting these efforts would undoubtedly pose a challenge since their purpose was to be evasive, to sustain and revitalize the Temple cult below the radar of Roman rule. We shall try to detect them nonetheless, tracking a fugitive Jewish tradition as it runs for cover in the Judean wilderness and in other even more remote hiding places.

~ 5

Flights of Fancy

One hesitates to draw on lessons about cultural persistence from the Holocaust when, as Primo Levi observed, the path to perdition was broad and the paths to salvation difficult and improbable. Precisely because those paths were so improbable, however, the concentration camp reveals the impulse to survive operating at the outermost limits of possibility. Most Jews interred in the camps did not survive this experience, of course, and those who did were usually far too preoccupied by the challenges of brute physical survival to attend to the demands of Jewish religious tradition. Very occasionally, however, someone managed to find a way to keep the Sabbath or mark a holiday. At Buchenwald, for example, a group of young men celebrated Hanukkah by procuring a can of machine oil and lighting an impromptu Hanukkah lamp under a bunk. Prisoners in other camps found ways to construct a *sukkah*, the temporary shelter built in observance of the Festival of Booths. At the camp in Plaszow, one was erected in a lumber yard and disguised as a storage bin; in Auschwitz, a sukkah was hidden between large barrels.[1] Under watch by ruthless guards, and in circumstances of complete exhaustion, deprivation, and terror, Jews were yet able to find opportunities to observe Jewish tradition, improvising with whatever materials were available, finding places in which to conceal ritual practice.

In this chapter, I argue that early Jews used analogous techniques to preserve the Temple cult under Roman rule, developing ways to relocate it in hidden or out of the way places beyond the enemy's reach. This tactic was introduced in Chapter 1 when looking at the legend of the hidden ark, but that story reflects a mythologized understanding of the First Temple's destruction, not what Jews actually did to salvage their cultic tradition. Did Jews ever really try to hide the Temple cult? Early Jews did imagine the Temple cult on the move. The Bible describes an age when the cult led what one recent scholar describes as a locomotive existence: the days of Israel wandering in the wilderness. In this period, the cult was housed in the Tabernacle, what Josephus describes as a "portable and a wandering temple," that could be packed up and carried from place to place.[2] Even after that cult was settled in Jerusalem, Jews could still envision it taking flight. Ezekiel depicts such a scenario, for example, alleging that God had abandoned the Temple on the eve of its destruction to join the Jews in exile, there establishing "a little sanctuary" (Ezekiel 11:16). The Hebrew Bible constrained the Temple's mobility by fixing it in Jerusalem, but some of its material also established the possibility of relocation, of moving the sanctuary or evacuating God to a new locale. Was there ever any effort to activate these options?

As far-fetched as it might seem, relocating the Temple to a new setting was a real possibility. In Greece, there is evidence of whole temples moved stone by stone from one place to another during the Roman period (a phenomenon referred to by classicists as "itinerant temples").[3] We have no evidence of Jews attempting to move the Temple in quite that way, but as we shall see below, we do know of at least one effort to relocate the Temple to Egypt by other means. That was with the permission of Egypt's ruler at the time, however. Relocating the Temple was a formidable undertaking because of the practical obstacles in the way, and to accomplish this without the knowledge of foreign rulers would have been all the more difficult, especially in the Roman period. Rome had the Temple under continuous surveillance by soldiers stationed in an adjacent tower known as the Antonia (*J. W.* 5.244–45), and in that tower the Romans kept the special vestments of the high priest, without which he could not perform his duties, under lock and key (*Ant.* 15.403–408; 18.91–95). In the hidden ark myth, Jeremiah has no difficulty finding a secure hiding place. It was far more difficult to deploy such a tactic when the enemy was as watchful as Rome. After the Second Temple's destruction, some Jews resorted to the same tactic to preserve their possessions that Jeremiah had used to safeguard the ark, hiding their wealth underground, but it did not take long for the Romans to find it (*J. W.* 6.432; 7.114–15).

As impractical as it was to relocate the Temple—and as difficult as it was to do so without being detected—Jews may nonetheless have found ways to smuggle their cultic tradition out of Jerusalem, not by actually moving the Temple but by using their imaginations to project it from one place to another. We know of just such a phenomenon in the age following the Temple's destruction, when Jews and Christians transferred the identity of sacred spaces located in Jerusalem to local synagogues and churches, a phenomenon to which Jonathan Z. Smith has called attention as a sign of the increasingly mobility of the sacred in late antiquity.[4] One means of effecting this relocation was through what Smith describes as *metonymy:* using something physically associated with the sacred place to transfer its essence to a new locale. Another means was what Smith calls *metaphor*—the forging of a resemblance between two unlike things that makes it appear as if the qualities of one have been transferred to the other. Jews in late antiquity used this tactic to transform the synagogue into a quasi-Temple, imitating aspects of the original—the *parokhet*, the *soreg*, et cetera—in the synagogue's design.[5]

While neither metaphor nor metonymy could do anything to transport the Temple in a literal sense, we should not for that reason underestimate their power to relocate its presence in other ways. Helpful for understanding Smith's argument here is Stanley Tambiah's study of magical speech.[6] Tambiah noted that metonymy and metaphor correspond to the two kinds of "sympathetic magic" identified by James Frazier, each a way of acting on objects without physically manipulating them. Contagious magic, like metonymy, operates through the principle of contiguity: an object that has been in contact with another—a person's garment for instance—is thought to have the power to influence the person even from a distance. Imitative or homeopathic magic, like metaphor, operates on a principle of similarity, allowing one to effect an object by acting on a likeness of it or an effigy. From the perspective of their practitioners, metonymic and metaphoric thinking (or contagious and imitative thinking in Frazier's parlance) can overcome distance, putting what is absent or inaccessible in normal reality within reach through what Frazier describes as a kind of magical telepathy: "Whatever doubts science may entertain as to the possibility of action at a distance," he observed, "magic has none." Smith suggests that the same processes can work as a form of virtual transport, moving a temple through space.

Smith and those who follow his analysis associate the emergence of these tactics with the shift in late antiquity from "locative" religiosity that pinpoints the sacred in a fixed place (e.g., the Temple) toward "diasporic" religiosity in which the sacred is ambulatory or diffuse. Without challenging this narrative, I would nevertheless argue that in the first century C.E., when Jews did not yet know that the Temple was doomed to obsolescence, they were employing these tactics for a different end, not to re-place the sacred but to protect it from displacement by the Roman Empire. By coincidence, perhaps, these tactics play a similar role in Rome's own struggle for cultural survival, or so suggests the epic poet Virgil in his account of how the Romans' Trojan ancestors preserved their culture after Troy's destruction. The pious Aeneas, the ancestor of the Romans, is said to have carried a portable symbol of Trojan tradition with him as he fled the city, the *Penates*, his family household gods. Rescuing the *Penates* was what allowed Aeneas and his descendants to continue the tradition of his lost city, to reestablish a new Troy in Italy. During the course of his journey across the Mediterranean, Aeneas encounters another group of Trojan exiles who have founded a "little Troy" in Epirus modeled on the original, having been drawn to the site because of its resemblance to the topography of their homeland (*Aen.* 3.349). Reflected in Virgil's epic, as Maurizio Bettini has recognized, are both of the tactics that Smith describes, Aeneas using a "metonymy," portable statues of the gods, as a vehicle to transport Trojan tradition from one place to another; the other Trojans relying on "metaphor" to recreate Troy through a likeness.[7] I propose that Jews in the Roman period endeavored to relocate the Temple using precisely these tactics.

Triggering these Jewish efforts at cultic relocation was the Roman Empire's displacement of the sacred. Noting its similar effect on the sacred spaces of Greece, Susan Alcock observes that the Romans carted off thousands of Greek cult statues to serve as public monuments or private trophies in Rome, or else moved them around within

Greece. From a famous sanctuary at Tegea, for example, Augustus removed images of the goddess Athena Alea and installed them in Rome; and Nero is said to have appropriated some 500 statues from Delphi, "some of gods, some of men" (Pausanias, *Description of Greece* (cf. 105), 8.46.1–5; 10.7.1).[8] Roman imperialism uprooted the gods of Egypt in the same ways, appropriating its divine images and symbols for urban display or imitating their appearance in Egyptianizing monuments.[9] Roman rule, in other words, tended to have an *unsettling* effect on the sacred places that it controlled, moving cult objects from one place to the other, or appropriating their qualities through imitation. I cannot prove it, but I suspect that the forced migration of the sacred that occurred under Roman rule played a catalytic role in the transition to the more ambulatory religiosity that Smith discerns in late antiquity, if only inadvertently, by undoing the fixity of sacred space and dislodging cult symbols from their places.

Like others in the Roman Empire, Jews also suffered cultic dislocation under imperial rule. After destroying the Temple in 70 C.E., the Roman army removed cult objects like the Temple's menorah and altar for display in an imperial temple in Rome, and may have relocated other sacred objects elsewhere in the empire (according to one sixth century chronicle, the cherubs in the Temple were set up in Antioch).[10] Through the telepathic tactics of metonymy and metaphor, Jews asserted a kind of imaginary control over their cultic tradition: preserving those vestiges of the Temple they did retain so as to reestablish the cult in a safer location, or creating a double that could serve in its place. Perhaps it is because these kinds of relocation are so fantastical that they never seem to quite work, falling short of rematerializing the Temple in a stable form. Though they may fail to meet our standards of reality, for those who believed in their power, these tactics effectively sustained the Temple as a viable counter-reality, under the surface of a Roman controlled reality, or in a realm beyond it.

So I shall attempt to argue with those vestiges that I have at my disposal. Compounding the challenge of detecting efforts that early Jews sought desperately to keep hidden is the nature of our sources. We know little of what Jews did in the Roman period outside of what we are told by Roman sympathizers like Philo and Josephus, Jews whose goal it was to reassure their Roman audience that they, and the tradition they represented, had nothing to hide. Recall that according to Philo, for example, Moses bid his disciples to allow "the clear sunlight to shine upon their own life" by displaying everything they do in public (*Spec. Laws* 1.319–322). One may well question whether it is possible to detect anything behind the surface of these sources, much less the furtive concealment of tradition that we are trying to uncover.

Thanks to another kind of evidence, however, we do know some of what Jews in this period were hiding from outsiders. Remote, inhospitable, and pocked with countless caves, the Judean wilderness was a natural refuge and hiding place long before the Romans arrived on the scene. (cf. *2 Macc.* 5:27). Jews in the Roman period took refuge there, not only hiding within its caves but also apparently creating new ones, one recent survey found over 40 caves or cave complexes dug out in the period of the Jewish Revolt.[11] I am not suggesting that we look for vestiges of the Temple itself concealed in these caves, but what has already been found there is of critical use to our investigation—the Dead Sea Scrolls. The scrolls afford an unexpected glimpse at the kinds of tactics that Jews in this period used to hide their activities from others. Some of the scrolls are written in a cryptic script; others, in a kind of coded terminology.[12] Both kinds of text, thought to have been produced by the Qumran sect, suggest a community seeking to conceal itself from outsiders, as does the apparent decision of this sect to settle in an isolated locale and hide their library in caves.

It may not be a coincidence that one of the Dead Sea Scrolls, the famously mysterious *Copper Scroll*, records an act of concealment, the hiding of a large amount of cultic vessels, gold and silver, and other kinds of precious objects. The scroll does not disclose why this treasure was hidden, but scholars of an earlier generation have made a connection to the hidden ark legend, arguing that the scroll was modeled in some way on Jeremiah's effort to safeguard the ark after the First Temple's destruction. Hardly any contemporary scholars now accept this interpretation, but before we dismiss it, we need to consider some previously neglected evidence, evidence of a similar tactic used by another culture seeking to sustain its traditions under Rome.

Smuggling the Temple to Safety

Given its name by scholars because it was inscribed on two copper sheets, the *Copper Scroll* records a set of instructions for how to find coins and other kinds of treasure hidden in various places around Jerusalem. Here is a sampling:

> In the ruin which is in the valley of Achor, under the steps leading to the East, forty long cubits: a chest of silver and its vessels with a weight of seventeen talents. KEN.[13] In the sepulchral monument, in the third course: one hundred gold ingots. In the great cistern of the courtyard of the peristyle, in a hollow in the floor covered with sediment, in front of the upper opening: nine hundred talents. (col. 1.1–8)[14]

Who hid these treasures and why? What circumstances led to their concealment, and who was intended to find them? The scroll itself provides no clear answers. Many believe that it was written in the time of the Second Temple's destruction on the basis of its paleography, but one cannot absolutely rule out a later date—130 C.E., for example, the time of the Bar Kochba Revolt. Some of the hiding places have been identified, but many remain obscure, and despite numerous treasure hunting expeditions, the treasure itself remains out of sight.[15] The last item mentioned in the list is a copy of the scroll hidden in a tunnel with graves at its entrance. Finding this copy could conceivably answer our questions since it may include an "explanation" (col. 12.11–13).[16] It too remains elusive, however, leaving scholars to puzzle over the copy in our possession.

Undeterred by the lack of evidence, some scholars have tried to solve the mystery of the *Copper Scroll* nonetheless, reading it carefully for clues about where the treasure comes from and why it was hidden. There is consensus on one point of relevance to our investigation: A good portion of the treasures are cultic in nature—tithe vessels, libation bowls, and priestly garments. By one count, approximately 25 percent of the list's 61 or so hiding places contain identifiably religious materials, with the possibility of a cultic provenance for the rest of the treasure as well, much of it coin hoards that could have come from the Temple treasury or been intended for deposit there.[17] This, and the fact that several of the hiding places are associated with priests or priestly names, has led many scholars to conclude that the treasures come from the Temple.[18] We know from Josephus that numerous Temple vessels and cultic implements were either destroyed by the rebels during the Jewish Revolt (*J. W.* 5.562) or handed over to the Romans (*J. W.* 6.387–91), but this did not preclude the possibility that other cult objects were smuggled out of Jerusalem without Roman knowledge. According to a number of scholars, the *Copper Scroll* is a record of their concealment from shortly before or just after the Second Temple's destruction.

The assumption that the *Copper Scroll* records a *real* treasure distinguishes these hypotheses from another way of reading the scroll that was first proposed by J. T. Milik. Milik argued that the scroll was not a record of actual buried wealth but a reflection of the hidden ark story.[19] Noting that the *Copper Scroll* does not enumerate any item clearly associated with the First Temple like the ark, Milik conceded that its author might have adapted the legend in light of the Second Temple, but he nonetheless maintained that the treasure itself was a mythical conceit. In support of this hypothesis, Milik produced an intriguing parallel, a Hebrew text called *Masseket Kelim* that was known in a medieval version and in a later version discovered in Beirut inscribed on two marble plaques.[20] Like the *Copper Scroll*, *Masseket Kelim* records a long list of cultic vessels hidden in various locations, but it also contains a prologue that explains that the vessels were hidden before the First Temple's destruction by Shimmur the Levite and other notables from the Bible. They were to remain hidden until the coming of the messiah and the return of the exiles to Israel when, presumably, the Temple would be rebuilt. *Masseket Kelim* obviously reflects the hidden ark legend, but it also shares traits with the *Copper Scroll*, not only in its list of cultic treasure but also in its reference to a "copper tablet." For Milik, *Masseket Kelim* confirmed the *Copper Scroll* as a reflection of the hidden ark myth, not a record of a real treasure but a figment of the imagination.

Milik's reasoning failed to convince the scholarly community, and today, most scholars believe that the scroll records a real treasure hidden for some reason during the Roman period.[21] It strikes them as implausible that someone would take the trouble to compose such a dry and precisely detailed record, and on such costly material, if what they were recording did not exist. As for *Masseket Kelim*, the parallel with the scroll is certainly intriguing, but its composition is too late to be taken seriously as a valid analogue. For these reasons, and perhaps also because of a lingering suspicion that Milik wanted to discourage others from hunting down a treasure he secretly knew to be real, most scholars dismiss the link between the scroll and the hidden ark story.

Despite this near consensus, however, it may be that the debate over whether the treasure was real or fictional polarizes two possibilities that may not have been fully distinct in the first century C.E., for we know that people in this period were capable of mistaking fictional buried treasure for the real thing. In 65 C.E., a Carthaginian named Bassus informed Nero that he had had a dream that revealed the location of an immense treasure of gold buried in a cave on his estate by Queen Dido at the time when she founded Carthage (*Ann.* 16.1–3). With Nero's men, he dug up his whole property, declaring this and that place the sites of the treasure, but he never found it. What is instructive about this incident for understanding the *Copper Scroll* is not just that Dido's treasure proved illusory but that its fictiveness was not apparent to the Romans or even to the unfortunate Bassus himself, who could only wonder how, after all his other imaginings had come true, this one alone had deceived him.

In a similar way, though we have come to think of the ark story as mythical, people in the first century evidently believed that the Temple's contents were actually hidden somewhere. During Pilate's administration, a certain man rallied a Samaritan mob to go with him to Mount Gerizim, their sacred mountain, where he promised to reveal the sacred vessels hidden there by Moses. The Samaritans followed him to the mountain only to find their way blocked by Pilate's forces (*Ant.* 18.85–87). For his part, Josephus is incredulous, accusing the Samaritan leader of mendacity, but he speaks as a hostile outsider to Samaritan culture—the Samaritans themselves clearly believed the vessels were really hidden somewhere under Mount Gerizim, so much so that, like Bassus, they were ready to put their lives on the line to recover them.[22]

It is possible, then, that the *Copper Scroll* treasure was mythical, as Milik argued, but was understood to be real by the author of the scroll who described it accordingly. Alternatively, the treasure might have been real, as so many scholars suspect, but the act of concealing it modeled on the hidden ark myth. If this were the case, one would expect the treasure to include the most prominent cult objects kept in the sanctuary at the time—objects that could serve as the seeds of cultic revival, just as the ark does in the myth. However, the contents of the sanctuary—the menorah, the golden altar, and other famous objects—were all taken by the Romans. In their absence, could less conspicuous cult vessels play a revitalizing role? What little evidence we have supports this possibility. According to *2 Maccabees* 1:19–36, some priests seeking to preserve the Temple cult from the Babylonians took fire from the altar and hid it in the hollow of a dry cistern. When the Jews returned from exile, the descendants of the priests were unable to retrieve the fire, but they did find some "thick liquid" which proved sufficient to re-ignite the sacrifice. That even a dormant residue of sacrificial oil was enough in the minds of some to revive the Temple sacrifice suggests that anything linked to the Temple could be seized upon to resuscitate cultic practice, including the kind of generic cult vessels listed in the *Copper Scroll.* What invested an object with this power was its identity as a physical remnant of the Temple, or in other words, its role as a metonym.

Further support for this hypothesis is a striking parallel from the Greek world, an analogue neglected in previous studies of the scroll. A Greek people known as the Messenians suffered a disruption of their culture, not unlike that inflicted upon the Jews by Babylonian conquest, when they were defeated by the Spartans and sent into exile. The Greek geographer Pausanias reports that the Messenian leader Aristomenes learned from a prophecy that his people were to be defeated and that the survival of their culture depended on their burying a "secret thing," something that Pausanias never describes clearly but is small enough to be contained within a bronze urn:

> If it were destroyed, Messene would be overwhelmed and lost for ever, but if it were kept, the oracles of Lycus the son of Pandion said that after lapse of time the Messenians would recover their country. Aristomenes, knowing the oracles, took it towards nightfall, and coming to the most deserted part of Ithome, buried it on the mountain, calling on Zeus who keeps Ithome and the gods who hitherto protected the Messenians to remain guardians of the pledge, and not to put their only hope of return into the power of the Lacedaemonians (*Description of Greece* 4.20.2)[23]

Classicists today understand this story as a myth. The age of Aristomenes probably never happened, Pausanias's story preserving a pseudo-history fabricated in the fourth century B.C.E. to supply a recently emergent Messenian state with a connection to Greece's heroic past.[24] The parallel with the hidden ark story is so patent that some scholars believe the Messenian myth was in fact its model.[25] What I find remarkable about the story is its association with a real object that bears a certain resemblance to the *Copper Scroll*, the Messenian mysteries—a sacred relic kept in Hellenistic Messenia before it was transferred to the nearby town of Andania, to be kept in some kind of wooden chest (4.33.5).[26] Pausanias tells us little about the mysteries themselves, but when he proceeds to describe their rediscovery in the days of the Theban general Epaminondas, it becomes clear that they bear at least a physical resemblance to the *Copper Scroll*. At this time, in 369 B.C.E., Epaminondas allowed the Messenians to return to their homeland under the leadership of Epiteles. The latter is said to have had a vision revealing where the lost mysteries were hidden, and digging there, he discovered a bronze urn, which he took to Epaminondas. When the latter opened its lid, he found the mysteries inscribed on "some tin foil, very thin, rolled up like a book" (4.26.8). Their recovery allowed the newly returned Messenians to revive the tradition that had been disrupted during their war with the Spartans and subsequent exile, and they, along with the urn in which they were found, were venerated as sacred objects. In Jewish tradition, *Masseket Kelim* makes a strikingly similar connection between object and story, mentioning a copper scroll among the treasures hidden in the time of the First Temple's destruction, but it is so chronologically remote that its testimony has proven easy to discount. It would render our argument that much more plausible to find an ancient text that connects a copper scroll with the hidden ark myth in the way that *Masseket Kelim* does, but short of finding such a missing link, the story of the Messenian mysteries is the next best thing, an *ancient* story that embeds a very similar object within a very similar myth.[27]

Since we do not know what the mysteries were exactly, it is impossible to compare them with the contents of the *Copper Scroll*, and there is no reason to think that they were especially similar. If the *Copper Scroll* treasure does come from the Temple, however, they may share at least one trait in common, for there is evidence that the Temple's vessels were also regarded as a mystery, something not to be seen by outsiders. According to biblical law, the Israelites were forbidden from seeing the objects in the Temple's inner sanctum (Num 4:20), and this prohibition seems to have been extended to the cult vessels of the Second Temple. This at least is the implication a fragment of a non-canonical gospel composed before 200 C.E. (P. Ox. V.840) that describes Jesus confronting this prohibition as he tries to glimpse the vessels:

> A certain Pharisee, a chief priest, whose name was Levi (?), met them and said to the Savior, "Who gave you leave to walk in this place of purification and to see these holy vessels, when you have not washed nor have your disciples bathed their feet? You have walked into the Temple defiled, a pure place, wherein no other man walk without washing himself and changing his garments, nor does he venture to see these holy vessels.[28]

As Daniel Schwartz has recognized, the scene suggests that the experience of seeing the Second Temple's vessels was barred to the impure and the uninitiated.[29] If the *Copper Scroll* is a list of such vessels—as scholarly conventional wisdom thinks it is—these treasures may have had a resonance similar to that ascribed to the Messenian mysteries, a "secret thing" whose sanctity is marked by its visual inaccessibility.

All this is to argue that what we have in the *Copper Scroll* is not merely an attempt to protect some treasure from Roman despoliation but an effort to preserve Jewish tradition itself in a latent form from which the Temple cult could later be rekindled. No amount of circumstantial evidence can prove such a hypothesis, but the Messenian myth shows that another culture in the Hellenistic-Roman period used, or imagined itself using, a similar tactic to preserve its tradition from the disruption of war and conquest. If we take Virgil at his word, the Romans' own ancestor Aeneas had used a similar tactic to preserve his culture, smuggling out the Penates so as to revive the religion of Troy in his new homeland. In these cases, the cult objects have already been salvaged and the tradition restored. The *Copper Scroll* may give us a glimpse of a culture in the act of preserving itself—after the concealment of tradition but before its rediscovery. Indeed, the scroll may have been intended as the key to that rediscovery, for the information it provides—not just the quantities and kind of objects hidden but where they are and how far down to dig for them—are analogous not so much to the mysteries themselves but to the cryptic dream that shows Epiteles where to look.

However one understands the *Copper Scroll*, there is evidence of a revived interest in the hidden ark myth during the Roman period, as reflected both in the Samaritans' quest for the vessels during Pilate's administration and in apocalyptic tellings like *Syriac Baruch* written shortly after the Second Temple's destruction. It was precisely during this period that Jews were increasingly losing control over the symbols of their cultic tradition, a trend that culminated with the plundering of the Temple in 70 C.E. but was already emerging in the preceding decades as Romans looted the Temple treasure and assumed intermittent control over the priestly vestments. The hidden ark story modeled a way to counter Rome's control over the symbols of Jewish tradition, a way of rendering cult symbols immune to appropriation—or rather, since the hidden ark story seems to have been construed in different ways by different communities in the first century C.E., we should say that it suggested several possible courses of action.

One path is reflected in the Samaritans' attempt to recover the vessels, an effort to reassert control over the symbols of their tradition by actively looking for them in defiance of Roman rule. This tactic faced an insurmountable obstacle when it confronted Pilate's army. A second option, possibly reflected in *Syriac Baruch*'s retelling of the story, was to wait the enemy out—to surrender control over the real contents of the Second Temple and cling to the hope that the lost contents of the First Temple will, with God's help, be recovered one day. Our reading of the *Copper Scroll* is worth considering, if only because it suggests a third option mediating between the brazenness of searching for the vessels in the present, and the passivity of fantasizing about their return in the eschatological future—a way to place the Temple's contents beyond the enemy's control without surrendering Jewish control over the timing of their recovery.

Duplicates and Decoys

Although it might be possible to hide the Temple's contents, doing so still entailed loss and risk. Metaphor offered an alternative vehicle of transport. My use of this term in this way may be confusing for readers accustomed to thinking of metaphor as a figure of speech. As I noted above, what I mean by metaphor is the "telepathic" process that Frazier referred to as imitative magic—conjuring the presence of something absent by mimicking its qualities or creating a likeness of it.[30] What makes "metaphor" an even more apt expression for our purposes is the meaning of its Greek ancestor—*metapherein*, to transfer or carry—a meaning that explains why Josephus uses a form of the word to describe the tabernacle as a "portable" temple (*Ant.* 3.103). By means of metaphoric thinking, Jews were indeed able to render the Temple portable, relocating it to places even less accessible to Rome than the Judean wilderness.

The process I have in mind seems to predate the Roman period, producing something like an effigy of the Temple in Hellenistic Egypt, an imitation Temple built by a priest named Onias after he fled to Egypt from Jerusalem at the time of Antiochus IV's conquest of the city. The story of its construction is told by Josephus in the *Jewish War* and the *Antiquities*. The first work reports that after receiving permission from Ptolemy VI and Cleopatra II, Onias settled in the area of Heliopolis where he "built a small town on the model of Jerusalem and a temple resembling ours" (*J. W.* 1.33). The *Antiquities* adds that this temple was constructed from a ruined Egyptian temple in a fortress known as "Bubastis-of-the-fields" (13.66, 70), cleansed by Onias and reconstructed in the image of Jerusalem. This resemblance is the most prominent characteristic of Leontopolis for Josephus, notwithstanding *J. W.* 7.427 where he seems to have second thoughts, claiming that the temple "was not like that in Jerusalem."[31]

Since we are speaking of an actual temple, it may seem strange to call it "metaphoric," but its construction does seem to have involved a metaphoric transference, projecting the qualities of Jerusalem and its temple onto an Egyptian fortress. This is exactly what the Trojan exiles did at Epirus to create a "new Ilium," relocating Troy in a new location by reproducing elements of its appearance. Virgil and Josephus even refer to their respective replicas in similar language, with Epirus described as "a little Troy" (*Aen.* 3.349); the Leontopolis temple, as "similar to that at Jerusalem, but smaller and poorer" (*Ant.* 13.72). Through this simulation, the Trojan exiles constructed a copy of Troy "better shielded from Greeks" (*Aen.* 3.495–9). Fleeing Jerusalem at the time of Antiochus's persecution, Onias may have had a similar consideration in mind when constructing a copy of Jerusalem, hoping thereby to establish a temple well insulated from the sacrileges being inflicted on the original. This is what Theodore of Mopsuestia (d. 428 C.E.) suggests in his account of the Leontopolis Temple: "Observing these things [the construction of a gymnasium and other outrages in Jerusalem], the blessed Onias was grieved, and lamented and protested. Since he saw that evil was increasing, he left the city and departed for Egypt where he raised an altar and constructed a temple."[32] While he could not literally move the Temple to Egypt (a refuge because it was outside the Seleucid kingdom, where Antiochus IV raged, falling under the protection of another kingdom), Onias did the next best thing, fabricating a copy that transposed Jerusalem's attributes onto an already existing Egyptian temple.

An ongoing debate about Onias's motives and the circumstances of Leontopolis's construction complicates this reconstruction. The problem traces back to Josephus, our principle source for the history of Leontopolis. His two accounts in the *Jewish War* and the *Antiquities* are simply inconsistent, ascribing to Onias different sets of motives and even identifying Onias himself differently. In the *Antiquities*, he is Onias IV, son of the Onias featured in the *Jewish War*; and his exile to Egypt is connected not to Antiochus's persecution but to his failed effort to attain the office of high priest in Jerusalem (*Ant.* 12.387). It is simply not possible to combine these contradictory accounts into a coherent historical narrative. As a result, some favor Onias III as the builder of the Temple, situating it against the backdrop of the Temple's desecration, but many others ascribe it to his son and place its construction later, after the Temple's restoration under the Maccabees.[33] There is no way to decide between these historical reconstructions.

What is important here, however, is not what really motivated the construction of this temple, but the tactical option that it exemplifies—it was possible for a Jew in the Hellenistic period to relocate the Jerusalem Temple by creating a likeness of it. Such a move flatly contradicts our understanding of biblical tradition, where the Temple seems well anchored in Jerusalem, and Jerusalem well anchored in Judea, but Onias's reading of scripture evidently allowed for the possibility of relocation, the priest believing that the prophet Isaiah had prophesied a temple in Egypt: "on that day there will be an altar to the Lord in the center of the land of Egypt" (Isa. 19:19. See *J. W.* 7.432; *Ant.* 13.68).

For those who have their doubts about Josephus (he also claims that the Samaritan Temple was "similar to that in Jerusalem"), there is evidence that the Qumran sect engaged in a similar kind of cultic relocation, projecting the attributes and role of the Temple onto its own community. The *Community Rule* (1QS), a text composed in the mid-to-late second century B.C.E., instructs its audience to leave the place of its residence, presumably Jerusalem, and establish a community that seems patterned on the Temple, forming a foundation for a "holy of holies":

> The Community council shall be founded on truth . . . to be an everlasting plantation, a holy house for Israel and the foundation of the holy of holies for Aaron, true witnesses for the judgment and chosen by the will (of God) to atone for the land . . . (col. 8.5–6)[34]

According to this passage, the organization of the community mimics the structure of the Temple. The community council, a group of 12 men, are identified as a "holy house for Israel" that will in turn establish a foundation for a metaphoric inner sanctum, a "holy of holies for Aaron," probably an inner circle of Aaronic priests. The Temple language returns in the next column:

> When these exist in Israel in accordance with these rules in order to establish the spirit of holiness in truth eternal, in order to atone for the guilt of iniquity and for the unfaithfulness of sin, and for the approval of the earth, without the flesh of burnt offerings and without the fats of sacrifice—the offering of the lips in compliance with the decree will be like the pleasant aroma of justice and the perfectness of behaviour will be acceptable like a freewill offering—at that moment the men of the Community shall set apart a holy house for Aaron, in order to form a most holy community [literally, a community of the Holy of Holies], and a house of the Community for Israel. (col. 9.3–6)

The language is confusing and arguably inconsistent,[35] but the thrust seems to be that, provided that the sect (or its council) conducts itself properly, it can serve as a virtual Temple, effecting atonement and making offerings of a sort. Like Onias's Temple, inspired by a prophecy in

Isaiah (19:19), the author of this text understands the formation of the community as a fulfillment of prophetic vision, specifically Isaiah 40:3: "In the wilderness prepare the way of the Lord, make straight in the desert a highway for our God." The difference is that the temple that this community constructs is not a physical replica, but one constituted through the community's prayer and conduct ("the offering of the lips in compliance with the decree will be like the pleasant aroma of justice and the perfectness of behaviour will be acceptable like a freewill offering").

Some scholars take this Temple language literally, imagining a full-fledged cult at Qumran replete with an altar and sacrifices.[36] No clear evidence of a temple or altar at Qumran has emerged, however, and most scholars now seem inclined to the view that the Temple language is closer to what we call a metaphor, referring to the community's efforts to substitute for the Temple at a time when it was considered defiled either because of Antiochus's desecration or as a result of incorrect priestly practice.[37] Even as a figure of speech, this temple still bears a resemblance to Onias's Temple, however, and not just because they arose in the same period and possibly under similar circumstances.[38] Each depends on the principle of similarity to construct an alternative to the Jerusalem Temple, a copy or a substitute, that serves the same function as the original *but somewhere different*, somewhere better protected or less accessible.

We have no direct evidence of such temple copies being fashioned in response to Roman rule, but there is evidence of a related tactic used to similar effect. In the wake of the Second Temple's destruction, some Jews came to consider the actual Temple, the one just destroyed, as the copy of an original located safely beyond reach. An apocalyptic text known as *4 Ezra*, set after the First Temple's destruction but like *Syriac Baruch* written after the destruction of the Second Temple, alleges that the Temple actually survived intact, unseen except to those to whom God revealed it.[39] Ezra himself is given a glimpse of this Temple, described as the fourth of seven visions reported in *4 Ezra*. He is ordered by an angel to go to an abandoned flower field, where, after praying to God, he sees a woman mourning for her son who had died on his wedding day. She is not what she appears to be and quickly transforms into an immense city-temple (10:27). The angel reveals that the woman was actually Zion in disguise, grieving for the destruction that befell her son Jerusalem (49).[40] Because Ezra tried to comfort her, God now desires to console him in return by showing him the city in its true form: "do not be afraid, and do not let your heart be terrified; but go in and see the splendor and vastness of the building as far as it is possible for your eyes to see" (10:55).

How does Jerusalem survive its destruction and by what means has it arrived in Babylon? Not in the way it survives in the hidden ark legend. In an earlier speech lamenting the Temple's destruction, Ezra reveals that nothing of the Temple's physical structure or contents has escaped the Babylonians, not even the ark: "For you see that our sanctuary has been laid waste, our altar thrown down, our temple destroyed . . . the ark of the covenant has been plundered, our holy things have been polluted."[41] All is not lost, however, for it turns out that the Jerusalem destroyed by the enemy is not the real Jerusalem, which will be revealed in the future: "behold the time will come . . . that the city which now is not seen shall appear" (7:6. Cf. 8:52; 13:36). This passage builds on an idea hinted at in Isaiah 6 and other biblical passages that the real sanctuary, the "true tent" of God as Hebrews calls it (8:1–2), lies in heaven.[42] Though the earthly copy is now lost, the heavenly prototype persists, invisible but no less real, as Ezra now discovers.

The Temple of *4 Ezra* is metaphoric in a different sense than the temples of Onias and the Qumran sect. Of course, Ezra's city-temple does not take the concrete form that Onias's temple does; it is more like a vision (indeed, in 10:34, Ezra wonders aloud whether his mind is deceiving him), but it is really there, the angel allowing Ezra to enter and look around. In fact, this celestial Temple is more real than the Jerusalem Temple just destroyed by the Babylonians ever was, since that Jerusalem was but a duplicate of the celestial cult in a material form. This duplicate Temple was vulnerable in a way that its heavenly model was not, but it was also expendable. According to *4 Ezra*, with the material Temple gone, Jews might be tempted to mourn as Zion herself does, but they can take comfort in the knowledge that the real temple persists.

4 Ezra is speaking of the biblical past, but as Michael Stone maintains, it may register the personal visionary experience of its author.[43] Such experience may have been common in the Roman period in the decades leading up to the Temple's destruction. Daniel Schwartz notes several incidents reported by Josephus in which Jews withdraw into the desert in pursuit of visions. Schwartz believes that these groups were hoping to glimpse or conjure an otherworldly Temple much as the Qumran sect, also withdrawing into the wilderness, seems to have done.[44] In one case, for example, a group heads into the wilderness in the hope of gaining "rest from troubles" (*Ant.* 20.188), a term that may allude to the Temple in its role as a "resting place" (cf. Isa. 66:1; Ps. 132:8; and *4 Ezra* 8:52). Schwartz does not cite *4 Ezra*, but its description of a visionary city-Temple revealed in a field is consistent with his reconstruction, perhaps registering in a fictionalized form what these groups saw, or hoped to see, in the desert.

None of the groups that Josephus describes ever seems to achieve the visionary experience that it seeks, however, each one stopped in its tracks by the Romans, just as the Romans had stopped the Samaritans from finding the vessels hidden under Mount Gerizim. The group seeking "rest from troubles," for example, was hunted down by the procurator Felix (*Ant.* 20.188). The hidden cults or celestial Temples that Jews sought in this period always stood at a distance, like a mirage, and blocking access to them was a Roman Empire that could be ruthless in its effort to find what Jews were hiding from it and to track down those who fled. This is precisely why the kinds of "telepathic" thinking we have described here were of such value, however, enhancing the options for controlling and relocating the Temple cult. Thinking metonymically—concentrating the Temple's identity in portable, concealable symbols—a Jew could slip the Temple cult under the surface of reality, keeping it in safekeeping for the time being. Thinking metaphorically—creating a double of the Temple—a Jew could move it to safer territory or turn the Temple itself into an expendable copy. Both techniques rely on "flights of fancy" but at their core, I am arguing, is a survival instinct responding to reality, the impulse of a people threatened by Roman predation, greatly constrained in their ability to hide or flee in any literal sense, but moved to take flight nonetheless.

Backed into a Corner

At the end of Chapter 3, we noted that submissiveness and flattery seemed to have little effect on Roman rule in the decades prior to the Revolt, working with rulers like Claudius but failing under local administrators like Florus, who responded with contempt to Jewish efforts to placate him. In this chapter, we have seen that Jews in this period also had reason to balk at the prospect of flight. With imperial rule difficult to placate, and with many escape routes blocked off, the options for cultural survival narrowed in the years just prior to the Jewish Revolt, which may help to explain why that revolt happened. In modern colonial societies, it has been argued, the oppressed turn to violence only when other options cease to work, when colonial rule fails to respond to petitions and intervenes to prevent escape or migration.[45] A similar dynamic can be detected in first century Palestine, with many Jews convinced that revolt was the only option left for preserving their tradition.

In fact, the Jewish Revolt of 66–70 began with an act that expressed an intense frustration with both appeasement and evasion as tactics of cultural survival. In 66 C.E., Eleazar ben Ananias, son of the high priest and perhaps a member of the Zealot party,[46] sought to prevent the Temple from being used in service to the Empire, persuading his fellow priests to interrupt the sacrifices for the emperor and the Roman people (*J. W.* 2.409).[47] The act not only rejected submissiveness; it also rejected evasiveness by openly asserting defiance of Rome. Indeed, the Zealots may have called themselves "Zealots" precisely to distinguish themselves from the sneakiness of other factions, for what distinguishes the zeal of a Phinehas or a Mattathias is not just its righteousness but its brazenness, its willingness to defend tradition *in the open.* The next chapter explores the Jewish Revolt as an attempt to make the most of this option.

To approach the revolt in this way, I hasten to note, is not to suggest that the survival of Jewish tradition was the only issue at stake for the rebels. Jews undoubtedly had multiple reasons for supporting the revolt—the maladministration of procurators like Florus, oppressive taxation that together with a severe famine in 48 C.E. greatly exacerbated poverty, class tensions within the Jewish community, and conflicts with non-Jewish neighbors (indeed, recent scholars argue that the concept of a single revolt conflates several converging uprisings motivated by different interests and ideologies).[48] What little we know of the belief system of the rebels suggests, however, that they saw the defense of tradition and the Temple as one of their chief objectives.[49] Josephus acknowledges as much if only by being so adamant that the rebels were more sacrilegious than the Romans (e.g. *J. W.* 6.99–102)—an apparent inversion of how the rebels saw themselves.[50] Without denying the array of grievances and ambitions that fueled the Jewish Revolt, this study shall take it as a given that one of its principle and most widely shared motives was the defense of a religious tradition threatened by Roman rule. The question we seek to illumine is why so many Jews in this period came to see rebellion as a viable way of sustaining this tradition, opting for it over other, less risky tactics like submission or flight. To note that these other tactics had ceased to work well in the years preceding the revolt is certainly part of the equation, but it is not sufficient. We also need to understand how Jews overcame the disadvantages of violence, the futility and peril of provoking a fight with an enemy as powerful as Rome.

This problem should not be confused with the issue of what made rebellion a justifiable tactic of cultural survival from a Jewish perspective. Even someone as empathetic to Rome as Philo acknowledged that Jews had an obligation to die for and even to kill in defense of their tradition, noting for example that the law required them to put to death any foreigner who encroached into the Temple's inner sanctuary (*Embassy* 212). What we are seeking to understand, rather, is what made rebellion a *practical* option in a political context in which one could almost predict its failure. To challenge Roman rule was to court destruction. Already in the Hasmonean period, the Romans had a reputation for invincibility, Judah seeking to make them friends because he knew that "they have subdued kings far and near, and as many as have heard of their fame have feared them" (*1 Macc* 8:12). Jews in the first century C.E. had all the more reason to fear Roman power given the catastrophic consequences of local uprisings undertaken in defense of Jewish tradition. When Pontius Pilate drew on sacred treasure to fund an aqueduct, many Jews rioted only to be slain by the Romans or trodden to death in the ensuing flight (*J. W.* 2.175–77). Another riot that broke out under the procurator Cumanus, sparked when a Roman soldier exposed himself to a Jewish crowd, resulted in the deaths of twenty or thirty thousand Jews, depending on which of Josephus's estimates one may believe (*J. W.* 2.223–27; *Ant.* 20.105–112). For rebellion against Rome to become a workable option, one whose likelihood of success outweighed the obvious risks, Jews would have to figure out a way to counter its enemy's seeming invincibility—its immense army, superior weapons, and legendary discipline. The next chapter explores the techniques by which Jewish rebels attempted to reverse this power imbalance—how they convinced themselves that war against Rome was not simply irrational, and how irrationality itself served them as an ally.

~ 6

Conjuring Power

To rebel against the Roman Empire, cautions Josephus, was to violate a fundamental law of nature: "Yield to the Stronger" (*J. W.* 5.367). He makes this point in a speech which he claims to have delivered before the walls of Jerusalem in an effort to convince the rebels in the city to surrender before it was too late, and it is a thesis he argues throughout his account of the Jewish Revolt, both in his own voice as a general who had recognized the wisdom of surrender and through speeches that he attributes to various moderates who had tried to stop the revolt. In a lengthy speech that he attributes to Agrippa II, for example, Josephus runs through a lengthy catalogue of all the nations that had submitted to Rome: the freedom-loving Athenians who once defeated Persia; the Macedonians who ruled a vast empire under Alexander; the Carthaginians, the Egyptians, the Gauls, all stronger than the Jews and with a greater claim to liberty (2. 358–87). Why should the Jews be any different when they lack the weaponry, the funds, and the allies to launch a proper revolt? "Will you alone disdain to serve those to whom the universe is subject?" Agrippa demands to know, "Will you shut your eyes to the might of the Roman empire?" (2.361–62). To challenge that might was such madness that even killing one's own family was a better option (2.395).[1]

According to Josephus, those who supported the rebellion were in fact afflicted with madness (*J. W.* 5.407; 6.328; 7.267). They did show a certain cunning in the battle stratagems they employed, gaining momentary victories, but in the end, their arrogance, impiety, and impetuousness led them, their people, and their tradition to destruction. As the war progresses, the rebels (as Josephus portrays them) seem to grow increasingly oblivious to reality, ignoring the repeated warnings of Titus, Josephus, and even God, who had been sending portents of the coming destruction (6.288). The historian claims at one point that God Himself had made the rebels impervious to reason, "blinding their minds because of their transgressions" (5.343). Soberminded Jews able to recognize the self-destructive folly of rebellion either join the Romans as Josephus does, or, as in the case of the high priest Ananus, are cut down by the rebels.

In reality, the rebels may not have been quite as deluded as Josephus claims. The *Jewish War* alludes to a number of considerations that may have made revolt against Rome seem a reasonable option. Despite Agrippa II's claim that the Jews had no one to help them, there were potential allies they probably tried to recruit, including Jews living beyond the Euphrates (*J. W.* 1.5), who might have been able in turn to recruit the Parthian kingdom in Iran, which had defeated the Romans on several occasions, even briefly conquering Jerusalem in 40 B.C.E. Another factor that probably made rebellion seem a feasible option was the upheaval within the Roman Empire, especially after the death of Nero in 68, a time when the Romans were distracted both by a violent, fast-changing contest over who would become emperor and by uprisings among the Celts and the Gauls (1.4–5). And as a last resort, the Jews could rely on the inaccessibility of Jerusalem, a city protected by three walls that made it nearly impregnable (5.136–55). Fighting against Rome was fraught with risk, but for those who supported the Jewish Revolt, it was not the irrational undertaking that Josephus alleges it to be.

The tactical advantage that I wish to focus on, however, was one that, from our vantage point, may seem irrational—the belief that the Jews had at their disposal a divine power far greater than Roman might. Mindful of biblical history in which God often defeated enemies far more powerful than Israel—the Egyptians, the Philistines, the Assyrians—Josephus acknowledges that if God had been on their side, the Jews would have been invincible (*J.W.* 2.390; 5.377–391). God was *not* on their side, he goes on to insist, because the sins of the rebels had driven

God to switch His allegiance to the Romans (taking Josephus with Him), but the rebels themselves evidently thought differently, claiming God as an ally even in the very final stages of the rebellion. When the Romans broke through the second of the city's three walls, the rebels were insisting that God would yet save the Temple (5.459). Even after the sacrifices had been interrupted—mere days before the Temple's destruction—one of the rebel leaders was still boasting that "he could never fear capture since the city was God's" (6.98).

This chapter is an attempt to reconstruct how those fighting the revolt recruited the protective power of God, the techniques they used to summon His assistance and render His power manifest in the battle. Like Josephus, we may opt to dismiss the rebels' reliance on God's power as self-delusional, knowing as we do that they lose the war in the end, but Jews in this period—and Roman strategists, too, for that matter—recognized the recruitment of divine support as a real advantage in a battle against a more powerful enemy. In what follows, we seek to understand the tactic of enlisting divine support, and how this option was put into practice in the heat of battle.

To guide our interpretation, I have drawn heavily on the study of modern peasant insurrections, especially as analyzed by Michael Adas in his study *Prophets of Rebellion*.[2] This title refers to the role played in the instigation of rebellion by what Adas labels the "millennial prophet"—a shamanistic-like leader who instills his followers with confidence by summoning otherworldly beings or preternatural powers to counter the enemy's superior weapons and organization. Although the conjuring of such power was not in the end sufficient for overcoming the technological and organizational advantages of colonial rulers, it did make their defeat *seem* plausible for indigenous communities, and that perception was tremendously empowering in its own right. Prophetic visions that forecast victory could instill warriors with the confidence to mount a fight they would otherwise seem destined to lose. Wearing a talisman as protection against superior weaponry could embolden a warrior to charge against an enemy despite the likelihood of being slain. Incantations could counter an enemy's superior numbers by summoning supernatural allies to the battle. However much such practices might seem to deviate from modern Western standards of rationality, Adas argues that within a belief system that embraces such practices as effective, they do in fact constitute a rational response to a situation of extreme power imbalance, helping rebels to mobilize and reassure followers otherwise too intimidated to fight.

For many Jews living at the time of the Jewish Revolt, supernatural power of this sort was believed to be within reach, rendered accessible through practices like prophesy, biblical interpretation, wonder-working, and exorcism. Josephus certainly took such practices seriously, claiming to have witnessed an exorcism performed by a magician who ordered demons to move objects around (*Ant.* 8.46–48). For lack of a better term, I describe such practices as "magic," a vexed term in the study of ancient Judaism but still a workable label.[3] One might expect a Jew committed to the preservation of Jewish tradition to have avoided any practice that violated the biblical law against sorcery and divination (Deut 18:10–11), and indeed, the practices I have in mind do not include what the Romans referred to as the *artes magicae*—spells, potions, necromancy, et cetera.[4] Jewish tradition offered its own ways to enlist divine power, however—prayer, prophecy, curses, and so forth—practices that, if not described as magic by Jews themselves, did function in the same way, recruiting the help of supernatural beings; revealing the future; or sapping the enemy of his supernatural power.

I refer to these practices as the arts of the irrational not just because they rely on supernatural beings and powers but because Jewish rebels used them to overcome the sort of rational calculation that might restrain their followers from attacking an invincible foe like the Roman army. As it happens, *this* sort of irrationality gave the Jews a real advantage in the revolt. As Josephus acknowledges, the rebels gained a number of unexpected victories against the Romans, and what made them so formidable—apart from their use of ambushes and other ruses—was a kind of reckless daring:

> (The Romans) found their opponents in no wise chastened by their severe misfortunes, while their own hopes were continually dashed, their earthworks mastered by the enemy's strategems, their engines by the solidity of the walls, their close combat by the daring of their antagonists. But worst of all was the discovery that the Jews possessed a fortitude of soul that could surmount faction, famine, war and such a host of calamities. They fancied the impetuosity of these men to be irresistible and their cheerfulness in distress invincible. (*J.W.* 6.12–14)

The rebels as depicted in this passage seem indifferent to the considerations and calculations that ought to have kept them from attacking the Roman army, cheerfully charging forward despite the futility of doing so. The Romans found this confidence so confounding that they began to imagine that the Jews more powerful than they were—a perception that, for a time, very nearly did reverse the power imbalance between the two sides. Jews mustered this mind-set, I want to propose, through the use of magic-like practices that allowed them to recruit the irrational—fantastical powers able to operate beyond the constraints of reason—as an ally against Roman power.

A Method for Madness

The insurgent movements that Adas analyzes developed a number of magical techniques or devices in an effort to offset the military might and superior technology of their European colonizers, techniques that could make followers feel so invincible that they were sometimes ready to charge the enemy directly, running at them over open terrain and in the face of machine guns.[5] Adas divides these techniques into several categories, three of which are relevant for reconstructing the role of magic-like practice in making revolt against Roman rule appear a viable option to many Jews:

1. *Preparatory Omens of Victory.* To overcome the fear of challenging a more powerful enemy, millennial prophets seized on strange or catastrophic occurrences—an earthquake, a famine, a comet—as portents of the enemy's eventual defeat. Spread through rumor, such portents helped to embolden the populace by puncturing the image of the European colonizer as invincible.
2. *Enlisting Otherworldly Assistance.* Through prayer and other pre-battle rituals, millennial prophets were able to kindle, or rekindle, the enthusiasm of warriors who might otherwise despair at the thought of challenging a far more powerful enemy. Before battle, for example, Maori warriors would transmit their prayers to heaven by means of a tall pole from which pennants and ropes were hung, the *niu* pole, through which angels were thought to descend in response to their call. Through ecstatic singing, dancing, and hypnotic techniques,

Maori warriors would enter a frenzied or trance-like state in which they believed themselves possessed by guardian spirits. The psychological effect of such practices was to reverse the power imbalance between the rebels and the enemy by drawing into the battle the most powerful of allies or endowing the warriors with superhuman ability.

3. *Supernatural Shielding.* Related to #2 is the use of chants, talismans, and other devices to gain protection from the enemy's weapons. In Java, for example, rebels carried slips of paper with Arabic inscriptions calling on supernatural agents to disable the Dutch invaders. The Pai Maire used special chants to summon fog or mist to conceal them, or to deflect the enemy's bullets. The intended or perceived effect of such practices was to neutralize the enemy's modern weaponry, weaponry against which there would be little defense otherwise.

Europeans often dismissed such practices as evidence of native irrationality, but for cultures that relied in their daily lives on divination, charms, and other magical practices to protect against illness and other threats, they constituted a real source of power, in fact, the greatest power that could be imagined. To enlist this power was not to deny reality but to find within indigenous tradition ways to compensate for the enemy's technological advantages, to counter them or neutralize them. And when tradition proved insufficient, these movements were often ready to appropriate the enemy's power by imitating the practices, symbols, and devices that seemed to generate it. Thus, the Maori are known to have worn pieces of European uniforms as protective patches, and the *niu* pole itself may be an attempt to capture some of the power transmitted through the mast-head of European ships or the telegraph pole.[6]

Many Jews in first century Palestine operated with a similar view of reality. This at least is the impression one gets from sources like the New Testament where Jesus and his disciples are able to draw on supernatural power to contend with illness, hunger, and other problems impossible to remedy in other ways. The most famous example is, of course, the use of exorcism to banish the evil spirits that afflict so many people in the world that the New Testament describes. Jesus is a master of this technique, expelling demons by the sound of his voice.

The New Testament ascribes this power to God, but the authors of the Gospel seem worried that it would seem demonic in its own right, acknowledging that the Pharisees attributed it to Beelzebub, ruler of the demons (Matt. 9:32–34; 12:22–30; Mark 3:22–27; Luke 11:14–23). As is well known, Jesus was thought capable of a number of other astounding feats as well—curing blindness, deafness, and other maladies, calming a storm, feeding thousands from a few loaves and small fishes, prophesying the future, and raising the dead—and he was not alone in his extraordinary powers, for we know of other figures in the decades preceding the Jewish Revolt who also laid claim to supernatural ability.[7] A prophet named Theudas promised his followers that he would part the Jordan River, for example, and an unnamed prophet from Egypt claimed that he had the power to command the walls of Jerusalem to fall down (*Ant.* 20.97–99; 169–72). Josephus himself may have been such a figure, claiming to have received divine dreams that foretold the future (3.351).[8]

Given that Jews in this period believed it possible to overcome disease, scarcity, bad weather, and even death through supernatural means, it is not surprising to find them using such means to combat Roman rule. Jesus as we know him from the New Testament did not attempt to incite a rebellion against Rome, but other prophets from this period did use their abilities to provoke insurrection. Josephus makes reference to a number of such figures, "deceivers and imposters" who "under the pretense of divine inspiration fostered revolutionary changes" (*J. W.* 2.259). Among these was the Egyptian prophet mentioned above who, beyond promising to break down the walls of Jerusalem, sought to overpower the Roman garrison stationed there and establish himself as ruler. Although we know very little about them, such figures are clearly similar to the millennial prophets Adas describes, laying claim to a prophetic or wonder-working power that emboldened their followers to take on the Romans.

Josephus's narratives reveal very little about these leaders or the techniques they employed to mobilize their followers. There is reason to suspect, however, that such techniques had grown fairly elaborate by this period. A particularly intriguing piece of evidence is a text found among the Dead Sea Scrolls known as the *War Scroll* or *War Rule*. Written in Hebrew during the Hellenistic or early Roman period, the scroll describes an eschatological battle between the

Children of Light, with whom the Qumran sect may have identified, and the Children of Darkness, dominated by a nation known as the *Kittim* that most scholars identify as the Romans.[9] The scroll falls somewhere between apocalyptic fantasy and a military manual, enumerating the trumpets and banners, battle formations, and weapons that the Children of Light are to utilize against their enemies, then laying out the course of the conflict itself, a 40-year war with preordained stages. Supernatural beings are present everywhere in the war. Joining the Children of Light in the battle are God and his angelic armies; on the side of the Children of Darkness are Belial, a Satan-like figure, and his demonic forces. Instructing Israel in how to enlist the former and combat the latter, the *War Scroll* is something like a how-to manual for fighting with (and against) supernatural power.

The *War Scroll's* chief tactical objective, one might say, is to draw the power of God and his angelic warriors into the battle. Toward this end, for example, it banishes unclean men from the military camp to accommodate the presence there of holy angels who will join Israel's army (col. 7.6).[10] It also provides the words of blessings that not only praise God for his help but seem designed to stir him up into action: "Rise up, rise up, Oh God of gods, and be exalted with power" (col. 14.16). Since the enemy also fights with the help of supernatural allies, Belial and other evil spirits, the Sons of Light are instructed to turn to God in order to neutralize their influence:

> . . . and his brothers, the [pri]ests and the levites and all the elders of the array with him. And in their positions they shall bless the God of Israel and all the deeds of truth and they shall damn there Belial and all the spirits of his lot. They shall begin speaking and say: "Blessed be the God Israel for all his holy plan and for all the deeds of his truth, and blessed be all who serve him in justice, who know him in faith [blank]. Accursed be Belial for his inimical plan, may he be damned for his blameworthy rule. Accursed be all the spirits of his lot for their wicked [blank] plan, may they be damned for their deeds of filthy uncleanness. . ." (col. 13.1–5)[11]

This ceremony reminds one of exorcistic texts also found at Qumran such as *1Q Apocryphal Psalms*, *4Q Songs of the Sage*, and *4Q Against Demons* that seek to protect against or counter the power of Belial,

Lilith, and other demons. The Children of Light are triumphant in the end, routing the *Kittim* and their allies, and the key to their victory—more important than any weapon or battle maneuver that Israel employs—is the support received from its supernatural allies. In fact, the scroll casts Israel itself as little more than a weapon through which God strikes at the enemy: "It is from you that power comes, and not from our own being. It is not our might nor the power of our hands which performs these marvels except by your great strength" (col 11.4–5).

None of this seems an especially realistic approach to war. In fact, commentators often note how *impractical* the scroll's battle plan is. The inspiration for many of its instructions is the Hebrew Bible, which in Deuteronomy establishes the protocols of battle (including pre-battle rhetoric to exhort the troops. See Deut 20:1–4). When the Maccabees found themselves under attack on the Sabbath, they realized they had to temporarily suspend or reinterpret the law to accommodate the exigencies of battle, pragmatically resolving to fight on the Sabbath if necessary (*1 Macc*. 2:40–41).[12] Not so the warriors of the *War Scroll*, who are bidden to halt the battle for the entire Sabbatical year (1QM col. 2.8–9). The war itself is expected to follow a predetermined course, without any surprises—indeed, even setbacks happen according to a pre-established timetable (1.13–14; 16.11)—imposing a rigidity of posture that seems at odds with the flexibility needed to maneuver in a field of operation controlled by the enemy. The scroll certainly offers no instruction in the kinds of tactics and tricks often resorted to by armies operating at a strategic disadvantage—the use of surprise, ambushes, feigned retreats, and other ruses to which Greek and Roman military manuals give attention.

What might strike even a Roman as shrewdly tactical about the *War Scroll*, however, is its focus on troop morale and how to boost it.[13] The scroll seems especially concerned that the Sons of Light will be intimidated by the danger of war, and much of its instruction seems designed to provide assurance by reminding the soldiers of God's presence alongside them. Thus, the trumpets, banners, and weapons that Israel uses are all to be inscribed with words suggesting God's role in the battle (cols. 3–6), and the scroll also supplies the words of various speeches to be delivered to the troops "to strengthen them with God's power" (col. 10.2–8; 15.6–16; 16.13–17.9). All this provides the Sons of Light with an asset that even the most pragmatic of Roman tacticians recognized as crucial for victory in situations when one was outnumbered or outgunned by the enemy, the confidence that comes from knowing that one fights with a god on one's side. As the Greek general Xenophon put it: "It is neither numbers nor strength which wins victories in war, but whichever of the two sides it be whose troops, *by the blessing of the gods*, advance to the attack with stouter hearts" (*Anabasis* 3.1.42).

Building on this insight, Greek and Roman generals developed ways to manipulate the psychology of soldiers, to instill them with a sense of elation and invulnerability by *simulating* acts of divine intervention. The Roman strategist Frontinus lists a number of cases in which cunning generals were able to turn the tide of the battle by convincing their men that the gods were fighting on their side. (*Strategems* 1.11–12). Pericles, noticing a thick grove near the battlefield where he was to fight, hid there a large man mounted on a chariot drawn by white horses. When the battle began, the man was to rush out and shout to the men that the gods were assisting them. The result was that a startled enemy fled almost before a single spear was thrown (1.11.10). Other generals faked favorable prophecies and portents to raise the morale of their soldiers. Thus, Alexander the Great once used a fake liver omen to reassure his men that the gods were with them (1.11.14), and the Roman general Gaius Marius took with him a Syrian wisewoman from whom he pretended to learn in advance the outcome of battles (1.11.12). Operating within the parameters of Jewish belief and ritual tradition, the *War Scroll* establishes an equivalent series of techniques to reassure Israel's solders of divine support—purification rituals to allow the angels to join their camp; weapons that manifest God's power in battle through the words inscribed on them; and prayers and battle-field speeches that summon God into action.

Evidence that Jews actually employed such tactics comes from *1* and *2 Maccabees*, composed in roughly the same period as the *War Scroll*, where Judah uses them to sustain the morale of his troops. Judah's men are intimidated by the enemy's army—according to *1 Maccabees* 9:6, many even deserted when they saw the huge number of the enemy's forces. What keeps Judah's army fighting nonetheless is their confidence in God's support, a confidence reinforced by the occasional otherworldly apparition:

> While they were still near Jerusalem, a horseman appeared at their head, clothed in white and brandishing weapons of gold. And together they all praised the merciful God and were strengthened in heart, ready to assail not only humans but the wildest animals or walls of iron. They advanced in battle, having their heavenly ally, for the Lord had mercy on them. They hurled themselves like lions against the enemy, and laid low eleven thousand of them and sixteen hundred cavalry, and forced all the rest to flee. (*2 Macc.* 11:8–11)

Because he was "effective in arousing valor and awakening courage in the souls of the young" (*2 Macc.* 15:17), Judah is able to instill such confidence even when God and His angels do not manifest themselves directly. In *1 Maccabees* 3:17, when Judah's men see the enemy approaching, they ask Judah: "How can we, few as we are, fight against so great and so strong a multitude?" Judah's response is to deliver a speech that assures his men that, with God on their side, it makes little difference how large the enemy's army is:

> It is easy for many to be hemmed in by few, for in the sight of heaven there is no difference between saving by many or by few. It is not on the size of the army that victory in battle depends, but strength comes from Heaven. (3:18–19)

Judah stages or leads many such performances over the course of his campaign to convince his men that God fights on their side: elaborate rituals supplicating God for help or seeking to learn from scripture about the outcome of the battle (*1 Macc.* 3:42–60; *2 Macc.* 10:25–26); pre-battle speeches and prayers that recall God's earlier intervention against more powerful enemies (*1 Macc.* 4:8–11; *2 Macc.* 8:16–20; 15:21–23); hymns recited in the midst of battle to encourage the men when they are weary (*2 Macc.* 12:36). In the course of his speech before the battle with Nicanor, for example, Judah urges his men "to keep in mind the former times when help had come to them from heaven and so to look for the victory that the Almighty would give them" (15:8). That alone was enough to raise their confidence, but Judah goes on, describing a vision in which the dead High Priest Onias III and the prophet Jeremiah present him with a golden sword from God to help defeat his enemies (15:8–16). His men are so buoyed by the speech that they put aside their fear for their families and resolve to engage the foe in hand-to-hand combat.

Long before the Jewish Revolt, these sources suggest, Jewish tacticians, like their Greek counterparts, had come to recognize that an army *convinced* that it fought with divine assistance could overcome a much larger foe. The techniques developed to instill this belief—a repertoire of ritual, prognosticatory, and rhetorical techniques inspired by the Bible—were different from those used by the Greeks because they were drawn from a different cultural tradition, but their intended effect was similar—to instill a sense of hopefulness, confidence, and invulnerability even in the face of much larger armies. In one case *1 Maccabees* itself seems aware of the similarity. Before their battle with the Seleucid commander Lysias, Judah and his brothers are said to have "opened the book of the law to inquire into those matters about which the Gentiles consulted the likenesses of their gods" (*1 Macc.* 3:48).[14] The reference may be to the sort of pre-battle divinatory practice illustrated by Frontinus: "Lucius Sulla, in order to make his soldiers readier for combat, pretended that the future was foretold him by the gods. His last act, before engaging in battle, was to pray, in the sight of his army, to a small image that he had taken from Delphi, entreating it to "speed the promised victory" (Strategems 1.11.11). I am not arguing that such performances were consciously and deceptively fabricated in the way that Pericles staged a simulated divine apparition—that would be to read against the grain of our sources. What I am arguing is that such techniques were developed in response to the same tactical problem to which Pericles was responding, giving Jewish military leaders a way to stimulate confidence at tactically opportune moments.

Did Jews involved in the revolt against Rome enlist divine support in such ways? We have just enough evidence to suggest a supernatural dimension to the war that is largely but not completely obscured in Josephus's writing. In his autobiography, Josephus notes an incident from his days as a revolutionary leader in Galilee when two of his associates, refugees from the court of Agrippa II, were accused of being sorcerers who had made it impossible for the Jews to defeat the Romans. Josephus makes light of the accusation by noting that the Romans would not have maintained so large an army if they could defeat their enemies with enchantments, but he was unable to convince the local population and had to help the nobles escape to Roman territory (*Life* 149–154). Jesus' exorcistic practice has been identified as an oblique mode of resistance against Rome, targeting not the empire itself but evil spirits associated with it, demons like "Legion" whose name derives from the most important unit of the Roman army.[15] Here we see Jews seeking to combat Rome's supernatural power in a more direct way, eliminating those who wielded magic on the Romans' behalf.

In another incident from the end of the Revolt, the rebel commander Simon ben Giora conjures a supernatural apparition to frighten the enemy off. Failing to escape from the Romans, Simon tries to intimidate them by dressing in white tunics and a purple mantle and rising out of a hole in the ground at the very spot where the Temple had stood—as if he were an angel or even a messianic figure. The ruse works for a time, rendering the frightened spectators immobile until someone fetches the Roman commander who puts Simon into chains (*J. W.* 7.26–31). The first episode gives the impression that Jews in this period attributed magical power to Rome, which they then endeavored to cut off at its source (an idea anticipated by the *War Scroll*, which, if its *Kittim* are the Romans, seeks to defeat them by combating their demonic allies). The second episode suggests a rebel leadership able to simulate otherworldly apparitions to frighten the enemy, much as Pericles did by dressing up a man as a divine messenger.

It is difficult to draw more out of Josephus precisely because one of his chief objectives is to deny the rebels any kind of supernatural power. Although God could defeat the Romans if He was so inclined, He had in fact deserted to the Romans' side, using his power to help them to defeat the Jews. To prove this point, Josephus notes various signs and portents sent by God just prior to and during the revolt to warn the Jews of the coming disaster: a sword-shaped star and comet hovering over Jerusalem for a year; a bright light appearing around the sanctuary and altar during the feast of Passover; a cow that gave birth to a lamb in the Temple; an immense and all but immoveable Temple gate opened of its own accord; and most remarkable of all, chariots and armed battalions hurtling through the clouds (*J. W.* 6.289–299).[16] Portents of the Romans' victory were also found in the Bible, including an oracle that predicted that one from Judea would become ruler of the world—according to Josephus, a reference to Vespasian who was in fact designated emperor during his campaign in Palestine (312–314).[17] Even as he insists that God was using these signals to warn the Jews of impending disaster, however, Josephus acknowledges that most Jews, under the influence of "prophets" seeking to convince them that God was coming to help them, construed them as signs of divine support or portents of victory. The symbolism of several of the portents supports such an interpretation. Thus, the appearance of a sword-like star and comet resonates in light of the famous oracle in Numbers 24:17 promising Israel victory over its enemies: "a star shall come out of Jacob, and a scepter shall rise out of Israel" (*War Scroll* col. 11.6–7 interprets this same oracle as a prophesy of Israel's success against the army of Belial). Similarly, the appearance of a celestial army recalls the celestial horseman seen by Judah and his men as they head into battle (2 Macc 11:8–11). Anticipating Adas, Josephus recognizes these portents as influential morale-boosters during the revolt, preventing desertions and sustaining the hope of dispirited fighters (*J. W.* 6.286–87). One portent, the oracle interpreted by Josephus as a prediction of Vespasian's emperorship but read by many Jews before the war as referring to one of their own, played a leading role in inciting the revolt (6.312).

Josephus's counter-interpretation of these portents, his claim that they signaled God's support not for the Jews but for the Romans, thus inverts one of the techniques used to mobilize support for the revolt: the use of preparatory omens. In a similar way, the historian may also invert some of the battlefield oratory used to encourage rebellion. The speech with which we began this chapter, delivered by Josephus before the walls of Jerusalem, is the antithesis of the kind of battle exhortations we have seen in the *War Scroll* and Maccabean literature, uttered not to embolden Jews in their fight but to induce them to surrender, and yet its appeals share a number of motifs with the battle oratory of the *War Scroll* and Maccabean literature. Like the battlefield speeches of the *War Scroll* and Judah the Maccabee, Josephus recalls earlier divine victories from the Bible where God had fought on the side of the Jews, including events like the Exodus (*J. W.* 5.383. Cf. *War Scroll* col. 11, 9–10; *1 Macc.* 4:9), the defeat of the Philistines (*J. W.* 5.384–86. Cf. *War Scroll* col. 11.2–4; *1 Macc.* 4:30), and the defeat of Sennacherib's army (*J. W.* 387–88. Cf. *1 Macc.* 7:41; *2 Macc.* 8:19; 15:22). In contrast to these other speeches, the lesson that Josephus draws from these precedents is that the Jews should leave it *entirely* to God to defeat their foes rather than fight themselves. But even this point he makes in a way that parallels the *War Scroll* and *2 Maccabees*. Compare:

> God's leadership it was that brought our fathers this triumph (over the Philistines), because, without resort to hand or weapon, they committed the issue to his decision (*J. W.* 5.396)
>
> Goliath from Gath, gallant giant, you delivered into the hands of David, your servant, for he trusted in your powerful name and not in sword or spear (*War Scroll*, col. 11.2)
>
> Maccabeus . . . stretched out his hands toward heaven and called upon the Lord who works wonders; for he knew that it was not by arms, but as the Lord decides, that he gains victory for those who deserve it (*2 Macc.* 15:21)

Also redolent of earlier battlefield oratory is Josephus's mention of a miracle that his audience could see themselves, the sudden swelling of the Siloam and other springs around Jerusalem. Occurring just as Titus and his army arrived to the city, the portent is interpreted by Josephus as a sign of God's support for the Romans (*J. W.* 5. 409–411). One of Judah's speeches also reports a recent marvel as proof of God's support, God's gift to him of a golden sword (*2 Macc.* 15:12–16). The point Josephus makes with these examples is identical to that of the rhetoric in the *War Scroll* and *1* and *2 Maccabees:* God has entered the fray and ensures victory. The only difference is that he seeks to sap Jews of the will to fight by placing God on the *other* side, fighting for Rome against the Jews.

We have no direct evidence of the battlefield exhortations used by Jews during the revolt, but what little we can glean from Josephus's narrative supports the idea that they were indeed the mirror image of Josephus's speech. On one occasion, the Romans tried to induce the Jews to surrender by cutting off the hands of captives and sending them into Jerusalem, with an appeal to the rebel leaders to spare themselves and the Temple. The rebel leaders' defiant response mirrors the central thrust of Josephus's speech above and calls to mind the earlier battlefield oratory of the *War Scroll* and Maccabean literature: "(the Temple) would yet be saved by Him who dwelt therein, and while they had Him for their ally, they would deride all menaces unsupported by action, for the issue rested with God" (*J. W.* 5.459). Josephus is not an especially trustworthy informant, especially when it comes to his description of the rebels from whom he was so eager to distance himself, but given what we have seen, it seems possible that rebel leaders actually made such claims to allay their troops' anxiety and to ignite their resolve to fight.

In the end, of course, Josephus was proven right: the Roman Empire was simply unbeatable. Along the path to this perhaps inevitable outcome, however, the Romans did suffer a number of unexpected setbacks and surprises. A key factor in making the rebels so hard to defeat, as we have noted, was their unshakeable confidence and imperviousness to fear, a frame of mind that allowed them to overcome the Romans' superior technology and discipline on several occasions, and to sustain the hopes of their following through a difficult siege (*J. W.* 5.280, 285, 306; 484–5). What we have seen here suggests how Jews were able to summon and sustain these emotions. By this point, Jewish leaders had at their disposal a variety of techniques by which to convince their following that God was fighting on their side. They certainly did not rely on these techniques alone to offset Rome's might—they poached its weapons (*J. W.* 2.553–4); copied its organization (*J. W.* 2.577–82); and otherwise did what they could to level the playing field. As even the rationalism of Roman military strategy acknowledged, however, relying on divine support could make all the difference against a larger army if only by generating irrational behavior that could panic or demoralize the enemy.

Conjuring divine help was a tactical measure, but it was artful as well, appealing to Jewish imaginations. It may not have taken much to activate those imaginations. In the period of the revolt, Jews seem prone to believe just about anything, including events that ought to have been impossible. Rebel leaders and their prophetic allies intervened in these imaginations, using the "arts of the irrational" to expand their assessment of what it was possible to achieve against a seemingly invincible enemy. Adrian Goldsworthy has described the pre-battle rituals of the Roman army—the general's speeches and ceremonial performances—as a kind of theatre used to generate the needed emotion in troops.[18] That is an apt description for the art form that I am describing here, a kind of battlefield theatre that relied on ritual, exegetical, and rhetorical performance to mobilize the imagination's capacity to believe in the impossible, to support a war that reason alone might deem impossible to win.

Defiance Dispelled

The efficacy of these techniques is corroborated by the fact that so many other opposition movements used them to challenge Roman domination. One such movement was the Druids, a priestly group that played a key role in fomenting resistance against the Roman Empire among the Celts. The Druids enlisted the supernatural in much the way Jewish rebels did. When the Capitoline Temple in Rome burnt down in 69 C.E., the Druids interpreted it as a sign of Rome's downfall (Tacitus, *Histories* 4.54). In an attack on the island of Mona, the center of Druidism, the Druids were present at the frontlines, raising their hands to heaven and screaming dreadful curses, a spectacle that so awed the Romans that they were momentarily paralyzed (Tacitus, *Annals* 14.30). One recent study has compared the Druids to the millennial prophets described by Adas, and similar figures can also be identified at the helm of other uprisings against Rome.[19] Jewish rebels were not the only ones to resort to supernatural measures to offset the might of a seemingly invincible Roman Empire.

Nor were they the only ones to fail in their use of this power: the Druids were suppressed as were most of the other prophets, magicians, and would-be gods that helped to incite rebellion against the Romans. Much of the Romans' success in vanquishing their supernatural enemies, as Josephus tried to explain to his superstitious countrymen, was the size of their army, but the Romans also recognized the degree to which the irrational could offset that advantage and sought ways to protect itself against it. One of the most famous of these countermeasures was known as *evocatio*, a ritual by which the Romans sought to encourage the enemy's protective deity to defect to their side by offering it a home and cult at Rome.[20] It is not clear that this ritual was still practiced in the first century C.E., much less that it was directed at God during the Jewish Revolt, but Josephus himself engages in something similar, using his speech before the walls of Jerusalem to assert that God had allied with the Romans: "My belief, therefore, is that the Deity has fled from the holy places and taken his stand on the side of those with whom you are now at war" (*J. W.* 5.412). Nowhere do the

Romans or Josephus offer God a cult in Rome, but Josephus does come close to suggesting that God might have been better off with the Romans than with the rebels in Jerusalem: "It is the Romans who may well be found to have been the upholders of our laws while their enemies were within the walls" (4.184). Reflected in the *Jewish War* is the rhetorical equivalent to *evocatio*, Josephus seeking to deny the rebels the aura of divine protection by encouraging them to imagine God defecting to the Romans.

In addition to this and other ways of demoralizing the Jews, the Romans also developed ways to protect their own morale. The Romans recognized that while irrationality could give an army an advantage, it could also render it susceptible to recklessness and panic. For this reason, Roman military strategists like Julius Caesar preferred to cultivate a sober and steady calm that made the Roman soldier impervious to terror, surprise, or dejection.[21] Josephus reports that both Vespasian and Titus sought to instill calm in their men during the Jewish Revolt, deliberately avoiding the impetuosity that characterized their enemy. After a particularly difficult battle with the Jews of Gamla, for example, Vespasian upbraided his soldiers for being too emotional:

> As it is the mark of vulgarity to be over-elated with success, so it is unmanly to be downcast in adversity; for the transition from one to the other is rapid, and the best soldier is he who meets good fortune with sobriety . . . Incautiousness in war and mad impetuosity are alien to us Romans; who owe all our success to skill and discipline (*J. W.* 4.42, 45 .Cf. 5.121–23).

To help sustain this calm in the face of ominous events or unexpected reversals, Roman tacticians recommended using rational or empirical explanation to help soldiers understand what was really happening and dispel any illusion of divine intervention against them. As an example, Frontinus cites Pericles's response when a thunderbolt struck his camp and terrified his army. To reassure his soldiers that the incident was not a supernatural omen of defeat, Pericles called an assembly and, before all his men, knocked two stones together to produce a spark, explaining that the thunderbolt had been produced by a similar process in the clouds (Frontinus, *Strategems* 1.12.10). According to Josephus, both

Vespasian and Titus are similarly clearheaded in their efforts to sustain the morale of their men. Titus was able to reassure his men after they were panicked by the loud collapse of a battle tower in the middle of the night, for example, by learning what had really happened and giving orders to make the explanation known (*J. W.* 5.291–95). Together with discipline and careful planning, appealing to soldiers' reason could overcome the dangerous swings of irrationality—reckless elation, surprise, terror—that might undermine the Romans' other military advantages.

Josephus's account of the Jewish Revolt pits these stratagems against the impetuous madness of the Jews, and it is the former that wins out. At least this is the impression that Josephus gives as he reflects on the revolt in retrospect. It is possible that the stratagems of disenchantment described here do not reflect what happened during the revolt itself as much as they do Josephus's rhetorical goals as an agent of Roman rule seeking to discourage future insurrection. In a lengthy description of the Roman army camp, Josephus admits that one of his goals is to discourage those who might still be contemplating rebellion: "If I have dwelt at some length on this topic, my intention was not so much to extol the Romans as . . . to deter others who may be tempted to revolt" (*J. W.* 3.108). The description of the Roman army in this and other passages serves that end by stressing how the discipline and sobriety of its leaders shielded it from disruptive emotions like confusion, panic, and enthusiasm (3.74; 100–101). One reason that it may be so difficult to reconstruct the arts of the irrational from Josephus's narrative of the revolt is that it was written precisely to counter these arts, either denying their efficacy as a viable mode of resistance or enlisting them on Rome's behalf to reinforce its image of invincibility.

Despite Josephus's efforts to ally divine power with Roman rule, however, Jewish rebels may once again have enlisted it for their cause during the Bar Kochba, or Second Jewish Revolt, fought some six decades after the Jewish Revolt (132–35 B.C.E.). According to rabbinic legend—formulated long after the revolt but perhaps reflecting traditions originating among the rebels themselves—the nickname given to the rebel leader Bar Kozeba by Akiba (Bar Kochba = "son of a star") was inspired by the prophecy in Numbers 24:17—"A star shall come out of Jacob" (see y. Taan. 68d; Lam. Rab. 2.2 § 4). The same oracle had been cited in the *War Scroll* and, as has been noted, it may even have inspired one of the portents seen during the Jewish Revolt, the appearance of a sword-shaped star over Jerusalem (*J. W.* 6.289). Later legend also claims that Bar Kochba was endowed with supernatural powers such as the ability to catch catapult missiles and throw them back.[22] Bar Kochba's reputation as a supernatural warrior raises the intriguing possibility that the magical/rhetorical techniques that had done so much to make rebellion seem a realistic option during the time of the Jewish Revolt—the circulation of preparatory omens and the claim to a wonder-working power—were revived decades after Josephus tried to disarm them, conceivably helping Bar Kochba to mobilize his followers against Rome.

The Bar Kochba rebels may have been more effective in combating this army than their predecessors were. According to the Roman historian Dio Cassius, they killed so many Romans that the emperor Hadrian did not begin his report to the Senate with the customary phrase "I and the legions are in health."[23] Still, the Bar Kochba revolt was eventually quashed as well, a defeat signaled in advance by a supernatural portent according to Dio—the collapse of Solomon's tomb. The futility of revolt did not foreclose other ways of sustaining Jewish tradition, however, the struggle to sustain it continuing so long as there were imaginations committed to its survival. Josephus allows us to explore one more effort to sustain Jewish tradition in the decades after the Second Temple's destruction, an effort that turned dying itself into a survival tactic.

~ 7
Playing Dead

JOSEPHUS NOTED THAT as the Temple was burning to the ground, two individuals chose to plunge into the fire and perish with the Temple rather than surrender (*J. W.* 6.280). Josephus says nothing more, but rabbinic legend from a later period supplies the words that those dying with the Temple supposedly uttered as they threw themselves into the flames:

> When the sons of the high priests saw that the Temple was destroyed and the sanctuary was burning, they picked up the keys (of the sanctuary), ascended to the top of the Temple, and threw them upward, saying, "Here are the keys that you gave us, for we were not reliable guardians that we should partake of the king's hidden things (perhaps a reference to the proceedings or vessels hidden from view in the sanctuary)." And taking hold of one another, they were drawn into the fire and burned.[1]

As rabbinic imaginations recall the incident, the decision to die was rooted in a sense of failed stewardship, the priests returning the Temple's keys to God because they had failed in their duty to defend it. But another source, written by the Roman historian Dio Cassius (ca. 160–230 C.E.), allows for a different interpretation, hinting at something tactical about the act of voluntary death:

> The Jews defended themselves much more vigorously than before, as if they had discovered a piece of rare good fortune in being able to fight near the Temple and fall in its defense . . . though they were but a handful fighting against a far superior force, they were not conquered until a part of the temple was set on fire. Then they met death willingly, some throwing themselves on the swords of the Romans, some slaying one another, others taking their own lives, and still others leaping into the flames. And it seemed to everybody, and especially to them, that so far from being destruction, *it was victory and salvation and happiness* to them that they perished along with the temple (*Roman History 66.* 6.2–3) (italics mine).[2]

What rabbinic sources interpret as an act of failure and remorse, Dio recognizes as self-empowerment, the Temple's defenders achieving victory by dying with it.

Of the two interpretations, I would venture to suggest that it is the latter that more likely captures the mindset of those choosing to perish with the Temple. The rabbinic legend employs a recognizably fictional motif, the priests' return of the Temple keys, that surfaces in earlier apocalyptic texts like *Syriac Baruch* (10:18).[3] It also seems influenced by the biblical story of the priests Nadav and Abihu who were consumed in a fire at the sanctuary's inauguration (Lev 10:1–2), a parallel that brackets the cult's history between two fatal fires.[4] Dio's account, on the other hand, is consistent with earlier Jewish depictions of the act of voluntary death, or "dying for the law" as Tessa Rajak refers to it, scenes where Jews willingly suffer pain and death rather than allow some violation of Jewish law or the Temple.[5] A brief survey of these scenes can help us to reconstruct—to the extent it is possible to penetrate the minds of the dying—what the Temple's defenders understood themselves to be doing at the moment they chose to die with the Temple, what victory they believed they had won.

The origins of dying for the law can be traced back to the Seleucid period. During Antiochus's persecution, some Jews accepted death rather than comply with the king's command compelling them to eat unclean swine's flesh. So reports *2 Maccabees*, which narrates in graphic detail the deaths of the scribe Eleazar and an unnamed mother and her seven sons, all of whom choose to suffer excruciating torture and execution rather than pollute themselves (*2 Macc.* 6–7). Their willingness to die for the law sets "an example of nobility and a memorial of courage" (6:31)—it also guarantees the immortality of the martyred (7:9; 11; 14; 23; 36)—and *2 Maccabees* intimates that it does more than that. As he goes to his death, the last of the seven sons expresses the hope that, through his and his brothers' death, the people's misfortunes will come to an end: "I, like my brothers, give up body and life for the laws of our ancestors, appealing to God to show mercy soon to our nation . . . and through me and my brothers to bring to an end the wrath of the Almighty" (7: 30–33, 37–38). Just a few verses later, Judah the Maccabee makes his first appearance in the story, gaining such quick success against the enemy according to *2 Maccabees* because "the wrath of the Lord had turned to mercy" (8:5). Noting that the latter phrase echoes the seventh brother's prayer, Jan van Henten argues that the deaths of Eleazar and the others was seen by the author of *2 Maccabees* as the turning point in the Maccabean Revolt, laying the groundwork for the defeat of Antiochus by helping to soften God's anger against Israel and redirect it against the enemy.[6]

A later source from the first or second century C.E., *4 Maccabees*, is even more explicit in making the deaths of Eleazar and the others the key to Israel's salvation during Antiochus's persecution:

> When he (Eleazar) was now burned to his very bones and about to expire, he lifted up his eyes to God and said, "You know, O God, that though I might have saved myself, I am dying in burning torments for the sake of the law. Be merciful to your people, and let our punishment suffice for them. Make my blood their purification and take my life in exchange for theirs (*4 Macc.* 6:26–29)

According to this passage, the act of voluntary death operated like sacrifice, specifically the Yom Kippur sacrifice, the blood of which was used to purify the sanctuary and ransom or expiate Israel's sins. In normal circumstances, when the Temple was operative, Jews would use animal sacrifice to serve these roles, but Antiochus's disruption of the cult had made it impossible to mollify God's anger in this way. Jews were nonetheless able to compensate for the absence of sacrifice, *4 Maccabees* suggests, by offering their own deaths in its stead:

> Because of them, our enemies did not rule over our nation, the tyrant was punished, and the homeland purified—they having become, as it were, a ransom for the sin of our nation. And through the blood of those devout ones and their death as an atoning sacrifice, divine Providence preserved Israel that previously had been mistreated (17:20–22)

This is also the implication of another source that was probably composed earlier in the Maccabean period, the expanded version of Daniel 3 in Greek versions of Daniel.[7] Here Daniel's three friends, thrown by Nebuchadnezzar into a fiery furnace because they refuse to bow down to a statue, offer their deaths in lieu of the offerings they might have offered had the Temple been standing. When the only options left were betraying the law of Moses or accepting death, the choice of death was thought to offer one last chance to enlist God's help against the enemy. This at least is the impression given by stories that show this tactic working to save Israel in the very moments that salvation seems impossible.

By an interesting coincidence—if it is a coincidence—the Romans had developed a very similar tactic, a practice known as *devotio*. When a general saw that things were going badly for his army, he could offer to sacrifice his life, or the life of his troops, in return for victory, making good on his vow by throwing himself into the battle.[8] In a famous instance recounted by the historian Livy, the consul Decius, seeing his troops pushed back before the enemy, uttered a prayer in which he offered the lives of his army and himself to the gods in exchange for victory (*History of Rome* 8. 9–10.14). As described by Livy, Decius's actions had a powerful emotional impact, terrifying the enemy and bolstering the spirits of his men who believed it stirred up the gods against the enemy. The Jewish conception of voluntary death mirrors this battle tactic, and the fact that it emerges in roughly the period when Jews first come into contact with the Romans leads one to suspect that the tradition of *devotio* may have helped to foster its development.[9]

When the Romans themselves began to threaten Jewish tradition, and other ways of deflecting them failed to work, Jews again turned to voluntary death, or threatened to do so. According to Philo, the leaders of the Jewish community were ready to sacrifice their lives if Caligula could not be persuaded to leave the Temple alone: "We gladly put our throats at your disposal . . . fine priests, we ourselves will conduct the sacrifices" (*Embassy* 233–234). In the *Jewish War* and the *Antiquities*, Josephus reports dozens of cases of voluntary death, many during the Roman period.[10] Jews seem especially willing to die in defense of the Temple, even a peaceable moderate like the high priest Ananus professing that "it were a noble end to die at the sacred portals, and to sacrifice our lives . . . for God and for the sanctuary" (*J. W.* 4.191). In *Against Apion*, an apologetic work written near the end of Josephus's life, he insists that the Jews were ready to give their lives to avoid changing even a single letter of the law:

> It is an instinct with every Jew, from the day of his birth, to regard (the Scripture) as the decrees of God, to abide by them, and, if need be, cheerfully to die for them. Time and again, ere now the sight has been witnessed of prisoners enduring tortures and death in every form in the theatres, rather than utter a single world against the laws and the allied documents (1.43; 2.218–19; 33).

Elsewhere Josephus gives the impression that Jews were willing to die for the law because they believed they would gain immortality as a result. Thus, for example, when the Romans subjected the Essenes to all manner of excruciating torture in an effort to compel them to blaspheme God and eat forbidden food, the latter refused to submit, cheerfully surrendering their lives because they were "confident that they would receive them back again" (2.152–53; Cf. *J. W.* 1.653; *Ag. Ap.* 2.218). Personal survival may not have been the only consideration, however. Another text from the first century C.E., the *Assumption of Moses*, suggests that those dying for the law might also have seen their deaths as a way of gaining victory over the enemy, as in *2* and *4 Maccabees*. Also known as the *Testament of Moses*, this text purports to record the prophet's last words, including his vision of an age in which Israel will be persecuted by "the king of the kings of the earth" (the Roman emperor?) who will "crucify those who confess their circumcision," and commit other sacrileges (Chapter 8). What will save the Jews, it seems, is the piety of a Levite named Taxo and his seven sons who withdraw to a cave to perish rather than transgress the law. Their willingness to die is rooted not in despair but in a desire to incite divine vengeance, a tactic that the author of the *Assumption of Moses* evidently expected to work since the very next scene that he chose to record portrays God exacting vengeance against His enemies.[11]

With the help of these sources, we can plausibly reconstruct what was going through the minds of the defenders of the Temple at the time of its destruction. As they watched the Romans enter the Temple and then saw fire begin to consume it, they found themselves in the desperate straits of Daniel's friends and the Maccabean martyrs. Both flight and resistance were impossible: the Jews were cornered in a burning Temple with no way out. God was not stepping in to defend His house as the rebels had expected—perhaps, as Josephus would later claim, because He was angry with them for their sins—and the cultic mechanism through which they might mollify Him, the sacrificial cult, was going up in smoke. There were no options left except for death, but in death as imagined in this period there was one last opportunity. More than just an escape-hatch to immortality, death offered a final chance to expiate sin, appease God and incite His anger against the enemy—and in this way to save the nation and the law, as happened after the voluntary deaths of the Maccabean age. Perhaps the searing heat of the flames only reinforced the parallel in their minds with Daniel's friends and the Maccabean martyrs. Of course we can never know whether the Temple's defenders actually thought such things before deciding to die, but if Dio is to believed, they had the demeanor of someone who did, exuding a cheerful hopefulness *empowered* by the act of dying with the Temple.

Even at the moment of the Temple's destruction, then, the struggle for Jewish cultural survival persisted, not only overcoming death but also enlisting it as a resource. That moment is nearly unrecoverable, however. What is accessible, and what allows us to push our narrative forward a bit further, is the literary accounts of voluntary death like those produced by Josephus. Writing a few years after the Temple's destruction, Josephus records the voluntary deaths of the Temple's defenders without ascribing to them any expiatory or salvific role. In fact, Josephus is famously ambivalent about the act of dying for the law. He alleges that the impulse to die for the law was innate to his people, and in his account of the mass suicide at Masada, he records a lengthy speech, ascribed to the rebel leader Eleazar, casting suicide at the end of the revolt as a noble rejection of servitude. He claims to have felt the impulse to die himself, tempted to take his own life when trapped by the Romans in a cave at Yodefat (*J. W.* 3.350–91), and later, in his appeal to the rebels in Jerusalem, professing a willingness to sacrifice his life if it would save the city (5.419). And yet, Josephus clearly had second thoughts about voluntary death. Ultimately rejecting suicide at Yodefat, he delivers a speech there that is the mirror image of Eleazar's speech at Masada, interpreting self-killing as a violation of natural and divine law. Many of his suicide reports seem to reflect this judgment as well, depicting voluntary death as an act of madness (e.g., 1.151; 7.389). What precisely he thought about those who chose to perish with the Temple is unclear, but elsewhere he is clearly suspicious of voluntary death, or at least deeply ambivalent about it.

Although it is impossible to get beyond Josephus's narrative to what really happened, that narrative itself may reflect the struggle for Jewish cultural survival as waged by Josephus himself a few years after the Temple's destruction. Daniel Boyarin proposes to think of martyrdom (the outgrowth in late antiquity of dying for the law) as a discourse, not just a practice but a way of talking about that practice that does its own cultural work.[12] In the cases that Boyarin examines, rabbinic stories from the Amoraic period, Jewish imaginations use stories of dying for the law to mock Roman power and, if Boyarin's reading is correct, to define their relationship with Christianity. Josephus, writing in a different setting, puts the discourse of dying for the law to work in a different way. At Yodefat, as his men were poised to commit suicide, Josephus feigned the readiness to die so convincingly that his comrades went to their deaths believing he was dying with them (*J. W.* 3.390). He employed an analogous skill in the composition of his narratives, I propose, using his writing to simulate the act of voluntary death. How and why he did so is something I will be seeking to reconstruct in the remainder of this chapter, as I argue that Josephus developed an alternative to this tactic through his descriptions of dying for the law, an option beyond death that we might refer to as *thanatosis*, or playing dead.

The Suicidal Feint

Josephus's portrait of voluntary death is, as we have noted, confusingly inconsistent, sometimes extolling it, sometimes discrediting it. What are we to make of this apparent inconsistency? If Josephus admired the act of voluntary death, why stress its irrationality and impiety? If he disapproved of it, why accentuate its heroic dimension in so many scenes? Was he too careless or incompetent to smooth out the inconsistencies in his narrative? In the past, scholars characterized Josephus in just this way, and if they are right, there is little point to trying to resolve Josephus's inconsistent treatment of voluntary death.[13] The Josephus of contemporary scholarship is usually given more credit than this, however, recognized as a shrewd (if not completely original) rhetorician capable of irony, evasiveness, and ambivalence.[14] Under the influence of this conception, recent scholars have questioned whether the historian's treatment of voluntary death is as clumsily inconsistent as it appears, finding within it a philosophically nuanced and context-dependent view of voluntary death or arguing that its ambivalence reflects a deliberate effort to avoid taking a stand on an issue that was controversial in the Hellenistic-Roman period.[15]

This purposefully equivocal Josephus is the one we will summon for the present study, noting that it is consistent with how Josephus portrays his own character within the *Jewish War*. Consider the various poses that Josephus strikes when trapped with his men at Yodefat: first arguing against suicide and in favor of surrender to the Romans (*J. W.* 3.350–82); then, when his comrades insist that he take his own life, pretending to go along by proposing a lottery to determine who kills whom (387–390); then when he and one other find themselves the last men standing, repenting of his decision to die and escaping to the Romans (391)—and then telling the Romans to whom he surrenders that he would have chosen to die had God not sent him to tell Vespasian that he was destined to become emperor (400). The Josephus that we meet in this narrative in turn embraces and eschews death, professing a willingness to die even as he seeks to evade it. I would argue that the impulse to survive also animates his contradictory depictions of voluntary death in the *Jewish War* and the *Antiquities*, a thesis I will try to defend by situating these texts within the place and time in which they were written: Rome under the Flavian emperors Vespasian, Titus, and Domitian (69–96 C.E.). Reading Josephus's suicide accounts within this setting reveals a Jewish imagination drawing on the Romans' own tradition of voluntary death (as inflected in the Flavian period) to fashion a new tactic of cultural survival, one that adapts the act of dying for the law, or rather the discourse that it inspired, so as to realign Jewish tradition and Roman rule.

Josephus, it turns out, was not the only author in the Flavian period to equivocate on the topic of voluntary death. In his recent study of mythic and historical narratives composed by the poets Statius, Valerius Flaccus, and Silius Italicus, Donald McGuire finds that suicide is a central theme for all three writers, who often depict it as a noble gesture of defiance in the face of tyranny or conquest. All three are nevertheless equivocal in their depictions of the act, insinuating reservations about suicide even as they commemorate its heroism.[16] Consider by way of illustration Silius's epic the *Punica*, which tells the story of the second Punic War between the Romans and Hannibal. Early in the poem, Silius recounts Hannibal's conquest of the city of Saguntine in southern Spain, a battle that culminates in a mass suicide that calls to mind Josephus's description of the mass suicide at Masada. Silius praises the Saguntines for their heroic death that "glory in defeat keeps famous forever throughout the world" (2.612–13), an evaluation that reflects the traditional Roman esteem for suicide as a way of preserving one's autonomy and dignity in the face of defeat.[17] His actual description of the suicide evokes the crimes of civil war and parricide, however:

> Against their will men stain their hands with kindred blood; they marvel at the crime they have committed with loathing, and weep over the wickedness they have wrought. One man, distraught with rage and the madness of disaster and extreme suffering, turns a sidelong glance at the breast of his mother. Another, snatching an axe and aiming it at the neck of his loved wife, reproaches himself and curses his unfinished crime. (2.617–24)

Here Silius projects his ambivalence onto the actors within the narrative, the Saguntines themselves responding with horror to their deed.

McGuire concludes that this and other ambivalent suicide reports in the epics of Valerius Flaccus, Statius, and Silius accommodate a shift in Roman culture, whereby a deed once esteemed as an honorable act became increasingly suspect during the Flavian period. Writing about suicide was a risky undertaking in Rome at this time. As philosophers like Seneca stressed, suicide was the ultimate expression of one's autonomy, a form of freedom that no tyrant could compromise.[18] Precisely for that reason, the act constituted a potential challenge to imperial control, with nobles sometimes killing themselves in explicit protest against the emperor. There was nothing a ruler could do to punish those who chose to defy him in this way, but there was a way to keep people from celebrating the act's defiance: punish those who extolled suicide. Dio tells us that Junius Arulenus was executed under Domitian because he dared used the word "holy" to describe Thrasea Paetus, a Stoic who killed himself after being sentenced to death by Nero (*Roman History* 67.13).[19] Flavian authors still extolled suicide as an honorable mode of resistance to tyranny, and to this extent may have been venturing a kind of coded criticism of Flavian rule, but if so, they did this with extreme caution, also sending signals to their readers that called into question the rationality or ethics of those who committed the act. True, suicide allows a kind of freedom that no tyrant can suppress, but as these authors describe it, it also shares much in common with tyranny—its madness and brutality—and even does tyranny's work for it in a way by silencing those who would protest it.

A close inspection of Josephus's descriptions of voluntary death, composed in the same period, reveals the employment of similar literary devices to generate a similar ambiguity. Let us look more closely at the Masada story. A number of elements in the story give the mass suicide a heroic cast. Eleazar's speech is full of allusions to classical literature, including the *Phaedo* in which Socrates justifies his own voluntary death.[20] It also ascribes to the act the very motives associated with those noble suicides that Romans so admired—a passionate commitment to liberty and honor as a motive for the suicide (*J. W.* 7.325: "we have it in our power to die nobly and in freedom"). Indeed, Josephus explicitly registers Roman approbation by noting at the end of the episode that the Roman soldiers who found the bodies of the dead "admired the nobility of their resolve and the contempt of death displayed by so many in carrying it, unwavering, into execution" (406). At the same time, however, Josephus undercuts the heroism of the mass suicide in much the same way that the Flavian poets did: Flavian epic often stressed the irrationality of suicide, associating it with savage ferocity or frenzied madness. Josephus uses similar motifs. Though Eleazar's speech creates an initial impression of rational deliberation, his followers cut him off before he is finished, "overpowered by some uncontrollable impulse," and they rush about "like men possessed" (7.389).[21]

The same ambivalence can be discerned in other suicide accounts in the *Jewish War*: Josephus's account of Pompey's conquest of the Temple features a description of how those within the Temple allowed themselves to be killed or killed themselves rather than surrender to the Romans, a scene that fuses positive and negative elements in the same way that the Masada story does. The initial signals are quite favorable. Noting that the Jews were ready to risk their lives to continue with the sacrificial service, Pompey "was filled with admiration for (their) invariable fortitude" (*J. W.* 1.148). When the Romans break into the Temple, the priests there continue their ministrations unperturbed, "putting the worship of the Deity above their own preservation" (150). But then the narrative takes a turn into the realm of civil war and madness: "Most of the slain perished by the hands of their countrymen of the opposite faction . . . some, driven mad by their hopeless plight, set fire to the buildings around the wall and were consumed in the flames" (151). In another scene at the opposite end of the *Jewish War*, Josephus seems to waver between two interpretations of the act. In 7.417, he wonders about what it was that impelled Sicarii rebels in Egypt to endure a terrible death at the hands of the Romans with such fortitude: was it courage or insane desperation? The text raises the question without resolving it. Many of the dozens of suicide reports in the *Jewish War* and even the *Antiquities* are self-contradictory in this way, including his description of how his fellow soldiers killed themselves at Yodefat, acknowledging the courage and nobility of the act but in a way that associates it with rash impetuousness, sinfulness, or self-defeat.

All this resembles Flavian epic so closely that one cannot help but suspect that Josephus was responding to the same pressure that led other contemporary authors to equivocate in their suicide accounts. Josephus was certainly vulnerable to such pressure, combating accusations that he was treasonous against the Romans into the reign of Domitian (*Life* 416; 424–425, 428–429). Simply to honor the act of suicide, an act clearly and repeatedly associated in the *Jewish War* with rebellion against Rome, would be to risk appearing subversive, which may explain why Josephus goes to such lengths to distance himself from the act through his account of the Yodefat episode. It might seem strange for an author as adamant about his own probity as was Josephus to have described himself behaving in the cowardly way that he does at Yodefat, pretending to go along with the mass suicide of his troops and then duplicitously switching sides to the Romans. As he himself admits, his own men accused him of treachery (*J. W.* 3.356–59), and when it became known among his fellow Jews that his death was a fiction, "the demonstrations of wrath at his being still alive were as loud as the former expressions of affection when he was believed to be dead" (3.438). Josephus does his best to minimize his treachery, claiming that God Himself wanted him to live so that he could deliver a message to Vespasian, but in the end his description of himself still remains puzzlingly self-shaming. For an author seeking to ingratiate himself with the Flavian emperors, however, the benefits of such a disclosure still outweighed any contempt it inspired, not only explaining how Josephus transitioned from rebel to imperial servant, but helping to distance him from an act likely to seem suspicious to his Flavian patrons.

At the same time that Josephus had reason to distance himself from voluntary death, however, he also had much to gain by describing it in laudatory terms. "Dying for the law" was well-established within Jewish tradition by this time as an heroic act. By eschewing it, Josephus risked alienating Jewish readers, just as he had alienated his fellow soldiers when he refused to take his own life. Suicide as a literary theme also gave him an opportunity to appeal to his Roman readers, and to align Jewish tradition with their cultural tradition. As we have already seen, Josephus's suicide narratives mirror those produced by the Romans themselves, rooting Jewish voluntary death in the same values that motivated the praiseworthy suicides of Socrates, Decius, or Seneca.[22] Josephus often makes Roman approval a part of his narrative in fact, noting the admiring response of Romans who witness the Jews taking their lives or readying themselves to do so—Pompey, Pilate, Petronius, the Romans at Masada (*J. W.* 1. 146; 2.174; 7.406).

To the extent that his suicide accounts stirred empathy or admiration in Roman readers, they could serve Josephus's literary agenda in a number of ways. For one thing, they could help to flatter the Romans. The Romans considered it shameful to vanquish an enemy easy to defeat, taking pride in their victories only when their foe equaled them in courage and skill.[23] As Josephus remarks in his introduction to the *Jewish War*, this was one reason that earlier accounts of the war were inadequate: by rendering the Jews a weak and puny people, they robbed the Romans of the glory of defeating an equal opponent (*J. W.* 1.7–8). Josephus's own description of the revolt is an attempt to magnify the Romans' accomplishment in defeating the Jews by casting the latter as an enemy worth defeating. His suicide accounts serve this end when they mimic the Roman tradition of "noble death," endowing Jews with the same fearlessness, honor, and uncompromised commitment to liberty Roman heroes like Decius displayed in battle. As if to emphasize the parallel, the *Jewish War* includes stories of Romans who mirror Jewish contempt for death, as in *J. W.* 6.186–187 where a soldier named Longinus chooses to slay himself rather than accept defeat.

Beyond expanding the Romans' accomplishment in defeating the Jews, such stories also played an important role in undergirding Josephus's own credibility. In Flavian epic, suicide signifies more than a love of freedom and defiance of tyranny; it is motivated by fidelity to self.[24] Remaining true to oneself to the point of death, sacrificing oneself rather than betraying one's core principles and commitments, was considered the surest proof of one's integrity, especially in Stoic thought but evidently for others as well. Apparently mindful of this idea, Josephus acknowledges that his own refusal to commit suicide at Yodefat looked like self-betrayal to his men, who say to him:

> How soon have you forgotten yourself! How many have you persuaded to die for liberty? False, then, was that reputation for bravery, false that fame for sagacity, if you can hope for pardon from those whom you have fought so bitterly, or, supposing that they grant it, can deign to accept your life at their hands. Nay, if the fortune of the Romans has cast over you some strange forgetfulness of yourself, the care of our country's honor devolves on us. (*J. W.* 3.357–59)

Josephus denies this accusation, but the only way he can really show that he has not compromised himself in a cowardly effort to save his skin is to insist that God had compelled him to stay alive to serve on a divine mission. Had it been his decision to make, Josephus maintains, he would have preferred to have died:

> For my part, I shall never pass over to the enemy's ranks, to prove a traitor to myself. I should indeed then be far more senseless than deserters who go over to the enemy for safety whereas I should be going to destruction—my own destruction. I pray,

> therefore, that the Romans may prove faithless; if, after pledging their word, they put me to death, I shall die content. (3.381–382)

Reflected here is a rhetorical technique that Agrippa I used to convince Caligula of his sincerity: invoking one's willingness to die as proof that one is telling the truth and not simply acting out of self interest (see Chapter 3). Elsewhere, Josephus adapts this topos to demonstrate the veracity of his historical claims. In *Against Apion*, one of the chief proofs that the Jews' records of their past are reliable is their readiness to die for them. Unlike the Greeks, who would not suffer the smallest injury to save their national library, the Jews would sooner suffer death than alter a single syllable of their law—evidence that the Jew Josephus, and not self-serving Greek rivals such as Apion, was telling the truth. In a world of competing narratives about the past, many of them fictions disguised as fact, Josephus invoked the Jewish tradition of voluntary death as the ultimate proof of not just his own personal integrity but of his narrative's authenticity as well.

By enlisting the tradition of "dying for the law" in this way, Josephus was almost certainly looking out for his own welfare, but he may also have been operating as an ambassador for Jewish culture, appealing to Rome to allow the continuation of Jewish tradition, if not the rebuilding of the actual Temple.[25] His effort to use dying for the law as proof of authenticity works in tandem with his assertions of Jewish antiquity to make a case for Jewish cultural survival under Roman rule. Rome had particular admiration for antiquity, so much so that according to Susan Alcock, the fate of a Greek temple in the Roman period—whether or not it attracted the imperial patronage it needed to persist—seems to have depended to a significant extent on Rome's perception of its antiquity.[26] The advantages of appealing to Rome's esteem for antiquity may explain why Josephus made the kinds of claims that we cited in the introductory chapter, asserting the changelessness of Jewish culture because he knew how much his Roman readers valued this trait. What *proved* these claims was precisely the Jews' willingness to die for their tradition, as during Antiochus's persecution, when the inauthentic Samaritans renounced the law (*Ant.* 12.257) while the Jews were willing to die for it (12.267). It has been noted that Josephus often alters his sources to emphasize the Jews' willingness to die for the law.[27] One reason he did this, it seems, was to strengthen a key thesis of the

Antiquities, that Jewish culture was as old as its practitioners claimed that it was, a trait that could make a life-saving difference in the struggle for cultural persistence under imperial rule.

The challenge for Josephus as he made such arguments was to emphasize the willingness of Jews to die for their traditions without appearing to endorse suicide as a form of resistance to imperial rule. What we have seen here suggests that he found a solution to this predicament in Roman literary practice, a cultivated ambivalence that conveyed the heroism of suicide while blunting its subversiveness at the same time. A model for the compromise Josephus tries to strike can be found within his narratives, in stories where the Jews save the law through an act that at first resembles suicide but swerves away at the last instant:

> The Jews, as by concerted action, flung themselves in a body on the ground, extended their necks, and exclaimed that they were ready rather to die than to transgress the law. Overcome with astonishment at such intense religious zeal, Pilate gave orders for the immediate removal of the standards from Jerusalem (*J. W.* 2.174).

By means of a similar performance, this time before the governor Petronius, the Jews were able to stall Caligula's order to install a statue in the Temple:

> At this the multitude cried out that they were ready to endure everything for the law. Petronius, having checked their clamor, said, "Will you then go to war with Caesar?" The Jews replied that they offered sacrifice twice daily for Caesar and the Roman people, but that if he wished to set up these statues, he must first sacrifice the entire Jewish nation; and that they presented themselves, their wives, and their children, ready for the slaughter. These words filled Petronius with astonishment and pity at the spectacle of the incomparable devotion of this people to their religion and their unflinching resignation to death. So for the time he dismissed them (*J. W.* 2.196–8).

Josephus did not make up either of these scenes from scratch. We have an earlier account of the Petronius incident narrated by Philo in his *Embassy to Gaius*. Philo also narrates an incident similar (though not identical) to the attempted sacrilege by Pilate (*Embassy* 299–305).[28] Among the differences between the two accounts, the most significant for our purposes concerns how the Jews stop Pilate: Josephus claims that the procurator was overcome by the awesome sight of Jews ready to die for their tradition, whereas Philo claims that what stopped Pilate was the Jews' threat to go over his head to the emperor. Daniel Schwartz, who sees the two stories as variant accounts of the same event, has argued that Josephus adjusted his telling to emphasize the theme of dying for the law.[29] Nuancing this conclusion, I would suggest that what we have inscribed into this story is something more complex, a reflection of Josephus's own efforts as an author to *exhibit* the readiness of the Jews to die for their tradition—and in this way align them with Roman values—without fully committing to death.

Josephus introduces a similar revision in his retelling of the Maccabean Revolt. There, the Maccabees are urged by their father Mattathias

> to remain constant as such and to be superior to all force and compulsion, being so prepared in spirit as to die for the laws, if need be, and bearing this in mind, that when the Deity sees you so disposed, He will not forget you, but in admiration of your heroism will give (the laws) back to you again, and will restore to you your liberty. (*Ant.* 12.281).

Notice a subtle change that Josephus has introduced by means of this speech (a paraphrase of *1 Macc.* 2:49–68): the Maccabees need to be ready to die for the law, but they do not actually have to follow through with the act in order to save the law: merely being "prepared in spirit as to die" insures God's protection. Josephus' ensuing history of the revolt bears this out, for when the general Lysias sees that the Maccabees are "prepared to die if they could not live as free men," he retreats—the victory which made it possible for the Maccabees to reclaim the Temple.[30] According to Josephus, the Romans respond in much the way that God is depicted doing in Mattathias's speech, so awed by the Jews' *exhibition* of their willingness to die for the law that they permit its survival.

What motivated these revisions, I propose, was Josephus's desire to accommodate the ambivalence about voluntary death characteristic of the Flavian age. It would have been extremely difficult for Josephus to simply have discredited the practice of dying for the law given its heroic resonance for Jews, but it also would have been difficult for him to endorse the act, if only because to do so would have been to court imperial suspicions of suicide as a form of resistance. Josephus's revisions develop an intermediate position, one that seems consistent with Jewish tradition but is far less self-destructive than full-fledged death. Dying for the law was noble, but as Josephus depicts it, it was also impetuous and, in many cases, unnecessary—especially in the Roman period when rulers like Vespasian and Titus were predisposed to respect Jewish tradition, provided that the Jews did not challenge Roman rule. By exhibiting their willingness to die but hesitating just long enough to give their audiences an opportunity to admire their resolve or pity their fate, Jews could save their tradition without destroying themselves, appealing to rulers whose own tradition of noble death perhaps predisposed them to admire similar behavior in others. Virtual death, the art of feigning suicide, thus offered a way to save Jewish law without suffering the irreversibly negative consequences of the act it simulated.

In developing this tactic, Josephus may have been influenced by the theatricalization of death in Roman culture of the first century C.E., a period that saw the emergence in Roman culture of what classicists refer to as the "fatal charade," the public execution of prisoners staged as the reenactment of a mythical or historical narrative.[31] Jews too were executed in this theatrical way. According to Philo, the governor Flaccus ordered Jews to be crucified in the theatre, an exhibition followed by "dancers and mimes and flute players and all the other amusements of theatrical competitions" (*Flaccus* 84–85). Many such executions occurred just a few years before Josephus wrote his narratives, in the aftermath of the revolt when on one occasion alone, a birthday celebration for Titus's brother, 2,500 Jews were slain in a manner typical of the fatal charade, killed in contests with animals or burned alive (*J. W.* 7. 37–39). Ironically, this terrible experience might have colored the experience of dying for the law in a way that was useful for Jewish cultural survival, helping Jews like Josephus to recognize its fascination for the Romans, its ability to stimulate their interest, and stir their emotions, only its dramatic potential was put to work in a different way. The not-quite-fatal charades crafted by Josephus dramatize the act of dying for the law not to entertain, but to trigger another set of reactions: admiration for the Jews' fearlessness and contempt of death, sympathy for their struggle to preserve their tradition, and perhaps a sense of recognition, of identification with the Jews as a people of equivalent virtue and values. Although these performances simulated the spectacles of death that so entranced the Romans, they used the histrionics of dying to make possible a different kind of denouement, one in which the performers are spared from actually having to die.

These stories of would-be suicide may or may not tell us much about how Jewish culture survived in the days of Pilate and Petronius—it is difficult to distinguish between what is real and fictional in Josephus's description of these events—but what they do reveal, I am suggesting, is a glimpse of Josephus's struggle for personal and cultural survival in the Flavian period. Wavering between suicide and survival, the Jews in these stories exhibit the impulse to die in a way that ends up rendering the act itself unnecessary because it stirs Roman admiration or sympathy. In doing so, they enact within the narrative the very tactic that Josephus was seeking to employ by telling this sort of story, appealing to a Roman tradition of voluntary death without arousing imperial suspicions of full-fledged suicide. This tactic looks like dying for the law but only deceptively so, actually sharing more in common with Josephus's virtual suicide at Yodefat. At least as Josephus tells that story (and it is possible that it too has been shaped by the narrative tactic identified here), the feigning of voluntary death makes possible a switch from one tactic to another, allowing Josephus to avoid what he regarded as a pointlessly self-destructive fate and to seek Roman protection instead. If what I have argued here is correct, the virtual deaths of Josephus's narratives were an attempt to make possible the same kind of tactical pivot, a turn from dying in defiance of foreign rule to living under its patronage.

Life After Death

From the vantage point from which Josephus was writing, dying for the law, though admirable perhaps, had done nothing to save the Jews or the Temple in their struggle against the Romans. Through his writing, he developed an option beyond that last resort, enlisting and adapting the memory of dying for the law in an effort to realign Jewish culture and imperial rule. While the results of Josephus's efforts to salvage Jewish tradition are unknown, perhaps having little impact on the fortunes of Jewish culture in subsequent decades, I would like to conclude by noting that Josephus's storytelling could have served as a prelude to the next chapter of Jewish culture, the age of the rabbis.

It is the rabbis who carry the story of Judaism forward in late antiquity, and the founding myth of their culture of study and prayer seizes from Josephus's death feint the tactic by which Jewish tradition was saved after the Temple's destruction. A legend circulated centuries after the Jewish Revolt tells of how the famous sage Rabbi Yohanan ben Zakkai escaped from Jerusalem just before its destruction. The Jewish rebels in control of the besieged city had decreed that only the dead should be allowed to leave the city, seeming to cut off escape but also providing Yohanan with an opportunity. In the most elaborate form of the legend, the version in the Babylonian Talmud, Rabbi Yohanan pretends that he is sick, placing something rotten next to him to give off the smell of decay, and when the rumor of his death becomes known, has his disciples carry him out of the city in a coffin. Having somehow escaped into the Romans' camp, he meets Vespasian who asks what he can do for him. In one version (preserved in the midrashic collection *Lamentations Rabbah*), Rabbi Yohanan asks that the Romans lift the watch on one of Jerusalem's gates so that some of its inhabitants might flee. In the version that has become better known (*Abot deRabbi Natan*, version A), Yohanan endeavors to "save a little" of Jewish tradition, not seeking to restore the Temple but asking the emperor's permission to practice the commandments and establish a prayer house and academy at the refugee camp of Yavneh. Rabbi Yohanan's academy in Yavneh came to be recognized as the center of rabbinic Judaism until the Bar Kochba revolt, linking the Judaism of Second Temple days with that perpetuated by the rabbis.

There might be some historical kernel to this story, but most of it is almost certainly fictional, bearing a suspicious resemblance to the story that Josephus tells about his own survival.[32] In all versions of the legend, Yohanan predicts that Vespasian will become emperor, a plot element that clearly parallels Josephus's self-description, either drawn directly from the *Jewish War* or from some intermediate source.[33] A more intriguing parallel for our purposes is the role of feigned death in both stories. While there are differences, of course—Yohanan does not pretend to kill himself but feigns full-fledged death—there is no mistaking the similarity. Surfacing only in the third or fourth century, this story has little value for reconstructing how Jewish culture actually survived the Temple's destruction, but it does tell us a lot about the rabbinic imaginations that told and retold it: how they sized up the challenges of cultural survival, and where they located opportunity. For them, as for Josephus, what made survival possible was not death but a fictional simulation.

As imagined by early Jews, dying for the law could salvage the most hopeless of circumstances, saving Jewish tradition even after it was too late, but it could only do so in an imagined realm beyond death, where Jews were completely liberated from political powerlessness and the fragility of their physical bodies. The suicidal feint offered a way to deploy death within the constraints of the real—showing the readiness to die, acting as if to commit it, even exuding the smell of decay without slipping beyond a world delimited by Roman rule and human mortality. It is here, in the efforts of Josephus and the rabbis to exploit death and skirt it at the same time, that we can observe early Jewish imaginations in the ultimate act of resourcefulness, creating opportunities to sustain their culture even from what would seem like the end of all possibility.

~ 8

The Art of Cultural Persistence

LOOKING BACK ON THE THREE or so centuries since the destruction of the Second Temple, the fourth century Christian preacher John Chrysostom pronounced Jewish ritual permanently extinct. It is true, he noted in his *Homilies against the Jews*, that Jews had recovered from earlier catastrophes—slavery in Egypt, the destruction of Solomon's Temple, Antiochus's persecution—but the present "captivity" was different, destined, as the prophet Daniel had foreseen, to "endure until the end" (5.10.899). That the Jews had repeatedly tried to rebuild a third Temple without success (Chrysostom notes three failed attempts of which only the last can be confirmed: the Bar Kochba Revolt, and attempts under the Roman emperors Constantine and Julian) was confirmation that Jewish ritual was dead. Whether or not Jews recognized its demise, their religious tradition had been eclipsed by Christianity's "lofty and spiritual way of worship."

It is true, of course, that Jews never did manage to rebuild a third Temple. While changes in the nature and priorities of our sources mean that we cannot trace the struggle for Jewish cultural persistence after Josephus in the way that we did for the Second Temple period, what little relevant evidence we do have hints at the continued use of some of the tactics we have considered in this book. In an environment transformed by Roman rule and Christianity, however, those tactics used to protect Jewish tradition while the Second Temple stood were no longer effective. It is possible, for example, that Jews attempted another major revolt in defense of their religious tradition, launching the Bar Kochba Revolt in response to a Roman attempt to ban circumcision or to prevent the reconstruction of the Temple.[1] Though the rebels mounted an extremely serious challenge to the Romans—they may even have recaptured Jerusalem for a time—in the end, this option proved just as self-destructive as it had in 66–70 C.E., resulting in the death and displacement of numerous Jews, the transformation of Jerusalem into a pagan city, and the apparent proscription of practices like circumcision, prayer, and Torah study.[2] The catastrophic reversals of the Bar Kochba Revolt may have been one of the considerations that gave later rabbis serious pause about promoting revolt, a turn famously reflected in the legend of Yohanan ben Zakkai's escape from a rebellious Jerusalem.

Relying on foreign rule was no more effective in restoring the Temple than the use of force, though particular rulers may have seemed promising in this regard. In 362 or 363, the Roman emperor Julian undertook to restore the Jewish Temple in an effort to refute Christianity, and perhaps also to ensure Jewish support in his war with the Persians.[3] The attempt collapsed, supposedly when a natural disaster, perhaps a fire or an earthquake, interrupted the building. Whether Julian subsequently changed his mind or whether he died too soon, the project never resumed, and the disenchantment that Jewish supporters of the initiative felt may be reflected indirectly in rabbinic stories that rebuke Cyrus for failing to make good on his promise to rebuild the Temple.[4] Still, some Jews may have hoped to do better when other rulers displaced the Romans. In 614 C.E. the Sassanid Empire captured Jerusalem from the Byzantine Empire, and this appears to have heightened an expectation that the Jews would soon recover the Temple. The *Book of Zerubbabel*, likely written during this period, though it is named for the Jew credited with rebuilding the Second Temple, foresees an "eternal temple" brought down from heaven.[5] So far as we know, however, the Temple was not rebuilt under the Sassanids, nor was it restored during the ensuing reign of Islam despite hints here and there in the sources that the caliph Umar made an attempt to do so.[6]

It is often said that in the aftermath of the Jewish and Bar Kochba revolts, Jews simply adapted to life without the Temple, accepting its reconstruction as impossible, at least in their present-day realities, and redefining Jewish tradition around new institutions and practices. The impulse to restore the Temple may have been more resilient than this view allows, persisting into the seventh century C.E. and beyond. In its struggle to assert itself, however, this impulse collided with an obstacle that proved insurmountable—foreign powers whom the Jews could neither defy nor recruit, at least not in the way that their ancestors had in their struggle to preserve the Second Temple.

And yet, Chrysostom's report of the death of Jewish ritual was greatly exaggerated. Jewish tradition did survive—and survives to this day. Through all the myriad, ramifying changes that Jewish tradition has undergone in the last two thousand years, even its most obsolete component, the Temple itself, can occasionally be glimpsed struggling to make a comeback. A few months after I began this book, I received a pamphlet from a local center of the Habad movement, a form of Hasidic Judaism recently infused with messianic fervor. The pamphlet offers various proofs for the late Lubavitcher Rebbe's messianic status, basing itself on Maimonides's criteria for what the Messiah would have to do to establish himself as real. One requirement is the Messiah's construction of "the Temple in his place." The Rebbe fullfilled this criterion, the pamphlet announces, when he identified his home at 770 Eastern Parkway in Brooklyn as an interim Temple. While the Temple has not yet returned to what you or I might call reality, a not insignificant number of Jews believe that it verges on becoming real again. And even in its absence, Jewish tradition persists, differing radically from what existed in antiquity, but still, improbably, transmitting elements of Jewish culture as old as or even older than the Second Temple: the Sabbath and festival cycle, circumcision, Torah study, the synagogue.

The present book is an attempt to illustrate the kinds of creativity that lie behind this sort of persistence. In the introduction, I challenged the characterization of early Jewish cultural persistence as a kind of inertia, an indisposition to exertion or change. We are now in a position to appreciate a more nuanced reason to reject inertia as an explanation for Jewish cultural persistence. "Inert" comes from the Latin meaning "lacking art," and that is the very antithesis of the artfulness demanded by the early Jewish struggle for cultural survival. Indeed, this struggle was artful in two senses of the word: in antiquity, the Latin *ars* denoted what we have been calling a tactic; in more recent parlance, of course, "art" also denotes works of imagination. What unites all the efforts examined in this book is precisely that they enlist both kinds of artfulness. Operating from a position of relative weakness, Jews had to be highly tactical, resorting to the sorts of practical defense mechanisms used by biological organisms in their struggle to survive. The survival tactics of early Jewish culture differed in a key respect from those found in nature, however: they used the imagination's powers to expand the parameters of reality, to overcome the limits of space, time, even death. What I mean by the *art* of cultural persistence is this ability to maneuver between the real and the imagined, to respond to and operate within the constraints of reality but also to transcend them.

I would like to close by pointing to the mastery of this double artfulness as an essential part of the story of early Judaism's survival. As I hope to have shown, early Jews were quite pragmatic in their struggles to sustain their traditions—cognizant of their powerlessness under foreign rule and able to adapt accordingly, quick to seize on available opportunities and resources, willing to shift from one tactic to another as circumstances required—but it is not clear to me that pragmatism alone would have been enough to see them through. In the Roman period in particular, as the practical options for sustaining the Temple—appeasement, resistance, flight—narrowed, Jews responded by creating opportunities simply not available within the parameters of the possible: shape-shifting and telekinetic power, the enlistment of supernatural allies, using death itself as a resource. All these responses emerged through the sorts of symbiotic interactions between pragmatism and the imagination that this book reconstructs. Admittedly, I cannot measure the impact of early Jews' dogged creativity, and I acknowledge the possibility that the life-span of their culture was not determined by what they themselves did, or imagined themselves doing, so much as by historical developments and chance events beyond their control. Still, until it can be proven otherwise, I for one prefer to think that early Jews did improve their chances of cultural survival through their artfulness—if only for the reassurance this notion offers as I recall the sacrileges of our own age and wonder whether we will have the imagination to survive them.

Abbreviations

Notes

Index

Abbreviations

ABD	Anchor Bible Dictionary. Edited by David Noel Freedman. 6 vols. New York: Doubleday, 1992.
AbrN	*Abr-Nahrain*
AIPHOS	*Annuaire de l'Institut de philologie et d'histoire orientales et slaves*
AJP	*American Journal of Philology*
AJSL	*American Journal of Semitic Languages and Literature*
BA	*Biblical Archaeologist*
BAR	*Biblical Archaeology Review*
BASOR	*Bulletin of the American Schools of Oriental Research*
Bib	*Biblica*
BibInt	*Biblical Interpretation*
BO	*Bibliotheca Orientalis*
CBQ	*Catholic Biblical Quarterly*
CPJ	*Corpus papyrorum judaicorum*. Edited by V. Tcherikover. 3 vols. Cambridge, 1957–1964.
DSD	*Dead Sea Discoveries*
ErIsr	*Eretz-Israel*
GR	*Greece and Rome*
GRBS	*Greek, Roman, and Byzantine Studies*
HCSP	*Harvard Studies in Classical Philology*
Hist.	Herodotus's *History of the Persian War*
HTR	*Harvard Theological Review*
IEJ	Israel Exploration Journal
JANES	*Journal of the Ancient Near Eastern Society*
JAOS	*Journal of the American Oriental Society*

JBL *Journal of Biblical Literature*
JEA *Journal of Egyptian Archaeology*
JHS *Journal of Historical Studies*
JJS *Journal of Jewish Studies*
JNES *Journal of Near Eastern Studies*
JQR *Jewish Quarterly Review*
JSJ *Journal for the Study of Judaism in the Persian, Hellenistic, and Roman Period*
JSOT *Journal for the Study of the Old Testament*
JSP *Journal for the Study of the Psuedepigrapha*
JTS *Journal of Theological Studies*
OLP *Orientalia lovaniensia periodica*
OTP *Old Testament Pseudepigrapha*. Edited by J. H. Charlesworth. 2 vols. New York: Doubleday, 1983.
PEQ *Palestine Exploration Quarterly*
RB *Revue biblique*
RevQ *Revue de Qumran*
SBLSP *Society of Biblical Literature Seminar Papers*
ScrHier *Scripta hierosolymitana*
SPhilo *Studia Philonica*
ST *Studia theologica*
TAPA *Transactions of the American Philological Association*
Transeu *Transeuphratène*
VT *Vetus Testamentum*
VTSup *Supplements to Vetus Testamentum*
ZA *Zeitschrift für Assyriologie und vorderasiatische Archäologie*
ZAW *Zeitschrift für die alttestamentliche Wissenschaft*

Notes

Introduction

1. See Shaye Cohen, *The Beginnings of Jewishness: Boundaries, Varieties, Uncertainties* (Berkeley: University of California Press, 1999).

2. See David Wilson, *Darwin's Cathedral: Evolution: Religion, and the Nature of Society* (Chicago: University of Chicago Press, 2002), 133–147, where he purports to identify the traits that have selected Judaism for long-term survival.

3. See Jacob Milgrom, *Studies in Levitical Terminology, I: The Encroacher and the Levite* (Berkeley: University of California Press, 1970).

4. When and why foreigners were banned from the sanctuary remains unclear. At some point they came to be perceived by Jews as a source of impurity, a kind of contagion banned from the sanctuary, but scholars differ over how early this perception emerged or whether it was in fact the reason Gentiles were excluded from the sanctuary. See Adolph Büchler, "The Levitical Impurity of the Gentile in Palestine before the Year 70," *JQR* n.s. 17 (1926–27): 1–79; Gedalia Alon, "Levitical Uncleanness of Gentiles," *Jews, Judaism and the Classical World: Studies in Jewish History in the Times of the Second Temple and Talmud* (trans. Israel Abrahams; Jerusalem: Magnes, 1977), 146–189; and more recently, Jonathan Klawans, "Notions of Gentile Impurity in Ancient Judaism," *Association for Jewish Studies Review* 20 (1995): 285–312; Christine Hayes, *Gentile Impurities and Jewish Identities* (Oxford: Oxford University Press, 2002).

5. See Elias Bickerman, "The Warning Inscriptions of Herod's Temple," *Studies in Jewish and Christian History*, vol. 2 (Leiden: Brill, 1980), 210–224; Peretz Segal, "The Penalty of the Warning Inscription from the Temple of Jerusalem," *IEJ* 39 (1989): 79–84. Two copies of this inscription have been found. See Jean Frey, *Corpus Inscriptionum Iudaicarum*, vol. 2 (Vatican City: Pontifical Institute of Christian Archaeology, 1936, 1952) #1400.

6. Michel de Certeau, *The Practice of Everyday Life* (trans. Steven Rendall; Berkeley: University of California Press, 1984), 35–36.

7. Ibid., 37.

8. See de Certeau, *Practice of Everyday Life*, 39—a reading of Greek culture based on Marcel Détienne and Jean-Pierre Vernant, *Les Ruses de l'intelligence. La mètis des Grecs* (Paris: Flammarion, 1974).

9. For a listing of Greek and Roman stratagems, see Everett Wheeler, *Stratagem and the Vocabulary of Military Trickery* (Leiden: Brill, 1988).

10. *Strom.* 1.24, 160.1–3. For a translation, see John Ferguson, *Stromateis: Books 1–3* (Washington, D.C.: Catholic University of America Press, 1991), 141–143.

11. de Certeau, *Practice of Everyday Life*, 66.

12. Ethel Person, "The Creative Role of Fantasy in Adaptation," *Imagination and its Pathologies* (ed. James Phillips and James Morley; Cambridge MA; MIT Press, 2003), 111–132.

13. Person, "Creative Role," 112.

14. John Sallis, *The Force of Imagination: The Sense of the Elemental* (Bloomington: Indiana University Press, 2000), 128.

15. For the archaeological evidence of Herod's Temple complex, see Meir Ben-Dov, *In the Shadow of the Temple: The Discovery of Ancient Jerusalem* (trans. Ina Friedman; New York: Harper and Row, 1985); For the evidence of synagogues as places of worship in the Second Temple period, see Lee Levine, "The Second Temple Synagogue: the Formative Years," *The Synagogue in Late Antiquity* (ed. Lee Levine; Philadelphia; American Schools of Oriental Research, 1987), 7–31; Donald Binder, *Into the Temple Courts: The Place of the Synagogues in the Second Temple Period* (Atlanta: Society of Biblical Literature, 1999). On Jewish ritual baths, see Ronny Reich, "The Hot Bath-House (Balneum), the Miqweh and the Jewish Community in the Second Temple Period," *JJS* 39 (1988): 102–107; Benjamin Wright III, "Jewish Ritual Baths: Interpreting the Digs and the Texts: Some Issues in the Social History of Second Temple Judaism," *The Archaeology of Israel: Constructing the Past, Interpreting the Present* (ed. Neil Silberman and David Small; Sheffield: Sheffield Academic Press, 1997), 190–214. On phylacteries and *mezuzot* from Qumran, see Jozef T. Milik, "Tefillin, Mezuzot et Targums (4Q128–4Q157)," *Qumran Grotte 4, II 2 I. Archaéologie, II. Tefillin, Mezuzot et Targums* (ed. Roland de Vaux and Jozef T. Milik; Oxford: Oxford University Press, 1977), 34–85.

16. On the perception of Judaism as a petrified culture, see James Pasto, "Islam's 'Strange Secret Sharer': Orientalism, Judaism, and the Jewish Question," *Comparative Studies in Society and History* 40 (1998): 437–474.

17. Tony Judt, "Israel: the Alternative," *New York Review of Books* vol. 15, no. 16 (October 23, 2003). The relevant statement reads: "The very idea of a 'Jewish state' . . . is rooted in another time and place. Israel, in short, is an anachronism." For the stereotype of Jews as lacking creativity and imagination, see Yacob Shavit, *Athens in Jerusalem: Classical Antiquity and Hellenism in the Making of the Modern Secular Jew* (trans. Chaya Naor and Niki Werner; London: Littman Library of Jewish Civilization, 1997), 220–224; Kalman Bland, *The Artless Jew* (Princeton: Princeton University Press, 2000), 26–33.

18. E.g., cf. Walter Burkert, *Structure and History in Greek Mythology and Ritual* (Berkeley: University of California Press, 1979), 45.

19. Catherine Bell, *Ritual: Perspectives and Dimensions* (New York: Oxford University Press, 1992), 145–150. Cf. Roy Rappaport, *Ritual and Religion in the Making of Humanity* (Cambridge; Cambridge University Press, 1999), 334–343.

20. Cf. Marshall Sahlins, "Structure and History, *Islands of History* (Chicago: University of Chicago Press, 1985), 136–156, especially 143ff.

21. See Eric Hobsbawm and Terence Ranger, ed., *The Invention of Tradition* (Cambridge: Cambridge University Press, 1983).

Chapter 1: After Babel

1. The biblical evidence bearing on the exilic period and restoration of the Temple raises far more questions than we can address adequately in this chapter. For reviews of the evidence and its problems, see Peter Ackroyd, *Exile and Restoration: A Study of Hebrew Thought of the Sixth Century* B.C. (London: SCM Press, 1968); Sara Japhet, "The Temple in the Restoration Period: Reality and Ideology," *Union Seminary Quarterly Review* 46 (1991): 195–251; Peter Bedford, *Temple Restoration in Early Achaemenid Judah* (Leiden: Brill, 2001).

2. See Bedford, *Temple Restoration*, 230–299.

3. See Hans Barstad, *The Myth of the Empty Land: A Study in the History and Archaeology of Judah During the "Exilic" Period* (Oslo: Scandinavian University Press, 1996); for recent responses to Barstad's thesis, see Lester Grabbe, ed., *Leading Captivity Captive: 'The Exile' as History and Ideology* (Sheffield: Sheffield Academic Press, 1998).

4. Like their counterparts in biblical studies, some archaeologists stress the evidence of destruction and depopulation in their reconstruction of the Babylonian/early Persian period, while others stress evidence of continuity. For the first view, see Ephraim Stern, "Israel at the Close of the Monarchy: An Archaeological Survey," *BA* 38 (1975): 26–54; idem, "The Babylonian Gap," *BAR* 26 (2000): 45–51, 76; idem, *Archaeology of the Land of the Bible Volume II: The Assyrian, Babylonian, and Persian Periods (732–332* B.C.E.*)* (New York: Doubleday, 2001), 321–326. For the second, see Gabriel Barkay, "The Iron Age II-III," *The Archaeology of Ancient Israel* (ed. Amnon Ben-Tor; trans. Raphael Greenberg; New Haven: Yale University Press; Tel Aviv: Open University of Israel Press, 1992), 372–373. The debate continues, as witnessed by the most recent contributions to the discussion in Oded Lipschitz and Joseph Blenkinsopp (ed.), *Judah and the Judeans in the Neo-Babylonian Period* (Winona Lake, IN: Eisenbrauns, 2003).

5. The biblical account of the plunder of the Temple vessels does have partial corroboration from the Babylonians' own account of their siege of Jerusalem in 598 B.C.E., which reports that after defeating Jerusalem Nebuchadnezzar carried off "vast tribute" to Babylon. See Albert Grayson, *Assyrian and Babylonian Chronicles* (Locust Valley, NY: J. J. Augustin, 1975), 102 (Babylonian Chronicle 5; reverse l. 13).

6. Peter Ackroyd, "The Temple Vessels—A Continuity Theme," *Studies in the Religion of Ancient Israel* VTSup. 23 (1972): 166–181.

7. George Steiner, *After Babel: Aspects of Language and Translation* (London: Oxford University Press, 1975), 227.

8. I draw the term "godnapping" from Alasdair Livingstone, "New Dimensions in the Study of Assyrian Religion," in *Assyria 1995: Proceedings of the 10th*

Anniversary of the Neo-Assyrian Text Corpus Project Helsinki, September 7–11, 1995 (ed. Simo Parpola and Robert Whiting; Helsinki: The Neo-Assyrian Text Project, 1997), 165–177. For other studies of cultic despoliation in Mesopotamia, see Mordechai Cogan, *Imperialism and Religion: Assyria, Judah and Israel in the Eighth and Seventh Centuries* B.C.E. (Missoula, MT: SBL and Scholars Press, 1974), 22–41; 119–121 (table 1); M. A. Brandes, "Destruction et Mutilation de Statues en Mésopotamie," *Akkadica* 16 (1980): 28–41, 31–32; Hermann Spieckermann, *Juda unter Assur in der Sargonidenzeit* (Göttingen: Vandenhoeck & Ruprecht, 1982), 344–362; S. Halloway, *The Case for Assyrian Religious Influence in Israel and Judah: Inference and Evidence* (Ph.D. diss., University of Chicago, 1992), 342–349, 547–557; John Kutsko, *Between Heaven and Earth: Divine Presence and Absence in the Book of Ezekiel* (Winona Lake, IN: Eisenbrauns, 2000), 101–123, 157–169.

9. Erving Goffman, *Frame Analysis: An Essay on the Organization of Experience* (Cambridge: Harvard University Press, 1974), 287–292.

10. See Rykle Borger, "Gott Marduk and Gott-König Sulgi als Propheten, Zwei prophetische Texte," *BO* 28 (1971): 3–24.

11. See Menahem Haran, "The Ark and the Cherubim: Their Symbolic Significance in Biblical Ritual," *IEJ* 9 (1959): 30–38, 89–94; Ronald Clement, *God and Temple* (Philadelphia: Fortress, 1965), 28–35.

12. For the similarity between the Ark Narrative and Mesopotamian stories of divine exile and return, see Mathias Delcor, "Jahweh et Dagon: ou le Jahwisme face à la religion des Philistins, d'après 1 Sam. V," *VT* 14 (1964): 136–164; Anthony Campbell, *The Ark Narrative (1 Sam 4–6; 2 Sam 6): A Form-Critical and Traditio-Historical Study* (Missoula, MT: SBL and Scholars Press, 1975), 179–191; Patrick Miller and J. J. M. Roberts, *The Hand of the Lord: A Reassessment of the "Ark Narrative" of 1 Samuel* (Baltimore: Johns Hopkins University Press, 1977).

13. For literary and redactional analysis of this episode, see Theodor Seidl, *Texte und Einheiten in Jeremia 27–29: Eine literaturwissenshaftliche Untersuchung 1* (St. Ottilien: Eos Verlag, 1977); idem, *Formen und Formeln in Jeremia 27–29* (St. Ottilien: Eos Verlag, 1978).

14. On Ezra 1 as an historical source, see Peter Ackroyd, "Problems in the Handling of Biblical and Related Sources in the Achaemenid Period," *Achaemenid History. III. Method and Theory* (ed. Amelie Kuhrt and Heleen Sancisi-Weerdenburg; Leiden: Dutch Institute for the Near East, 1987), 33–54; Hugh G. M. Williamson, "The Composition of Ezra i-vi," *JTS* (1983): 1–30; Baruch Halpern, "A Historiographical Commentary on Ezra 1–6: Achronological Narrative and Dual Chronology in Israelite Historiography," *The Hebrew Bible and Its Interpreters* (ed. William Henry Propp, Baruch Halpern, and David Noel Freedman; Winona Lake, IN: Eisenbrauns, 1990), 81–142; Sara Japhet, "'History' and 'Literature' in the Persian Period: The Restoration of the Temple," *Ah Assyria!: Studies in Assyrian History and Ancient Near Eastern Historiography Presented to Hayim Tadmor* (ed. Mordechai Cogan and Israel Eph'al; Jerusalem: Magnes, 1991), 174–188; Lester Grabbe, "Reconstructing History from the Book of Ezra," *Second Temple Studies 1. Persian Period* (ed. Philip Davies; Sheffield: Sheffield Academic Press, 1991), 98–106; Bedford, *Temple Restoration*, 87–132.

15. For arguments in favor of the decree's authenticity, see Elias Bickerman, "The Edict of Cyrus in Ezra 1," *JBL* 65 (1946): 249–275; Roland de Vaux, *The Bible and the Ancient Near East* (trans. Damian McHugh; Garden City: Doubleday,

1971), 63–96. For a different view, see Kurt Galling, "Die Proklamation des Kyros in Esra 1," *Studien zur Geschichte Israels im persischen Zeitalter* (Tübingen: J. C. B. Mohr [Paul Siebeck], 1964), 61–77.

16. See Bedford, *Temple Restoration*, 115.

17. Nabonidus may have had other motives for removing the statues to Babylon, protecting them from the enemy or insuring the loyalty of Babylonian cities. See Paul-Alain Beaulieu, *The Reign of Nabonidus, King of Babylon, 556–539* B.C. (New Haven: Yale University Press, 1989), 220–224.

18. For the text of the *Cyrus Cylinder*, see Paul-Richard Berger, "Der Kyros-Zylinder mit dem Zusatzfragment BIN II Nr. 32 und die akkadischen Personennamen in Danielbuch," *ZA* 64 (1975): 193–203. The translation here is drawn from James Pritchard, *The Ancient Near East: An Anthology of Texts and Pictures* (Princeton: Princeton University Press, 1958), 206–228.

19. Amelie Kuhrt, "The Cyrus Cylinder and Achaemenid Imperial Policy," JSOT 25 (1983): 83–97.

20. Sources hostile to Persian rule could stress its sacrilegious character. See, for example, Aeschylus, *The Persians*, ll. 808–902: "When they (Xerxes and his army) went to the land of Greece, they were not ashamed to steal images of gods, nor set fire to temples; altars vanished from sight, and the shrines of gods were uprooted from their foundations and turned upside down in total chaos." For a story of Persian sacrilege in Babylon, see Amelie Kuhrt and Susan Sherwin-White, "Xerxes' Destruction of Babylonian Temples," *Achaemenid History II. The Greek Sources* (ed. Amelie Kuhrt and Heleen Sancisi-Weerdenburg; Leiden: Dutch Institute for the Near East, 1987), 69–78. For a story of Persian sacrilege in Egypt, see Leo Depuydt, "Murder in Memphis: The Story of Cambyses's Mortal Wounding of the Apis Bull (ca. 523 B.C.E.)," *JNES* 54 (1995): 119–126.

21. See Alan Lloyd, "The Inscription of Udjahorresenet: A Collaborator's Testament," *JEA* 68 (1982): 166–80, esp. 171–2. Joseph Blenkinsopp, "The Mission of Udjahorresnet and those of Ezra and Nehemiah," *JBL* 106 (1987): 409–421.

22. For the text of the petition, see Arthur Cowley, *Aramaic Papyri of the Fifth Century B.C.* (Oxford: Clarendon, 1923), no. 30, 111–114. For more on Persia and the Elephantine temple, see Thomas Bolin, "The Temple of Yahu (Hebrew) at Elephantine and Persian Religious Policy," *The Triumph of Elohim: From Yahwisms to Judaisms* (ed. Diana Edelman; Grand Rapids: Eerdmans, 1995), 127–142.

23. See Heleen Sancisi-Weerdenburg, "Gifts in the Persian Empire," *Le Tribut Dans l'Empire Perse* (Pierre Briant and Clarisse Herrenschmidt; Louvain-Paris: Peeters, 1989), 129–146; Pierre Briant, *From Cyrus to Alexander: A History of the Persian Empire* (Winona Lake, IN; Eisenbrauns, 2002), 302–323.

24. Briant, *From Cyrus to Alexander*, 241.

25. For modern scholarly speculation about the fate of the ark, see Menahem Haran, "The Disappearance of the Ark," *IEJ* 13 (1963): 46–58.

26. *2 Maccabees* may be preceded chronologically by Eupolemus's *On the Kings of Judaea*, probably composed in the second century B.C.E. and now preserved only in five brief citations by Eusebius and Clement. One of these fragments reports that Nebuchadnezzar "took as tribute the gold and silver and bronze in the Temple and sent them to Babylon except for the ark and the tablets. This Jeremiah preserved" (F.GrH 723 F5; cf. Eusebius *Praep.ev.* 9.39.5). See Carl Holladay, *Fragments from Hellenistic Jewish Authors, vol. 1 Historians* (Chico: Scholars Press, 1983), 93–156.

27. For studies of the hidden Ark legend in this period, see George Nickelsburg, "Narrative Traditions in the Paralipomena of Jeremiah and 2 Baruch," *CBQ* 35 (1973): 60–68; Isaac Kalimi and James Purvis, "The Hiding of the Temple Vessels in Jewish and Samaritan Literature," *CBQ* 56 (1994): 649–685; Marilyn F. Collins, "The Hidden Vessels in Samaritan Traditions," *JSJ* 3 (1972): 97–116.

28. For the translation of *2 Baruch*, see A. Frederik Klijn, "2 (Syriac Apocalypse of) Baruch: A New Translation and Introduction," *OTP* 1: 615–52. Klijn dates its composition to around 100 C.E.

29. See Felix von Luschan, *Ausgrabungen in Sendschirli*, vol. IV (Berlin: Georg Reimer, 1911), 363; David Ussishkin, "The Syro-Hittite Ritual Burial of Monuments," *JNES* 29 (1970): 124–128 (who interprets the burial somewhat differently). Recently, Ussishkin has added another example: three fragmentary Egyptian statuettes, including one of a high official of the 12th Dynasty embedded in a platform wall of a temple tower at Late Bronze Age Megiddo. See David Ussishkin, "The Destruction of Megiddo at the End of the Late Bronze Age and its Historical Significance," *Mediterranean Peoples in Transition: Thirteenth to Early Tenth Centuries BCE* (ed. Seymour Gitin, Amihai Mazar, and Ephraim Stern; Jerusalem: Israel Exploration Society, 1998), 197–219, esp. 211–212.

30. Most scholars places *1 Esdras* in the third or second century B.C.E. See Jacob Myers, *I and II Esdras* (Garden City: Doubleday, 1974); 8–15; Anne Gardner, "The Purpose and Date of 1 Esdras," *JJS* 37 (1986): 18–27.

31. See Richard Laqueur, "Ephoros" *Hermes* 46 (1911): 161–206, esp. 168–72. For possible Greek antecedents, see Wilhelm Rudolph, "Der Wettstreit der Leibwächter des Darius, 3 Esr 3, 1–5, 6," *ZAW* 61 (1945–1948): 176–190, esp. 178–179.

32. Cf. A. Hilhorst, "The Speech on Truth in 1 Esdras 4, 34–41," *The Scriptures and the Scrolls: Studies in Honor of A. S. van der Woude on the Occasion of his 65th Birthday* (VTSupp 49; ed. Florentino Garcia-Martínez, A. Hilhorst, and C. J. Labuschagne; Leiden: Brill, 1992), 135–151.

33. See Erich Gruen, *Heritage and Hellenism: The Reinvention of Jewish Tradition* (Berkeley: University of California Press, 1998), 166–167.

34. Cf. A. Hilhorst, "Speech on Truth," 143–145.

35. The translation is that of Elizabeth von Voigtlander, *The Bisitun Inscription of Darius the Great: Babylonian Version* in *Inscriptions of Ancient Iran, part I, vol. 2 Texts I* (London: published on behalf of Corpus Inscriptionum Iranicarum by Lund Humphries, 1978), 46, col. 5, 10.65.

36. Briant, *From Cyrus to Alexander*, 125–126.

Chapter 2: Maccabean Maneuvers

1. For Maccabean-Roman relations, see Wolf Wirgin, "Judah Maccabee's Embassy to Rome and the Jewish-Roman Treaty," *PEQ* 101 (1969): 15–20; Thomas Fischer, "Rom und die Hasmonäer: Ein Überblick zu den politischen Beziehungen 164–137 v. Chr.," *Gymnasium* 88 (1981): 139–150; Tessa Rajak, "Roman Intervention in a Seleucid Siege of Jerusalem?" *Greek, Roman and Byzantine Studies* 22 (1981): 65–81; Menahem Stern, "The Treaty between Judah and Rome in 161 B.C.E.," *Zion* 51 (1986): 3–28 (in Hebrew).

2. Eric Gruen, *Heritage and Hellenism: The Reinvention of Jewish Tradition* (Berkeley: University of California Press, 1998), 253–268.

3. See Elias Bickerman, "La charte séleucide de Jérusalem," *Studies in Jewish and Christian History*, vol. 2 (Leiden: Brill, 1980), 44–85; idem, "Une proclamation séleucide relative au temple de Jérusalem," *Studies*, 86–104; Jorg-Dieter Gauger, *Beiträge zur jüdischen Apologetik: Untersuchungen zur Authentizität von Urkunden bei Flavius Josephus und im 1. Makkabäerbuch* (Köln-Bonn: Peter Hanstein Verlag, 1977), 23–151.

4. On the letters' authenticity and original significance, see Victor Tcherikover, *Hellenistic Civilization and the Jews* (Philadelphia: Jewish Publication Society of America/Jerusalem: Hebrew University, 1959), 213–219, 225–226; Otto Mørkholm, *Antiochus IV of Syria* (Copenhagen: Gyldendal, 1966), 152–157, 162–165; Menahem Stern, *The Documents on the History of the Hasmonaean Revolt* (Tel Aviv: Kibbutz Hameuchad, 1972), 56–60, 66–73 (in Hebrew); Christian Habicht, "Royal Documents in Maccabees II," *HSCP* 80 (1976): 1–18; Robert Doran, *Temple Propaganda: The Purpose and Character of 2 Maccabees* (Washington, D.C.; Catholic Biblical Association of America, 1981), 64–67; Jonathan Goldstein, *II Maccabees* (New York: Doubleday, 1983), 408–428; Klaus Bringmann, *Hellenistische Reform und Religionsverfolgung in Judäa: Eine Untersuchung zur jüdisch-hellenistischen Geschichte (175–163 v.Chr.)* (Göttingen: Vandenhoeck & Ruprecht, 1983), 40–51; David Flusser, "The Dedication of the Temple by Judas the Maccabeus: Story and History," *The Jews in the Hellenistic-Roman World: Studies in Memory of Menahem Stern* (ed. Isaiah Gafni, Aharon Oppenheimer, and Daniel Schwartz; Jerusalem: Zalman Shazar Center for Jewish History/Historical Society of Israel, 1996), 55–82 (in Hebrew).

5. Gruen, *Heritage and Hellenism*, 1–40; John Ma, "Seleukids and Speech-Acts: Performative Utterances, Legitimacy and Negotiation in the World of the Maccabees," *Scripta Classica Israelica* 19 (2000): 71–112.

6. See Angelos Chaniotis, "Conflicting Authorities: Asylia between Secular and Divine Law in the Classical and Hellenistic Poleis," *Kernos* 9 (1996): 65–86.

7. See Kent Rigsby, *Asylia: Territorial Inviolability in the Hellenistic World* (Berkeley: University of California Press, 1996).

8. Ibid., 481–531.

9. Ibid., 22–25.

10. See *Ant.* 13.51. The garbling of the formula may have occurred in the course of translation, for the present form of *1 Maccabees* is a Greek translation of a presumably Hebrew work which was itself probably citing a Greek document in this instance.

11. *2 Maccabees* 3:12 and Philo (*Embassy to Gaius* 346) claim inviolable status for the Temple, but these are *Jewish* assertions of inviolability; there is no evidence of the Seleucid kingdom or Roman rule formally recognizing the claim. For the Greek Lysimachus, in fact, Jerusalem not only lacked inviolable status, it was the antithesis of that status, its name having been derived from the Greek for "sacred violation," *Hierosyla*. See Menahem Stern, *Greek and Latin Authors on Jews and Judaism* (Jerusalem: Israel Academy of Sciences and Humanities, 1980), vol. 1: 384–385.

12. Cf. Rigsby, *Asylia*, 527–531.

13. Although they were a priestly family, the Hasmoneans were not a family in line for the high priesthood, a position traditionally confined to descendants of the high priest Zadok. See Daniel Schwartz, "On Two Aspects of a Priestly View of Descent at Qumran," *Archaeology and History in the Dead Sea Scrolls: The New York*

University Conference in Memory of Yigael Yadin (ed. Lawrence Schiffman; Sheffield: Sheffield Academic Press, 1990), 157–179. Regarding charisma, see Max Weber, *On Charisma and Institution Building* (ed. S. N. Eisenstadt; Chicago: University of Chicago Press, 1968), 48–65.

14. On opposition to the Hasmoneans, see Jonathan Goldstein, *I Maccabees*, (Garden City: Doubleday, 1976), 64–72; Joseph Sievers, *The Hasmoneans and Their Supporters: From Mattathias to the Death of John Hyrcanus I* (Atlanta: Scholars Press, 1990), 86–92, 146–147.

15. Erich Gruen, "Seleucid Royal Ideology," *SBLSP* (1999): 24–53, esp. 25–26. See also Oliver Hoover, "Striking a Pose: Seleucid Types and Machtpolitik on the Coins of John Hyrcanus I," *The Picus* 3 (1994): 40–57, which notes other ways in which Hyrcanus's coins emulate those of the Seleucids.

16. See Niels Hyldahl, "The Maccabean Rebellion and the Question of 'Hellenization'," *Religion and Religious Practice in the Seleucid Kingdom* (ed. Per Bilde et al; Aarhus: Aarhus University Press, 1990), 188–203, esp. 201.

17. The following comparison is indebted to Robert Doran, "Independence or Co-Existence: The Responses of 1 and 2 *Maccabees* to Seleucid Hegemony," *SBLSP* 1999: 94–103. I have also drawn many insights from Elias Bickerman, "Héliodore au Temple de Jérusalem," *Studies in Jewish and Christian History*, vol. 2, 159–191; J. G. Bunge, *Untersuchungen zum zweiten Makkabäerbuch: quellenkritische, literaische, chronologische und historische Untersuchungen zum zweiten Makkabäerbuch als Quelle syrisch-palästinensischer Geschichte im 2. Jh v. Chr.* (Bonn: Rheinmische Friedrich-Wilhelms-Universität, 1971); Christian Habicht, *2 Makkabäerbuch* (Gütersloh: G.Mohn, 1976).

18. As argued by Seth Schwartz, "Israel and the Nations Roundabout: 1 Maccabees and the Hasmonean Expansion," *JJS* 42 (1991): 16–38.

19. See Doron Mendels, "A Note on the Tradition of Antiochus IV's Death," *IEJ* 31 (1981): 53–56.

20. Both the original composition of *2 Maccabees* and its subsequent abridgement could fall at any point between the life of Judah, who died in 160 B.C.E., and 124 B.C.E., the date of the prefatory letter in *2 Maccabees* 1:1–9. See Felix-Marie Abel, *Les livres des Maccabées* (Paris: J. Gabalda, 1949), xli–xliii.

21. See Amelie Kuhrt and Susan Sherwin-White, "Aspects of Royal Seleucid Ideology: The Cylinder of Antochus I from Borsippa," *Journal of Hellenic Studies* 111 (1991): 71–86.

22. According to *J. W.* 1.54–60; *Ant.* 13.228–35, here is what really happened: After murdering Hyrcanus's father Simon, Ptolemy son of Abubus took Hyrcanus's mother hostage, torturing her in front of him and threatening to throw her down from the city's walls. Undisturbed by the threats, Hyrcanus's mother bravely urged her son to take revenge, and Ptolemy put her to death.

23. See Solomon Zeitlin, *The Book of Judith* (Leiden: Brill, 1972), 26–71; Carey Moore, *Judith* (Garden City; Doubleday, 1985), 67–70 (who dates it to the end of reign of John Hyrcanus, around 104 B.C.E.). Many scholars have opted for an earlier dating in the Persian period. See, for instance, Michael Heltzer, "The Persepolis Documents, the Lindos Chronicle, and the Book of Judith," *Parola del passato* 44 (1989): 81–101. Their arguments only establish that the narrative draws on names and other details from the Persian period, however (e.g., the Persian general Orophernes, a possible model for Holofernes, who served in an Egyptian

campaign launched by Artaxerxes III), not that it was actually written in this period. For an attempt at a compromise between the two datings, see Doron Mendels, *The Land of Israel as a Political Concept in Hasmonean Literature: Recourse to History in Second Century B.C. Claims to the Holy Land* (Tübingen: J. C. B. Mohr [Siebeck], 1989), 81–101. For the medieval identification of Judith as a sister of the Maccabees, see Andre-Marie Dubarle, *Judith: Formes et sens des diverses traditions*, vol. 2 (Rome: Pontifical Biblical Institute, 1966), 170–171.

24. Moore, *Judith*, 67–70.

25. Ibid., 208–209.

26. See Stanley Burstein, "Cleitarchus in Jerusalem: A Note on the Book of Judith," *The Eye Expanded. Life and the Arts in Greco-Roman Antiquity* (ed. Frances Titchener and Richard F. Moorton, Jr.; Berkeley: University of California Press, 1999), 105–112.

27. See Sidnie White, "In the Steps of Jael and Deborah," *No One Spoke Ill of Her: Essays on Judith* (ed. James Vanderkam; Atlanta: Scholars Press, 1992), 5–16.

28. Dubarle, *Judith*, vol. 2, 112.

29. Cf. Mikhail Rostovtzeff, *The Social and Economic History of the Hellenistic World* (Oxford: Clarendon Press, 1941), 35.

Chapter 3: Friends in High Places

1. For analysis of these documents, see Miriam Pucci Ben Zeev, *Jewish Rights in the Roman World: The Greek and Roman Documents Quoted by Josephus Flavius* (Tübingen: J. C. B. Mohr [Siebeck], 1998).

2. See Gerhard Delling, "Philons Enkomion auf Augustus," *Klio* 54 (1972): 171–192; Ray Barraclough, "Philo's Politics: Roman Rule and Hellenistic Judaism," *ANRW* II.21:418–551; Maren Niehoff, *Philo on Jewish Identity and Culture* (Tübingen: J. C. B. Mohr [Siebeck], 2001), 111–136.

3. Clifford Ando, *Imperial Ideology and Provincial Loyalty in the Roman Empire* (Berkeley: University of California Press, 2000), 362–373.

4. See Andrew Erskine, "The Romans as Common Benefactors," *Historia* 43 (1994): 70–87.

5. See David Konstan, "Patrons and Friends," *Classical Philology* 90 (1995): 328–342.

6. All translations of Philo follow that of Francis Colson, George Whittaker, and Ralph Marcus, *Philo, with an English Translation* (Loeb Classical Library; Cambridge: Harvard University Press/London: Heinemann, 1929–1962)—checked against the original text in Roger Arnaldez, Jean Pouilloux, and Claude Mondésert, *Les Oeuvres de Philon d'Alexandrie, vols. 1–36* (Paris: Éditions du cerf, 1961–1992). For commentary on the *Embassy to Gaius*, see E. Mary Smallwood, *Philonis Alexandrini Legatio ad Gaium* (Leiden: Brill, 1961).

7. For the fullest discussion of the imperial cult, see Simon Price, *Rituals and Power: The Roman Imperial Cult in Asia Minor* (Cambridge: Cambridge University Press, 1984).

8. For the emergent religious functions of the synagogue in Hellenistic-Roman antiquity, see Steven Fine, *This Holy Place: On the Sanctity of the Synagogue during the Greco-Roman Period* (Notre Dame: University of Notre Dame Press, 1997).

9. For the synagogue as a site of euergetic exchange, see Tessa Rajak and David Noy, "Archisynagogoi: Office, Title and Social Status in the Greco-Roman Synagogue," *JRS* 83 (1993): 75–93; Tessa Rajak, "Jews as Benefactors," *Studies on the Jewish Diaspora in the Hellenistic and Roman Periods* (ed. Benjamin Isaac and Aharon Oppenheimer; Tel Aviv: Tel Aviv University Press/Ramot, 1996), 17–38; L. Michael White, *Building God's House in the Roman World: Architectural Adaptation among Pagans, Jews and Christians* (Baltimore: Johns Hopkins University Press, 1990), 60–101.

10. Eventually, some synagogues were named for emperors. See Arnaldo Momigliano, "Severo Alessandro archisynagogus: Una conferma alla Historia Augusta," *Athenaeum* 12 (1934): 151–153. For synagogues dedicated to the safety or the welfare of the emperor, see Rajak and Noy, "Archisynagogoi," 92 no. 27; L. Michael White, "Synagogue and Society in Imperial Ostia: Archaeological and Epigraphic Evidence," *Judaism and Christianity in First-Century Rome* (ed. Karl Donfried and Peter Richardson; Grand Rapids: Eerdmans, 1998), 30–68, esp. 53–57.

11. For analysis of this riot and the political and social issues at stake for the rioters, see E. Mary Smallwood, *The Jews under Roman Rule: From Pompey to Diocletian* (Leiden: Brill, 1976), 220–255; Aryeh Kasher, *The Jews in Hellenistic and Roman Egypt: The Struggle for Equal Rights* (Tübingen : J. C. B. Mohr [Siebeck], 1985); Koen Goudriaan, "Ethnical Strategies in Graeco-Roman Egypt," *Ethnicity in Hellenistic Egypt* (ed. Per Bilde; Aarhus: Aarhus University Press, 1992), 74–99; Joseph Modrzejewski, *The Jews of Egypt: From Rameses II to Emperor Hadrian* (Philadelphia: Jewish Publication Society, 1995), 161–225; Dorothy Sly, *Philo's Alexandria* (London and New York: Routledge, 1996); Miriam Pucci Ben Zeev, "New Perspectives on the Jewish-Greek Hostilities in Alexandria During the Reign of Emperor Caligula," *JSJ* 21 (1990): 227–235.

12. See John Fitzgerald, "Philippians in the Light of Some Ancient Discussions of Friendship," *Friendship, Flattery and Frankness of Speech* (ed. John Fitzgerald; Leiden: Brill, 1996), 141–160, esp. 145–147.

13. See Geoffry Sumi, "Impersonating the Dead: Mimes at Roman Funerals," *American Journal of Philology* 123 (2002): 559–585.

14. For more on *prosopopoiia* and its use by another Jew in the first century C.E. (Paul), see Stanley Stowers, *A Rereading of Romans: Justice, Jews and Gentiles* (New Haven: Yale University Press, 1994), 264–284.

15. Niehoff, *Philo*, 118–128.

16. Philo echoes this tradition elsewhere in the *Embassy* when he notes that Augustus "never wished anyone to address him as a god but was annoyed if anyone used the word" (*Embassy* 154). Claudius too refuses divine honors in his famous letter to the Alexandrians of 41 B.C.E. "But the establishment of a high priest and temples of myself I decline . . . in the belief that temples and the like have been set apart in all ages for the gods alone." See Martin P. Charlesworth, "The Refusal of Divine Honours: An Augustan Formula," *Papers of the British School of Rome* 15 (1939): 1–10; Niehoff, *Philo*, 89–90.

17. For the translation and original text, see *Plutarch's Moralia* (trans. Frank Babbitt; Loeb; London: William Heinemann, 1927), 278–279.

18. Shadi Bartsch, *Actors in the Audience: Theatricality and Doublespeak from Nero to Hadrian* (Cambridge: Harvard University Press, 1994), 148–187.

19. See Solomon Zeitlin, "Did Agrippa Write a Letter to Gaius Caligula?" *JQR* 56 (1965–1966): 21–31; Daniel Schwartz, *Agrippa I: The Last King of Judaea* (Tübingen: J. C. B. Mohr [Siebeck], 1990), 178–180, 200–202.

20. See Erwin Goodenough, *Politics of Philo Judaeus: Practice and Theory* (New Haven: Yale University, 1938), 19. Smallwood, *Legatio*, 182. For a different view of the purpose and intended audience of the *Embassy*, see Niehoff, *Philo*, 39–44, who argues that it was addressed to a Jewish audience.

21. Goodenough, *Politics*, 5–7.

22. For the connection between friendship and frankness of speech, see David Konstan, "Friendship, Frankness and Flattery," *Friendship, Flattery and Frankness of Speech*, 7–19; Clarence Glad, "Frank Speech, Flattery, and Friendship in Philodemus, *Friendship, Flattery and Frankness of Speech*, 21–59.

23. Caligula's ability to detect disloyalty in seemingly innocuous speech seems to be corroborated by other accounts. See Suetonius, *Caligula* 27.4.

24. See Frederick Ahl, "The Art of Safe Criticism in Greece and Rome," *AJP* 105 (1984): 174–208.

25. Homi Bhahba, "Of Mimicry and Man: The Ambivalence of Colonial Discourse," *The Location of Culture* (London: Routledge, 1994), 85–92.

26. For a recent summary of the philological and historical issues raised by these documents, see Schwartz, *Agrippa*, 99–106; Pucci Ben Zeev, *Jewish Rights*, 294–342. For the third edict, see *CPJ*, vol. 2: 153, lines 73–104 (and 36–37 for additional bibliography); Harold Bell, *Jews and Christians in Egypt* (London and Oxford: Oxford University Press, 1924), 1–37.

27. See Herbert Musurillo. *The Acts of the Pagan Martyrs. Acta Alexandrinorum* (Oxford: Clarendon 1954), 18–26, 117–140; *CPJ*, vol. 2:156.

28. For this identification, see Schwartz, *Agrippa*, 96–98.

Chapter 4: Optical Elusions

1. See Thomas Sebeok, "Pandora's Box in Aftertimes," *I Think I Am a Verb: More Contributions on the Doctrine of Signs* (New York: Plenum Press, 1986), 149–173.

2. On the phenomenon of scoptophilia, see Karl Abraham, *Selected Papers of Karl Abraham* (trans. Douglas Bryan and Alix Strachey; London: Hogarth, 1948), 169–171.

3. Carlin Barton, *The Sorrows of the Ancient Romans: The Gladiator and the Monster* (Princeton: Princeton University Press, 1993), 85–95.

4. See Kathleen M. Coleman, "Launching into History: Aquatic Displays in the Early Empire," *JRS* 83 (1993): 48–74; Andrew Feldherr, "Ships of Stage: Aenead 5 and Augustan Circus Spectacle," *Classical Antiquity* 14 (1995): 245–265; Alison Futrell, *Blood in the Arena: The Spectacle of Roman Power* (Austin: University of Texas Press, 1997); Donald Kyle, *Spectacles of Death in Ancient Rome* (London: Routledge, 1998); and the essays in Bettina Bergmann and Christine Kondoleon, *The Art of Ancient Spectacle* (Washington, D.C.: National Gallery of Art, 1999).

5. See Victor Tcherikover, "The Third Book of Maccabees As a Historical Source of Augustus' Time," *ScrHier* 7 (1961): 1–26.

6. For analysis of the triumph, see Hendrik S. Versnel, *Triumphus: An Inquiry into the Origin, Development and Meaning of the Roman Triumph* (Leiden: Brill, 1970); Claude Nicolet, *The World of the Citizen in Republican Rome* (Berkeley and

Los Angeles: University of California Press, 1980), 352–356; Richard Brilliant, "'Let the Trumpets Roar!' The Roman Triumph," *The Art of Ancient Spectacle*, 221–229.

7. See Douglas Domingo-Forasté, ed., *Claudii Aeliani: Epistulae et Fragmenta* (Stuttgart: B. G. Teubner, 1994), 43.

8. Cf. Lee Levine, "Josephus' Description of the Jerusalem Temple: War, Antiquities, and Other Sources," *Josephus and the History of the Greco-Roman Period* (ed. Fausto Parente and Joseph Sievers; Leiden: Brill, 1994), 233–246, who suggests that Josephus's two descriptions of the Herodian Temple capture it at two different historical periods, in 20 C.E. and just before the Jewish Revolt.

9. See Donald Strong, *Roman Museums: Selected Papers on Roman Art and Architecture* (London: Pindar Press, 1994), 13–30.

10. Some of the Temple's visual impressiveness has been recovered through the excavation of the southwest corner of the Temple mount. See Meir Ben-Dov, *In the Shadow of the Temple: The Discovery of Ancient Jerusalem* (trans. Ina Friedman; New York; Harper and Row, 1985); Bahat, "The Herodian Temple," *The Cambridge History of Judaism, Volume 3 The Early Roman Period* (ed. William Horbury; William D. Davies, and John Sturdy; Cambridge: Cambridge University Press, 1999), 38–58.

11. Pierre Benoit, "The Archaeological Reconstruction of the Antonia Fortress," *Jerusalem Revealed: Archaeology in the Holy City 1968–1974* (ed. Yigael Yadin; Jerusalem: Israel Exploration Society, 1975), 87–89; Gregory Wightman, "Temple Fortresses in Jerusalem Part II: The Hasmonean Baris and Herodian Antonia," *BAIAS* 10 (1990): 7–33. For a study of Herod's building program that emphasizes Roman influence (although it does not describe it in detail), see Duane W. Roller, *The Building Program of Herod the Great* (Berkeley: University of California Press, 1998).

12. Samuel Wolff, *Greek Romances in Elizabethan Prose Fiction* (New York: Columbia University Press, 1912), 177.

13. See Graham Zanker, "Enargeia in the Ancient Criticism of Poetry," *Rheinisches Museum für Philologie* 124 (1981): 297–311; Andrew Walker, "Enargeia and the Spectator in Greek Historiography," *TAPA* 123 (1993): 353–377; Andrew Feldherr, *Spectacle and Society in Livy's History* (Berkeley and Los Angeles: University of California Press, 1998).

14. Cf. Richard Davis, *The Lives of Indian Images* (Princeton: Princeton University Press, 1997), 176–179.

15. Rabbinic literature also exults in the luster of the Temple (e.g., *b. B. Bat.* 4a), but descriptions like that in the Mishnaic tractate *Middot* reflect representational priorities distinct from that in earlier Jewish-Greek sources.

16. Jas Elsner, *Art and the Roman Viewer: The Transformation of Art from the Pagan World to Christianity* (Cambridge: Cambridge University Press, 1995), 145–150.

17. For a list of these passages, see Elsner, *Art and the Roman Viewer*, 345 n. 69.

18. See Jas Elsner, "From the Pyramids to Pausanias and Piglet: Monuments, Travel and Writings," *Art and Text in Ancient Greece (ed. Simon Goldhill and Robin Osborne; Cambridge / New York: Cambridge University Press, 1994)*, 224–254, esp. 244–252.

19. Elsner, *Art and the Roman Viewer*, 146.

20. Cf. Feldherr, *Spectacle and Society in Livy's History*, 15–16, 24–25.

21. For an attempt to identify the objects pictured in this scene, see Leon Yarden, *The Spoils of Jerusalem on the Arch of Titus: A Re-investigation* (Stockholm: Svenska Institutet i Rom, 1991). For bibliography on the arch, see Louis Feldman, *Josephus and Modern Scholarship (1937–1980)* (Berlin: de Gruyter, 1984), 375–377.

22. See Diana Kleiner, *Roman Sculpture* (New Haven: Yale University Press, 1992), 190–191.

Chapter 5: Flights of Fancy

1. For these and other examples of covert ritual practice in the concentration camps, see Irving Rosenbaum, *The Holocaust and Halakhah* (New York: Ktav, 1976), 91–119.

2. Benjamin Sommer, "Conflicting Constructions of Divine Presence in the Priestly Tabernacle," *BibInt* 9 (2001): 41–63, esp. 48.

3. Susan Alcock, *Graecia Capta: The Landscapes of Roman Greece* (Cambridge: Cambridge University Press, 1993), 192–196.

4. See Jonathan Smith, *To Take Place: Toward Theory in Ritual* (Chicago: University of Chicago Press, 1997), 86–88.

5. For the imitation of the Temple in synagogue architecture, see Steven Fine, *This Holy Place: On the Sanctity of the Synagogue during the Greco-Roman Period* (Notre Dame: University of Notre Dame Press, 1997), 49–55, 79–94, 132–134.

6. Stanley Tambiah, *Culture, Thought and Social Action: An Anthropological Perspective* (Cambridge: Harvard University Press, 1985), 35–37.

7. Maurizio Bettini, "Ghosts of Exile: Doubles and Nostalgia in Virgil's parva Troia (Aenead 3.294ff.)," *Classical Antiquity* 16 (1997): 8–33.

8. Alcock, *Graecia Capta*, 175–180.

9. Anne Roullet, *The Egyptian and Egyptianizing Monuments of Imperial Rome* (Leiden: Brill, 1972).

10. John Malalas, Chronicle X, 260–261, cited in Fergus Millar, *The Roman Near East 31 B.C.–AD 337* (Cambridge: Harvard University Press, 1993), 79.

11. Joseph Patrich, "Hideouts in the Judean Wilderness," *BAR* 15 (1989): 32–42, reports the results of a survey of caves in the Judean wilderness under the auspices of the Institute of Archaeology of the Hebrew University in Jerusalem.

12. For the use of cryptic scripts, see Stephen Pfann, "The Writings in Esoteric Script from Qumran," *The Dead Sea Scrolls. Fifty Years after Their Discovery: Proceedings of the Jerusalem Congress, July 20–25, 1997* (ed. Lawrence Schiffman, Emanuel Tov, and James VanderKam; Jerusalem: Israel Exploration Society in cooperation with The Shrine of the Book, Israel Museum, 2000), 177–190. For the scolls' use of coded terminology, see William Schniedewind, "Qumran Hebrew as an Antilanguage," *JBL* 118 (1999): 235–252, esp. 250–251.

13. Here and in six other places, the list is punctuated by a series of two or three Greek letters, the meaning of which are unknown. See Edward Ullendorff, "The Greek Letters of the Copper Scroll Code," *VT* 11 (1961): 227–228; Judah Lefkovits, *The Copper Scroll-3Q15: A Reevaluation* (Leiden: Brill, 2000), 498–504.

14. I draw on the text and translation in *The Dead Sea Scrolls Study Edition*, vols. 1–2 (ed. Florentino García Martínez and Eibert Tigchelaar; Leiden: Brill, 1997). See also Al Wolters, *The Copper Scroll: Overview, Text and Translation* (Sheffield: Sheffield Academic Press, 1996). The text was originally made public by

Jozef Milik in *Les 'Petites Grottes' de Qumrân: Textes* (ed. Maurice Baillet, Jozef Milik and Roland de Vaux; Oxford: Clarendon, 1962), 201–302.

15. For attempts to decipher the topographic names listed in the Copper Scroll, see Bargil Pixner, "Unravelling the Copper Scroll Code: A Study of the Topography of 3Q15," *RevQ* 11 (1983): 323–365, esp. 325–358; Stephen Goranson, "Sectarianism, Geography and the Copper Scroll," *JJS* 43 (1992): 282–287.

16. But see Paul Mandel, "On the 'Duplicate Copy' of the Copper Scroll (3Q 15)," *RevQ* 16 (1993): 69–76.

17. See M. Lehmann, "Identification of the Copper Scroll Based on Its Technical Terms," *RQ* 5 (1964): 97–105; P. Kyle McCarter, Jr., "The Copper Scroll Treasure as an Accumulation of Religious Offerings," *Methods of Investigation of the Dead Sea Scrolls and the Khirbet Qumran Sitel: Present Realities and Future Prospects* (ed. Michael O. Wise et al.; New York Academy of Sciences, 1994), 133–148.

18. See Cecil Roth, *The Historical Background of the Dead Sea Scrolls* (Oxford: Blackwell, 1958), 44–45, 67; John Allegro, *The Treasure of the Copper Scroll* (Garden City, NY: Doubleday, 1960), 120–129; McCarter, "Copper Scroll," 140 (as one of two scenarios he considers possible); Regarding hiding places with priestly associations, note 1) the ford of the high priest in col. 6.14–7.1; 2) the name Zadok, the most influential priestly clan in Jerusalem, in 11.3 (Zadok's tomb) and 11.5–6 (Zadok's garden); and 3) mention of "Hakkoz" in 7.9, the name of another priestly family (cf. 1 Chr 24:10). Milik, (*'Pettite Grottes'*, 258) cites evidence that the latter family may have been entrusted with guarding the Temple treasury in the Second Temple.

19. Milik, *Pettite Grottes*, 275–284. For a recent attempt to revive this view, see Hanan Eshel and Zeev Safrai, "A Sectarian Composition Documenting Where the Treasures of the First Temple Were Hidden," *Cathedra* 103 (2002): 7–20 (Hebrew).

20. See Jozef Milik, "Notes d'épigraphie et de topographie palestiniennes," *RB* 66 (1959): 567–575.

21. The reasons for this consensus are summarized in Al Wolters, "Apocalyptic and the Copper Scroll," *JNES* 49 (1990): 145–154.

22. Some Jewish sources concede that there was something buried on Mt. Gerizim—not treasures, but idols. See Pseudo-Philo, *Biblical Antiquities* 25.10 which identifies the objects in question as seven golden images hidden by the tribe of Asher.

23. For text and translation, see the Loeb edition, W. H. S. Jones, *Pausanias' Description of Greece* (London: Heinemann, 1917–1935).

24. See Andrea Jordens and Gereon Becht-Jordens, "Ein Eberunterkiefer als 'Staatssymbol' des Aitolischen Bundes (IG XII 2,15), Politische Identitätssuche im Mythos nach dem Ende der spartanischen Hegemonie," *Klio* 76 (1994): 172–184; Susan Alcock, "The Pseudo-History of Messenia Unplugged," *TAPA* 129 (1999): 333–341.

25. See Yisrael Gutman, "Philo the Epic Poet," *Scripta Hierosolymitana* 1 (1954): 36–63.

26. The relocation of the mysteries in Andania is attested by an inscription dated to 92/91 B.C.E. For an English translation, see Marvin Meyer, *The Ancient Mysteries: A Sourcebook* (San Francisco: HarperSanFrancisco, 1987), 51–59. For the original text, see Wilhelm Dittenberger, *Sylloge Inscriptionum Graecarum* (3rd edition; Leipzig: Hirzel, 1915–1924), vol. 2, 401–411 (#736).

27. Pausanias's description of Greece, a work completed between 143 and 161 C.E., is less than a century removed from the time of the *Copper Scroll*, and may draw on a much earlier Messenian source.

28. Adapted from the translation in Bernard Grenfell and Arthur Hunt, *Fragment of an Uncanonical Gospel* (London: Oxford University Press, 1908), 16–17.

29. Daniel Schwartz, "Viewing the Holy Utensils (P. Ox. V, 840)," *NTS* 32 (1986): 153–159.

30. See James Frazier, *The Golden Bough: A Study in Magic and Religion* (abridged edition; New York: Macmillan, 1922), chapter 3, §2.

31. The inconsistency is puzzling. Most scholars suspect that book 7 of the *Jewish War*, or a portion of it, was written long after the rest of the book. If so, the denial of a similarity between Leontopolis and Jerusalem may represent a belated attempt by Josephus to deny what he had claimed in earlier writing, but it is not clear why he changed his mind, or did not smooth out the contradiction.

32. From his introduction to his commentary on Psalm 54 (55). See Robert Devreesse (ed.), *Le commentaire de Théodore de Mopsueste sur les psaumes* (Vatican City: Apostolic Vatican Library, 1939), 353, sec. C. According to Fausto Parente ("Le temoignage de Theodore de Mopsueste sur le sort d'Onias III et la fondation du temple de Leontopolis," *REJ* 154 [1995]: 429–436), Theodore refers to a passage in *2 Macc* suppressed in the version which now survives.

33. Most scholars endorse Onias IV as the builder of Leontopolis, but for an attempt to argue that the founder was Onias III, see Fausto Parente, "Onias III's Death and the Founding of the Temple of Leontopolis," *Josephus and the History of the Graeco-Roman Period: Essays in Memory of Morton Smith* (ed. Fausto Parente and Joseph Sievers; Leiden: Brill, 1994), 69–98. For other attempts to construct the history of Leontopolis, see Mathias Delcor, "Le Temple d'Onias en Égypte: Réexamen d'un vieux problème," *RB* 75 (1968): 188–203; Daniel Schwartz, "The Jews of Egypt between the Temple of Onias, the Temple of Jerusalem, and Heaven," *Zion* 62 (1997): 5–22 (Hebrew); Robert Hayward, "The Jewish Temple at Leontopolis: A Reconsideration," *JJS* 33 (1982): 429–443; Erich Gruen, "The Origins and Objectives of Onias's Temple," *Scripta Classica Israelica* 16 (1997): 47–70; Paul Rabinow, "The Last Oniad and the Teacher of Righteousness," *JJS* 48 (1997): 30–52; Joan Taylor, "A Second Temple in Egypt: The Evidence for the Zadokite Temple of Onias," *JSJ* 29 (1998): 297–321.

34. For text and translation, see James Charlesworth, *The Dead Sea Scrolls: Hebrew, Aramaic and Greek Texts with English Translations, Volume I. Rule of the Community and Related Documents* (Tübingen: J. C. B. Mohr [Siebeck]/Louisville: Westminster John Knox Press, 1993).

35. Note that this column's claim that the "men of the community shall set apart a *holy house* for Aaron" is different from col. 8.5 where the community council is to establish a "holy house" not for Aaron but for Israel. How one resolves this discrepancy depends on how one views the *Community Rule*'s redactional development. For two recent attempts to sort this development out, see Sarianna Metso, *The Textual Development of the Qumran Community Rule* (Leiden: Brill, 1997); Markus Bockmuehl, "Redaction and Ideology in the Rule of the Community (1QS/4QS)," *RevQ* 18 (1998): 541–560.

36. See, for example, Frank Moore Cross, *The Ancient Library of Qumran* (Minneapolis: Fortress, 1995), 85–86. For a period, some scholars claimed that an altar had been found at Qumran, a view now rejected. See Robert Kugler, "Rewriting Rubrics: Sacrifice and the Religion of Qumran," *Religion in the Dead Sea Scrolls*

(ed. Joan Collins and Robert Kugler; Grand Rapids: Eerdmans, 2000), 90–112, esp. 90–92. For a modified form of the altar theory, that the sect constructed prayer houses without sacrifice but modeled on the Temple cult, see Annette Steudel, "The Houses of Prostration *CD* xi, 21-xii, 1—Duplicates of the Temple (1)," *RevQ* 16 (1993): 49–68.

37. See Joseph Baumgarten, "Sacrifice and Worship among the Jewish Sectarians of the Dead Sea (Qumran) Scrolls," *HTR* 46 (1953): 141–159, reprinted in *Studies in Qumran Law* (Leiden: Brill, 1977), 39–56; Hermann Lichtenberger, "Atonement and Sacrifice in the Qumran Community," *Approaches to Ancient Judaism: Theory and Practice*, vol. 2 (ed. William Green; Chico: Scholars Press, 1980), 159–171; Johann Maier, "Temple," *Encyclopedia of the Dead Sea Scrolls* (ed. Lawrence Schiffman and James Vanderkam; Oxford: Oxford University Press, 2000), 921–927, esp. 924.

38. The Onias of the *Antiquities* leaves Jerusalem after losing the high priesthood to a rival priest. According to an influential reconstruction of the Qumran sect's history, the founder of the Qumran sect was also a high priest forced from office during the Hasmonean period. For more on the parallels between Leontopolis and Qumran, see Solomon Steckoll, "The Qumran Sect in Relation to the Temple of Leontopolis," *RevQ* 6 (1967–1968): 55–69.

39. A citation in Clement of Alexandria establishes that *4 Ezra* existed by 190 C.E. Since the Temple's destruction is central to the book, it was almost certainly written after 70 C.E. See Michael Stone, *Fourth Ezra: A Commentary on the Book of Fourth Ezra* (Minneapolis: Fortress Press, 1990), 9–10, which places it in Domitian's reign between 81–96 C.E.

40. For discussion of the word "likeness" as used in *4 Ezra* (*similitudo* in the Latin), see Stone, *Fourth Ezra*, 338.

41. The translation is that of Stone, *Fourth Ezra*, 316–317.

42. See Hans Bietenhard, *Die himmlische Welt im Urchristentum und Spätjudentum* (Tübingen: J. C. B. Mohr [Siebeck], 1951); Johann Maier, *Vom Kultus zur Gnosis* (Salzburg: Müller, 1964), 106–148; Harold Attridge, *The Epistle to the Hebrews: A Commentary on the Epistle to the Hebrews* (Philadelphia: Fortress, 1989), 222–224.

43. See Stone, *Fourth Ezra*, 33; idem, "A Reconsideration of Apocalyptic Visions," HTR 96 (2003): 167–180.

44. Daniel Schwartz, "Temple and Desert: On Religion and State in Second Temple Period Judaea," *Studies in the Jewish Background of Christianity* (Tübingen: J. C. B. Mohr [Siebeck], 1992), 29–43. For criticism of Schwartz' argument, see Bruce Longenecker, "The Wilderness and Revolutionary Ferment in First-Century Palestine: A Response to D. R. Schwartz and J. Marcus," *JSJ* 29 (1998): 322–336 and for Schwartz's rejoinder, Daniel Schwartz, "Whence the Voice? A Response to Bruce W. Longenecker," *JSJ* 31 (2000): 42–46.

45. See Michael Adas, "From Avoidance to Confrontation: Peasant Protest in Precolonial and Colonial Southeast Asia," *Colonialism and Culture* (ed. Nicholas Dirks; Ann Arbor: University of Michigan Press, 1992), 89–126.

46. See Aharon Oppenheimer, "Zealots," *The Encyclopedia of the Dead Sea Scrolls*, vol. 2 (ed. Lawrence Schiffman and James VanderKam; Oxford: Oxford University Press, 2000), 1007–1010, who notes a Talmudic tradition (Babylonian Talmud *Gittin* 56a) associating this act with a Zechariah ben Euqolos who

can be identified with Zacharias son of Amphicalleus, a Zealot leader according to Josephus (*J. W.* 4.225).

47. Note also that during the revolt itself, the rebel leader John of Giscala attacked another symbol of Rome's symbiotic relationship with the Temple cult, melting down vessels sent by Augustus and his consort (*J. W.* 5.562–63).

48. See the studies in Andrea Berlin and J. Andrew Overman, *The First Jewish Revolt: Archaeology, History and Ideology* (London: Routledge, 2002).

49. For the revolt as an attempt to defend the Temple and the law, see William Farmer, *Maccabees, Zealots and Josephus. An Inquiry into Jewish Nationalism in the Greco-Roman Period* (New York: Columbia University Press, 1956); Helmut Schwier, *Tempel und Tempelzerstörung: Untersuchungen zu den theologischen und ideologischen Faktoren im ersten jüdisch-römischen Krieg (66–74 n. Chr.)* (Schweiz: Universitätsverlag Freiburg/Göttingen: Vandenhoeck & Ruprecht, 1989), 55–145.

50. Cf. David Rhoads, *Israel in Revolution: 6–74 C.E.: A Political History Based on the Writings of Josephus* (Philadelphia: Fortress, 1976), 166–170.

Chapter 6: Conjuring Power

1. For analysis of Agrippa II's speech against revolt as a reflection of Josephus's own views about the war, see Tessa Rajak, "Friends, Romans, Subjects: Agrippa II's Speech in Josephus's *Jewish War*" *Images of Empire* (ed. Alexander Loveday; Sheffield: Sheffield Academic Press, 1991), 122–134.

2. Michael Adas, *Prophets of Rebellion: Millenarian Protest Movements against the European Colonial Order* (Chapel Hill: University of North Carolina Press, 1979).

3. Scholars differ on whether "magic" is a useful term in the study of ancient Judaism and Christianity, some noting that Jews and Christians avoided this label to describe their own practices; others stressing the heuristic advantages. See Peter Schäfer, "Magic and Religion in Ancient Judaism," *Envisioning Magic: A Princeton Seminar and Symposium* (ed. Peter Schäfer and Hans Kippenberg; Leiden: Brill, 1997), 19–43.

4. Having said this, I would note evidence from the Dead Sea Scrolls that some Jews did employ practices typically thought of as magical. See Matthias Albani, "Horoscopes in the Qumran Scrolls," *The Dead Sea Scrolls after Fifty Years: A Comprehensive Assessment*, vol. 2 (ed. Peter Flint and James VanderKam; Leiden: Brill, 1999), 279–330; and cf. William Lyons and Andy Reimer, "The Demonic Virus and Qumran Studies: Some Preventative Measures," *DSD* 5 (1998): 16–32.

5. Adas, *Prophets of Rebellion*, 147–159.

6. Ibid., 156–159. For a description of the *niu* ceremony, see James Cowan, *The New Zealand Wars: A History of the Maori Campaigns and the Pioneering Period*, vol. 2 (repr.; New York: AMS Press, 1969), 6, 9–10, 11–12.

7. On these figures, see Richard Horsley, "'Like One of the Prophets of Old': Two Types of Popular Prophets at the Time of Jesus," *CBQ* 47 (1985): 435–463; Rebecca Gray, *Prophetic Figures in Late Second Temple Jewish Palestine* (Oxford: Oxford University Press, 1993), esp. 112–144.

8. Gray, *Prophetic Figures*, 35–79.

9. The chief advocate of a Roman dating was Yigael Yadin, *The Scroll of the War of the Sons of Light against the Sons of Darkness* (Oxford: Oxford University Press, 1962), 244–246, who pointed to a number of parallels with Roman military practice.

Others place the composition of the *Rule*, or at least of parts of it, in the second century B.C.E., shortly after the Maccabean Revolt. See most recently, Russell Gmirkin, "Historical Allusions in the War Scroll," *DSD* 5 (1998): 172–214. Ultimately, the evidence for any particular dating is inconclusive, and the compositional history of the *Rule* may very well span the Hasmonean and Roman periods, as argued by Philip Davies, *1QM, The War Scroll from Qumran: Its Structure and History* (Rome: Pontifical Biblical Institute, 1977), 123–124. The meaning of *Kittim* may have evolved accordingly. In the Maccabean period, Jews identified them with their Hellenistic rulers, but the term came to be identified with the Romans after they conquered Palestine, the most likely meaning of most Qumran references. See Hanan Eshel, "The Kittim in the *War Scroll* and in the Pesharim," *Historical Perspectives: From the Hasmoneans to Bar Kokhba in Light of the Dead Sea Scrolls* (ed. David Goodblatt, Avital Pinnick, and Daniel Schwartz; Leiden: Brill, 2001), 29–44.

10. For the enlistment of angelic support in the battle described in the *War Rule*, see now Crispin Fletcher-Loius, *All the Glory of Adam: Liturgical Anthropology in the Dead Sea Scrolls* (Leiden: Brill, 2002), 375–395.

11. The translation is that of Florentino Martínez and Eibert Tigchelaar, *The Dead Sea Scrolls Study Edition*, 1: 133–135. For a critical edition, see Yadin, *Scroll*.

12. For Sabbath rest as a tactical problem for the Jews, see M. D. Herr, "The Problem of the Laws of War on the Sabbath in the Second Temple and Mishnaic Periods," *Tarbiz* 30 (1961): 242–256, 341–356 (Hebrew).

13. For other similarities with Greco-Roman military manuals, see Jean Duhaime, "The *War Scroll* from Qumran and the Greco-Roman Tactical Treatises," *RevQ* 13 (1988): 133–151.

14. Admittedly, the Greek of this statement is obscure and other interpretations of its significance are possible. See Jonathan Goldstein, *1 Maccabees* (New York: Doubleday, 1976), 261–262.

15. See P. Hollanback, "Jesus, Demoniacs and Public Authorities: A Socio-Historical Study," *JAAR* 49 (1981): 567–588; Brent Shaw, "Josephus: Roman Power and Responses to it," *Athenaeum* 83 (1995): 357–390, esp. 364–365; John Dominic Crossan, *The Historical Jesus: The Life of a Mediterranean Jewish Peasant* (San Francisco: Harper, 1991), 314–318.

16. Cf. Tacitus, *Histories* 5, 13.1–2, reproduced in Menahem Stern, *Greek and Latin Authors on Jews and Judaism*, vol. 2 (Jerusalem: Israel Academy of Sciences and Humanities, 1980), 23, 31.

17. This oracle is also mentioned by Suetonius (*Vespasion* 4.5) and Tacitus (*Histories* 5.13). It is not clear to what oracle these sources are referring exactly. Perhaps a scriptural passage is its source, but its apparent circulation throughout the Near East, mentioned by Seutonius, has led some scholars to conjecture that it derived from a syncretic prophesy broadly circulated under the name of Hystaspes. See Ramsay MacMullen, *Enemies of the Roman Order: Treason, Unrest and Alienation in the Empire* (Cambridge: Harvard University Press, 1966), 148.

18. Adrian Goldsworthy, *The Roman Army at War 100 BC–AD 200* (Oxford: Clarendon, 1996), 145–149.

19. Jane Webster, "At the End of the World: Druidic and Other Revitalization Movements in Post-Conquest Gaul and Britain," *Britannia* 30 (1999): 1–20. See also MacMullen, *Enemies of the Roman Order*, 95–162; Arnaldo Momigliano, "Some Preliminary Remarks on the 'Religious Opposition' to the Roman

Empire," *Opposition et résistances a l'empire d'Auguste a Trajan* (ed. Adalberto Giovannini and Denis van Berchem; Geneva: Fondation Hardt, 1987), 103–133; Glen Bowersock, "The Mechanics of Subversion in the Roman Provinces," *Opposition*, 291–320.

20. See Gabriella Gustafsson, *Evocatio Deorum: Historical and Mythical Interpretations of Ritualised Conquests in the Expansion of Ancient Rome* (Uppsala: Uppsala University Press, 2000).

21. See Jon Edward Lendon, "The Rhetoric of Combat: Greek Theory and Roman Culture in Julius Caesar's Battle Description," *Classical Antiquity* 18 (1999): 273–329.

22. See Lamentations Rabbah 2.2 § 4.

23. Cassius Dio, *Roman History* 69, 12:1–14:3, cited in Stern, *Greek and Latin Authors*, vol. 2, 391–393.

Chapter 7: Playing Dead

1. Solomon Schechter, *Avot de-Rabbi Natan* (New York and Jerusalem: Bet ha-midrash le-rabanim be-Amerika, 1997; originally published in 1887), 20–21 (Version B, chapter 7). Other versions of the story appear in *Avot de Rabbi Natan*, Version A, chapter 4; the Palestinian Talmud *Sheqalim* 6:3, 50a; Babylonian Talmud *Taanit* 29a; *Pesikta Rabbati* 26; *Targum Sheni* to Esther 1:3; and *Leviticus Rabbah* 19:6.

2. Menahem Stern, *Greek and Latin Authors on Jews and Judaism*, vol. 2 (Jerusalem: Israel Academy of Sciences and Humanities, 1980), 371–375.

3. See David Goodblatt, "Suicide in the Sanctuary: Traditions on Priestly Martyrdom," *JJS* 46 (1995): 10–29, esp. 17–19. For additional analysis of this rabbinic legend see, Anat Yisraeli-Taran, *The Legends of the Destruction* (Tel Aviv: Hakibbutz Hameuchad, 1997), 91–94 (Hebrew).

4. See Goodblatt, "Suicide in the Sanctuary," 24–27.

5. See Tessa Rajak, "Dying for the Law: The Martyrs' Portrait in Jewish-Greek Literature," *Portraits: Biographical Representation in the Greek and Latin Literature of the Roman Empire* (ed. M. J. Edwards and Simon Swain; Oxford: Clarendon, 1997), 39–67.

6. See J. Willem van Henten, *The Maccabean Martyrs as Saviours of the Jewish People: A Study of 2 and 4 Maccabees* (Leiden: Brill, 1997), 140–156.

7. For analysis of this episode, see Ernst Haag, "Die drei Männer im Feuer nach Dan 3:1–30," *Die Entstehung der jüdischen Martyrologie* (ed. Jan Willem Van Henten; B. Dehandschutter, and H. van der Klaauw; Leiden: Brill, 1989), 20–50. For the date of the addition's composition, see Carey Moore, *Daniel, Esther and Jeremiah: The Additions* (Garden City, Doubleday, 1977), 65.

8. See Hendrik Versnel, "Self-Sacrifice, Compensation and the Anonymous Gods," *Le sacrifice dans l'antiquité: huit exposés suivis de discussions* (ed. Olivier Reverdin and Jean Rudhardt; Vandoeuvres-Genève: Fondation Hardt, 1981), 135–194.

9. J. Willem van Henten, *Maccabean Martyrs*, 146–150.

10. J. Willem van Henten, "Noble Death in Josephus: A Survey" (paper presented at the annual meeting of the Society of Biblical Literature in Denver Colorado, 2001).

11. See Jacob Licht, "Taxo, or the Apocalyptic Doctrine of Vengeance," *JJS* 12 (1961): 85–103.

12. Daniel Boyarin, *Dying for God: Martyrdom and the Making of Christianity and Judaism* (Stanford: Stanford University Press, 1999), 94–95.

13. For a survey of scholars with this view, see Per Bilde, *Flavius Josephus Between Jerusalem and Rome: His Life, His Works and Their Importance* (Sheffield: Sheffield Academic Press, 1988), 123–141.

14. Bilde, *Flavius Josephus*, 141–150.

15. See David Ladouceur, "Masada: A Consideration of the Literary Evidence," *GRBS* 21 (1980): 245–260; Arthur Droge and James Tabor, *A Noble Death: Suicide and Martyrdom among Chrisitians and Jews in Antiquity* (San Francisco: Harper San Francisco, 1991), 93–95. For a more extended analysis of Josephus's ambivalence, see my "Josephus on How to Survive Martyrdom," *Journal of Jewish Studies* 55 (2004: 230–245).

16. See Donald McGuire, "Textual Strategies and Political Suicide in Flavian Epic," *The Imperial Muse. Ramus Essays on Roman Literature of the Empire*, vol. 2 (ed. A. Boyle; Victoria: Aureal, 1990), 21–45; idem, *Acts of Silence: Civil War, Tyranny and Suicide in the Flavian Epics* (Hildsheim: Olms-Weidman, 1997), 185–229.

17. For a survey of Roman attitudes toward suicide, see Anton van Hooff, *From Autothanasia to Suicide: Self-killing in Classical Antiquity* (London: Routledge, 1990).

18. For the philosophical justification of suicide in first century Rome, see Miriam Griffin, "Philosophy, Cato, and Roman Suicide," *GR* 33 (1986): 64–77 and 192–202.

19. McGuire, *Acts of Silence*, 63–85.

20. See Menahem Luz, "Eleazar's Second Speech on Masada and its Literary Precedents," *Rheinisches Museum für Philologie* 126 (1983): 25–43.

21. For these and other negative elements in the Masada story, frequently obscured in translation, see David Ladouceur, "Josephus and Masada," Josephus, Judiasm and Christianity (eds. L. Feldman and G. Hatal; Wayne State University Press, Detriot, 1987) pp. 95–113.

22. Many studies have noted the formal resemblance of Josephus's suicide accounts to Roman suicide accounts. See Raymond Newell, "The Suicide Accounts in Josephus: A Form Critical Study," *SBLSP* (1982): 352–369; idem, "The Forms and Historical Value of Josephus' Suicide Accounts," *Josephus, the Bible and History* (ed. Louis Feldman and Gohei Hata; Detroit: Wayne State University Press, 1989), 278–294; Shaye Cohen, "Masada: Literary Tradition, Archaeological Remains and the Credibility of Josephus,"*JJS* 33 (1982): 385–405.

23. For the concept of the "equal opponent," see Carlin Barton, *The Sorrows of the Ancient Romans: The Gladiator and the Monster* (Princeton: Princeton University Press, 1993), 182–183.

24. See François Ripoll, *La morale héroïque dans les épopées latines d'époque flavienne: tradition et innovation* (Louvain-Paris: Peeters, 1998), 387–390.

25. There is consensus among scholars of Josephus that one of his central goals was to reconcile his continuing commitment to Jewish tradition with loyalty to Rome. See Tessa Rajak, *Josephus: The Historian and His Society* (Philadelphia: Fortress, 1984), 185–222; Martin Goodman, "Josephus as Roman Citizen," *Josephus and the History of the Greco-Roman Period*, 329–338.

26. Susan Alcock, *Graecia Capta: The Landscapes of Roman Greece* (Cambridge: Cambridge University Press, 1993), 201–202.

27. Isaiah Gafni, "Josephus and *1 Maccabees*," *Josephus, the Bible and History* 116–131.

28. Many scholars conclude that Philo and Josephus are referring to separate incidents during Pilate's administration. See for example, E. Mary Smallwood, "Philo and Josephus as Historians of the Same Events," *Josephus, Judaism and Christianity*, 114–129.

29. Daniel Schwartz, "Josephus and Philo on Pontius Pilate," *Josephus Flavius: Historian of Eretz Israel in the Hellenistic-Roman Period* (ed. Uriel Rappaport; Yad Izhak Ben Zvi, Jerusalem, 1982), 217–236 (Hebrew).

30. Josephus produced this story through a revision of *1 Maccabees* 4:35: "When Lysias saw the rout of his troops and observed the boldness that inspired those Judas, and how ready they were to live or die nobly, he withdrew to Antioch."

31. Kathleen Coleman, "Fatal Charades: Roman Executions Staged as Mythological Enactments," *JRS* 80 (1990): 44–73.

32. For an attempt to reconstruct the historical background to the story, see Gedalyahu Alon, *Jews, Judaism, and the Classical World* (trans. Israel Abrahams; Jerusalem: Magnes, 1977), 269–313. More recent studies emphasize its fictional dimensions. See Jacob Neusner, *Development of a Legend: Studies in the Traditions Concerning Yohanan ben Zakkai* (Leiden: Brill, 1970), 228–239; A. J. Saldarini, "Johanan Ben Zakkai's Escape from Jerusalem: Origin and Development of a Rabbinic Story," *JSJ* 6 (1975): 189–204; Yisraeli-Taran, *Legends of the Destruction*, 51–75; Jeffrey Rubenstein, *Talmudic Stories: Narrative Art, Composition, and Culture* (Baltimore: Johns Hopkins University Press, 1999), 139–175.

33. Y. Baer ("Jerusalem in the Times of the Great Revolt," *Zion* 37 [1971]: 127–190, esp. 172–173) argued that Yohanan's concealment in a coffin reflects a topos common in the Hellenized Near East. One problem for this hypothesis is that no such parallel is attested in an ancient source. See Saul Lieberman, *Tosefta Ki-fshutah: A Comprehensive Commentary on the Tosefta* (New York: Bet ha-midrash le-rabanim ba-Amerika, 1955–1973), part 8, 990–992 (Hebrew).

Chapter 8: The Art of Cultural Persistence

1. On the possibility that the Revolt was triggered by a Roman ban on circumcision, see Peter Schäfer, "The Causes of the Bar Kochba Revolt," *Studies in Aggadah, Targum and Jewish Liturgy in Memory of Joseph Heinemann* (ed. Jakob J. Petuchowski and Ezra Fleischer; Jerusalem: Magnes and Hebrew Union College Press, 1981), 74–94; and Aharon Oppenheimer, "The Ban on Circumcision as a Cause of the Revolt: A Reconsideration," *The Bar Kokhba War Reconsidered: New Perspectives on the Second Jewish Revolt against Rome* (ed. Peter Schäfer; Tübingen: J. C. B. Mohr [Siebeck], 2003), 55–69. Oppenheimer and others reflected in this latter volume argue against such a ban as a cause of the revolt. Among those who believe that Temple restoration was a central goal of the Bar Kochba rebels, see B. Z. Luria, "The Temple in the Days of Bar Kochba," *Bet Miqra* 7 (1962): 240–256 (Hebrew); M. D. Herr, "The Causes of the Bar Kochba Revolt," *Zion* 43 (1978): 1–11 (Hebrew). Here too, however, the evidence is very shaky.

2. On rabbinic descriptions of the revolt's aftermath, see most recently Richard Kalmin, "Rabbinic Traditions about Roman Persecutions of the Jews: A Reconsideration," *JJS* 54 (2003): 21–50.

3. See Yochanan Lewy, "Julian the Apostate and the Building of the Temple," *Jerusalem Cathedra* 3 (1983): 70–96; Robert Wilken, *John Chrysostom and the Jews: Rhetoric and Reality in the Late 4th Century* (Berkeley: University of California Press, 1983), 128–164; Lena Cansdale, "Julian and the Rebuilding of the Jerusalem Temple," *AbrN* 34 (1997): 18–29. For a survey of the (mostly Christian) sources for this event, see David Levenson, "Julian's Attempt to Rebuild the Temple: An Inventory of Ancient and Medieval Sources," *Of Scribes and Scrolls: Studies on the Hebrew Bible, Intertestamental Judaism, and Christian Origins Presented to John Strugnell* (ed. Harold Attridge; John Collins, and Thomas Tobin; Lanham: University Press of America, 1990), 261–279.

4. See Babylonian Talmud *Megillah* 12a; and Ephraim E. Urbach, "Cyrus and his Decrees in the Eyes of the Sages," *Molad* 19 (1961): 403–410 (Hebrew).

5. See Robert Wilken, *The Land Called Holy: Palestine in Christian History and Thought* (New Haven: Yale University Press, 1992), 209–214. For the text of the *Book of Zerubbabel*, see Adolf Jellinek, *Bet ha-Midrasch*, vol. 2 (3rd ed.; Jerusalem: Sifre Vahrmann, 1967), 54–57. For an English translation with notes, see Martha Himmelfarb, "Sefer Zerubbabel," *Rabbinic Fantasies: Imaginative Narratives from Classical Hebrew Literature* (ed. David Stern and Mark Mirsky; Philadelphia: Jewish Publication Society, 1990), 67–90.

6. See Cyril Mango, "The Temple Mount, AD 614–638," *Bayt Al-Maqdis. 'Abd al-Malik's Jerusalem, Part One* (ed. Julian Raby and Jeremy Johns; Oxford: Oxford University Press, 1992), 1–16, esp. 1–2.

Index